Anonymous

Revival Sermons

Anonymous

Revival Sermons

ISBN/EAN: 9783337160814

Printed in Europe, USA, Canada, Australia, Japan

Cover: Foto ©Lupo / pixelio.de

More available books at **www.hansebooks.com**

EDITOR'S NOTICE.

In preparing for publication DAY'S REVIVAL SERMONS, we have endeavored to preserve, as much as possible, the Author's peculiar style of expression, and great plainness of speech; but in so doing, we have been under the necessity of paying less regard to literary taste and the usual theological phrases, and more to the literature of the Bible and the acumen of the Author. The thoughts in these sermons are clothed in words that burn into the very soul, when *preached;* but it is impossible to retain for the *reader*, the flashing eye, the benign countenance, or the native eloquence of the preacher. If the reader has been accustomed to hear from the pulpit literary performances without point in place of plain Bible truths, or smooth and scholastic *essays* in place of Gospel *sermons*, he is requested to bring these sermons to the Bible.

text, and compare them with the preaching and teaching of Christ and his Apostles, before condemning them for either their manner or matter.

That they are argumentative and logical, as well as pungent and practical, has been fully proved by the influence they have exerted over some of the best minds in the country, and the testimony of hundreds and thousands who have been converted under their delivery.

That they are evangelical in doctrine and catholic in spirit, is evident from the fact that they have been preached among all evangelical denominations of Christians, and followed by the outpouring of the Holy Spirit. The minor points, on which sects differ, give place to the fundamental truths of Christianity, as revealed in God's word, and as generally understood by Congregationalists, Baptists, Methodists, and others; consequently no objection obtains to their free circulation among all denominations of evangelical Christians. Of course they will be instrumental in doing good, in proportion to the zeal of Christians in circulating them.

Twenty-five years' experience as an evangelist, and the success which has thus far attended his preaching, has fairly entitled the Author to the credit of having been instrumental in leading as many souls to the Saviour as any other evangelist now in the field, and the multitudes who have urged the publication of his sermons, for the benefit of their families, while at the same time they would have the privilege of contributing to the support of him and his family, are now gratified.

J. W. ALDEN, Editor.

Boston, May 3, 1860.

CONTENTS.

I. PREPARE THE WAY... 9
   1. PREPARATION ON THE PART OF THE CHURCH NECESSARY. 2. WHEN MADE, A REVIVAL SURE TO FOLLOW.

II. LUKEWARMNESS... 47
   1. THE THREE STATES OF HEART, VIZ: 1. COLD. 2. HOT. 3. LUKEWARM.

III. IDLENESS 73
   1. DEFINITION OF TERMS IN THE TEXT. 2. IDLENESS INCONSISTENT WITH DUTY, AND FRAUGHT WITH GUILT. 3. WHY WE ARE IDLE. 4. CHRIST DEMANDS A REASON FOR SUCH CONDUCT.

IV. THE TITHES... 117
   1. THE DUTY TAUGHT IN THE TEXT. 2. THE SRENGTH AND MAGNITUDE OF THE PROMISE.

V. PRAYER... 145
   1. PRAYER A DUTY. 2. AN IMPORTANT DUTY. 3. A HIGH PRIVILEGE. 4. ASK, SEEK, AND KNOCK. 5. HOW TO PREVAIL IN PRAYER.

VI. POWER FROM ON HIGH..................................... 218
   1. POWER SPOKEN OF IN THE TEXT. 2. WHAT IT WILL ACCOMPLISH. 3. HOW OBTAINED. 4. GUILT OF THE CHURCH IN NOT OBTAINING IT.

VII. THE CARELESS ONES 247
   1. CARELESS ABOUT GOD. 2. CARELESS ABOUT GOD'S LAW. 3. CARELESS ABOUT CHRIST.

4. Careless about Death. 5. Careless about the Judgment, Heaven, Hell, Eternity, Salvation.

VIII. MORAL AGENCY.................................... 269

1. Attributes of a Moral Agent. 2. Proof of the Doctrine.

IX. GOD'S RIGHT TO GOVERN........................... 297

1. Definition of Government. 2. Two Departments in the Universe which need Governing. 3. Government supposes Power exercised over each Department. 4. But two kinds of Power used in Government. 5. Moral Agents not governed by Physical Power. 6. How far Physical Power is connected with Moral Government, and its Place. 7. The Necessity of Moral Agents being under Government. 8. The Being best qualified ought to Govern. 9. God the only Being qualified. 10. God's Right and Duty to Govern.

X. THE JUDGMENT DAY................................ 329

1. Its Appointment. 2. Its Objects. 3. Its Magnitude and Results.

SERMONS.

I.

PREPARE THE WAY.

Prepare ye the way of the Lord. — *Matt.* iii. 3.

1. PREPARATION ON THE PART OF THE CHURCH NECESSARY
2. WHEN MADE, A REVIVAL SURE TO FOLLOW.

JOHN THE BAPTIST, who uttered this text, was a wonderful man. His ministry was short but very effective. Few men ever moved the people so extensively in so short a time. His preaching seemed to electrify and arouse the whole region.

All Jerusalem were in an uproar, and they turned out in a mass to hear John preach, and were baptized of him in Jordan, confessing their sins. Nor was this movement confined to Jerusalem. The whole land of Judea was in a blaze, the work spread on every side, and in the short space of six months the inhabitants generally in that large region professed faith in his doctrine. So the history affirms, as the following language will show.

"Then went out to him Jerusalem, and *all* Judea, and *all* the region round about Jordan, and were baptized of him in Jordan, confessing their sins."

The probable secret of John's wonderful power over men, was the fact that he was filled with the Holy Ghost. He had been filled with the Spirit from a child up. His whole heart was in his work, his spirit was aroused and he poured forth the truth in great power upon the multitudes who flocked to hear him. Listen to him for a moment. "The kingdom of Heaven is at hand." It is now at your doors. The King in Zion is born and in your midst. He is about to enter upon his public work. Now, ye sleepy Jews, wake up and repent. I am the voice of one crying in the wilderness, sent before his face to call upon you to prepare his way. Wake up, wake up and make his paths straight. Set your houses in order, put every abomination from your hearts, and be in readiness for the ushering in of this new kingdom, which is ultimately to demolish all other kingdoms and to fill the whole world.

This text is figurative. To understand any portion of the Bible, where there is imagery used, we should adopt the following rule:—

We should first acquaint ourselves thoroughly with the literal thing referred to, whatever it may be. If it is an ancient custom we should learn what that custom was, so that the literal thing shall be distinctly before the mind. Then, by consulting the connection of the text, we can generally perceive the thought which the Spirit intended to convey by the use of the imagery. Or, in other words, we can get into our minds the very thought in the mind of the Spirit. When we get into our minds the exact thought that was in the mind of the Spirit we have the truth. And we have not the truth until that is the fact. The object of the Bible is to convey to us God's thought. It is a great storehouse of his thoughts. We should read it for the purpose of getting at those thoughts. The Bible contains his thoughts concerning himself, man, heaven and hell; concerning the way of life and salvation, and all the great things which are necessary for us to know to fit us for usefulness here, and for heaven hereafter. What a rich treasure! How infinitely valuable to man! How purifying and elevating in its tendency! It expands the soul and moulds it all over into God and heaven when it submits to be controlled by its great principles. Let us bring our hearts in warm contact with its heavenly truths, if we would become God-like.

But what is the custom referred to in this text? We reply, it was a custom frequently practised by monarchs, in that eastern portion of the world, in the days of John. As they were to pass into different portions of their dominions, they sent a messenger before their face, to call upon the people to prepare the roads. In some instances this was done at great expense. New roads were cut through entire; large hills were dug down; valleys filled up; the rough places were made smooth, and the crooked were made straight. The herald or crier went before the monarch's face, to see if this preparation for his reception was thoroughly done up. Now for the application. Jesus Christ, who is KING OF KINGS AND LORD OF LORDS, was about to make his appearance in Judea. He sent before his face his messenger, who was John the Baptist, to call upon the Jewish people to prepare for his reception. How this herald or forerunner of Christ pressed the duty in my text, upon the hearts of the Jews, everywhere. Hear him thunder all over Judea, "PREPARE YE THE WAY OF THE LORD!"— Wake up, one and all, shake off your stupidity, and wake up at once! The KING OF KINGS is at hand! Open your ears and listen to the rumbling of his chariot-wheels in the distance; open your eyes and behold his royal approach.

The text, in its application to us, contains two important practical truths.

I. Before Jesus Christ comes into any place to revive his work, a preparation is necessary on the part of the church.

II. In any place where and when the church will make this preparation, Christ will come to that people, and pour out his Spirit, and gather sinners into the kingdom.

Let us contemplate these truths for a few moments.

1. A PREPARATION IS NECESSARY ON THE PART OF THE CHURCH, IF SHE WOULD HAVE CHRIST COME. The text puts that matter at rest. God speaks to every individual in this church in the language of this passage. Hear him, my brethren, he is addressing you. *Prepare ye the way of the Lord.* This is his command to you. Here is a duty urged and you have not the right to neglect it. What! neglect to act when God commands! Have you a right to resist his will? For you to be indifferent when he speaks is the very height of wickedness. Hear him then and gird on your armor at once. But this is not the only place in the Bible where this truth is taught, and John is not the only teacher who understood and enforced it. Let us hear David for a moment. Ps. li. 12, 13: " Restore unto me the joy of thy salvation; and uphold me with thy free Spirit. *Then* will I teach transgressors *thy ways*, and sinners *shall be converted unto thee.*" David here introduces the true Bible theory of revivals. Did he fold up his arms and say " Let us wait God's time." Did he comfort himself in a wrong state of heart by saying " God's time to favor Zion is not yet come." He administered no such false comforts to his conscience. He knew that God's time would come when the joys of Jehovah's salvation are fully restored to his heart,

and he has prepared God's way. Where did David propose to commence? Did he say Lord I will go out and teach transgressors thy ways, and then you "restore unto me the joys of thy salvation"? Not one word of that. He knew his duty too well to undertake to move in that form. Look now, and look close, for here is a moral lesson to be learned from this passage, of vast importance to the ministry and the church. Where, then, did David propose to commence the work of God? I answer, *at his own heart*, where every Christian, and Christian minister on earth should always commence if he would have success. Mark how he cries out to God, " *Restore unto* me the joys of thy salvation." Then, ah, yes, then will I teach transgressors *thy ways;* not mine, but *thy ways*. And what shall be the result when the joys of God's salvation are fully restored to his own heart? Result? Let David answer. But note his words. Did he say, and *perhaps* sinners will be converted unto God? There is no *perhaps* in the case. How confidently he affirms, "And sinners SHALL BE CONVERTED UNTO THEE." David understood too well the influence he would have over others, to speak doubtingly, when his heart was full of God. He knew full well that to fill the church with God's Holy Ghost, the impenitent would feel her influence, and multitudes would flock to Christ.

Let this church begin where David proposed to

commence, and each member see to it that God's salvation is fully, FULLY restored to his own heart, and God will rock this whole community under his awful footsteps. *Sinners* SHALL *be converted* UNTO GOD. Will you do it? Will you begin to-day?

Let us now listen to Christ for a moment, and learn how he set men to work to promote a revival. No one can doubt but that he fully understood this matter, and if he has spoken let us hear him. Matt. vii. 5 : " First cast out the beam out of thine own eye ; and then shalt thou see clearly to cast out the mote out of thy brother's eye." How did the Saviour set his followers to work to save men? Did he say to them Go out with a beam in thine own eye, and take the mote from thy brother's eye? Particular attention should be given to this imagery. How impressive! The word translated beam in the text, says Dr. A. Clark, should have been rendered splinter. The eye, we all know, is the most delicate part of the human system. The least thing will affect it and put us in pain in a moment. If a man is to deal with this delicate organ, how important that his own vision be cleared up, as clear as heaven. A little blunder, and the eye is utterly spoiled, and the sight lost forever. Think of an individual, who, with a splinter in his own eye, should undertake, with a sharp instrument, to remove a mote from a brother's eye. How blundering! how foolish! He will most assuredly spoil the eye of the individual he undertakes to benefit.

Then again how hazardous! What consequences hang upon a little mistake! What would common sense dictate under such circumstances? · What would duty demand? Where should he commence? What hearer in this house hesitates for a reply? ALL, ALL exclaim, begin at home. Let his own vision be cleared up and then he can apply that instrument with skill and remove the mote without harming the eye. How impressive this imagery! How full of common-sense instruction! Think of the drunkard who would stand reeling over his cups, lecturing men on the subject of temperance. Who would hear him? How quick you would say, Wipe your own mouth, and break that decanter, before you lecture us. Cast first the beam out of your own eye. That thief gives an excellent lecture upon the subject of honesty, but during his lecture he slyly picks his neighbor's pocket who sits by his side. What influence would his lecture have over his audience think you? What would they say? I will not hear such a fellow. Let him first repent and become an honest man, and do works meet for repentance, before he exhorts us. Begin the work at his own heart and get that right, and then it will be time for us to hear him.

Now I affirm that this same common-sense

lesson is the very lesson the Saviour has given the church, in the passage under consideration. Let the church first set her own heart right, and the obstacles in the way of God's blessing will be removed; and, moreover, by so doing, she commends herself so perfectly to the conscience of every sinner, that they will listen with profit to her warnings, and invitations to come to Christ. She will then be in a state where she has power with God, and power over men, to move them to repent. This is the point urged in my text, " Prepare ye the way of the Lord."

If this church would have Christ come, she must make this preparation. Will you do it? God calls for an answer. He puts the question to you personally. *Will you do it?* What does your heart say? Does it respond, I will? If so, God will come. Let us now look at the second great truth taught in this text.

2. WHENEVER A CHURCH MAKES THIS PREPARATION, CHRIST WILL VISIT THAT PEOPLE, AND A REVIVAL WILL BE THE CERTAIN RESULT.

In this matter there can be no failure. I fully believe that the judgment will reveal one great truth, that whenever and wherever any church has sought God as he directed, he never failed them. How can he? He has committed himself, and he would sooner let the heavens fall than suffer his word to fail. Look at a few things as evidence on this point.

1. I present the text. Did the monarch send his herald to call upon the people to prepare his way, where he himself did not expect to come? When they heard the proclamation of the herald, they expected when the way was prepared to hear the rumbling of his chariot-wheels.

Now I affirm that the great Monarch of heaven and earth calls upon this church to prepare his way. When you will do it, you shall hear the sound of his going forth, in the tops of the mulberry-trees, and he will appear, to build up Zion gloriously. He does not call upon you to prepare his way for nought. He means something by this demand, and when it is fully met on your part, he will not disappoint your hopes and expectations. The Messenger of the Covenant will suddenly come to his temple, and you shall learn by happy experience that you have not sought the Lord in vain nor spent your strength for nought.

2. I offer for proof the fact that God has given direction in his Word how his people should seek him for a blessing. Why give direction how he should be sought, if he does not intend to bless. Does he thus mock his people by raising their expectations only to disappoint them?

God plays no such deceptive game with his

children. He is a Being of infinite sincerity, and as such he raises no expectations he does not intend to meet, and none he will not meet, even exceeding their highest anticipations, if they will come into perfect union with him.

3. But look at a few promises on this point. " Ask," says God, " and it shall be given, seek and ye shall find, knock and it shall be opened unto you." How absolute these promises. What encouragement they afford to look to God with the fullest confidence that he will come. Take another : " Open thy mouth wide and *I will fill it.*" What a promise! God does not wish us satisfied with *little* things. He wishes to do *great* things. Let your desires enlarge and become great, and I will satisfy them. Repent, labor, and toil for great things, and look to me for them, by faith, and I will more than meet your expectations. I might multiply promises to any extent, for the Bible is full of them. One more, however, shall close this branch of the subject. " Ye shall seek me and find me, when ye shall search for me with all your heart." This promise specifies the time when God will be found by any church, or individual. Just when ye seek me with all the heart is my set time to favor Zion.

I have now given you God's testimony on this point. He is ready to bless this people if they will prepare the way of the Lord. Will you do it?

Keep in view, if you neglect this duty, God will hold you responsible for every soul that would be converted if you came up to his help. Will you go up to the judgment, and have the blood of these sinners on your hands, or will you repent and prepare the way of the Lord? What does your conscience say, and what is your decision?

Do I hear one raising the question, "What can I do to prepare the way of the Lord? I am not willing to meet the fearful responsibility of living as I have done. I must awake. Tell me what I can do?" I would to God that every professing Christian in this place were ready to raise that question honestly. With what delight I would answer it. "What!" says one, "can you show us how we can secure a revival in this place?" Most certainly we can. That is our work as ministers, to show men how they can secure God's blessing. Will you listen to me if I will undertake it? Does your heart respond, "*Yes*, most gladly; we will do anything, if God will only come." Very well; you keep that promise, and make it good while I proceed, and he will come. He will come to your heart and your family, perhaps; and oh! how Heaven will rejoice over the conversion of those children or that husband or wife or neighbor. "But what can we do?" I answer, —

1. You must be willing to be told of your faults.

This looks like a simple step to start with, but

much hangs upon it. God cannot and will not bless you until you are willing to know your heart. As a general thing, when men are in a wrong state of mind, they are not willing to know their true state. The Saviour affirmed concerning such, that they hate the light, and neither come to the light, lest their deeds should be reproved.

Men love to be flattered in their sins; they do not love that kind of preaching which lays open their wrongs; and this is the state of things in many of our churches at the present day. They have their idol sins, and they are determined to cling to them. They do not wish ministers to meddle with such matters. How liberal some men will be to support ministers, if they will only be cautious, and not probe their hearts with God's truth. Preach the truth in general terms, so as not to hit any particular sin or sinner, and that is the kind of preaching that suits this age. Now mark, if this church is in that state of mind, God will not bless, unless you repent. You must be willing to know your heart. Will you sit down here, and let me point out your sins faithfully, as far as I know them, and as I learn them from time to time? Do not deceive yourself on this point. It will cost you an effort to become honest enough to be willing to let the full blaze of truth in upon your hearts. You will be patient, perhaps, while I point out *some* of your sins; but when I come to put my hand on that idol so dear to you, how that heart will rebel.

Remember, my brother, if you would have God's blessing you must be willing to know your whole heart. Think, for a moment, why should you be unwilling? Are your wrongs a blessing, that you should cling to them or cover them up? Some men seem to guard and fortify themselves in their wrongs, as though their eternal life hung upon that course. My dear hearer, pause for a moment and reflect. Your wrongs are your only curse. They are the cause of all your wretchedness, and they are *the* things that will sink your soul deep in hell unless you see and put them away. What separates between your soul and your Maker, and shuts his blessing from your heart just *now?* God answers, "Your iniquity."

What grieves the Holy Spirit from you, shuts heaven's door in your face, and your poor spirit out of heaven? I answer, nothing but your unrepented iniquities. This you cannot deny. With these acknowledged facts, then, staring you in the face, will you still persist in being unwilling to know your wrongs? Will you call ministers hard, severe, and unreasonable, who faithfully point them out? Shall I become your enemy if I tell you the truth, and the whole truth? I should be your enemy in reality if I should cover up and hide from your eye your wrongs. To do it, would be to take the direct course to damn both your soul and my own.

God declares that he will require the blood of the lost at the hands of the unfaithful minister, who has refused to show the people their sins, and warn them of their danger. Let me ask, therefore, Do you wish us, as ministers, to bring the curse of God upon ourselves and the people to whom we minister? Do you answer, no? Then I ask, Will you sit here and let us search you with great faithfulness, with God's truth? and while we do it, will you cry out to God with an honest heart, "' Search me, O God, and try my ways.' Go to the bottom of my heart, and make me to know the worst of my case"?

Coming into this honest state of mind is one important step gained towards preparing the way of the Lord. Keep this in view: If you begin to fight, reject and cavil with God's truth, he will curse you with barrenness and leanness of heart, and give you over to pursue your own chosen way to hell.

2. If you would prepare the way of the Lord you must make up your mind to reduce to practice, at once, the instruction imparted from time to time, as far as that instruction is in harmony with the Bible

I do not ask you to practise any instruction I may impart, any farther than it harmonizes with God's truth. But as far as it is in harmony with the Bible, we have a right to ask you to practise it

God demands it at your hands, and you have not the right to refuse to do it. If we are what we profess to be, we are ambassadors for Christ. We come in his name to expound and enforce the claims of *God upon you*. What right have you then to reject and refuse to practise *God's* claims?

Do you think you can prepare the way of the Lord while you refuse to practise God's truth? What! secure God's blessing while you refuse obedience? Think of it. What does any impenitent sinner do more than to refuse to obey his Maker? Nay, more, what does the Devil but disobey? Now if you put yourself on a level with the Devil and impenitent men, do you expect you can prepare the way of the Lord in that state of heart? It is impossible! Infinitely ridiculous to think you can prepare God's way without giving yourself up to practise his demands. Here lies the secret why this community are not saved. It is not because you have not had the Gospel. You come and go, like the door upon its hinges, and hear the Gospel, but you do not intend to practise it. God looks down from heaven and proclaims " BE YE DOERS OF THE WORD, and not *hearers only*." Up to this hour many of you have been hearers only. You have made no calculation to practise the Gospel. God demands *practice*, you withhold the practice and then think it strange you do not have a blessing. How many of you here to-day are expecting to practise what you hear? Supposing I should now request all in this congregation to stand up, who would solemnly promise to reduce this sermon to practice, how many do you suppose would rise? Do you reply "I do not want to promise." Ah! that lets out the heart. When you are determined to do a thing, you are not afraid to promise. Now keep before your minds this truth and think of it as you go out and as you come in. God never will bless you in that state of heart. You must make up your minds to practise instructions. You must come here to hear, to learn your duty and then go out and *do* it. What is the object of preaching? What is the object of hearing? If you had Paul with all his faithfulness, or an angel from heaven, they could not benefit a man of you, unless you would reduce their instructions to practice. What say you? Will you obey? Will you begin now? Now, while on your seats, promise God? Promise him this moment you will give yourselves up to practise the truth? Do you do it? If you say yes, keep in view you give that pledge to God, not to me. Oh! may Heaven record, and help you to keep it.

3. If you would prepare the way of the Lord you must commence and pursue a rigid course of self-examination.

Much depends upon this step. This duty neglected and all is a failure. If I knew I could not persuade one in this community to attend to this duty, I would leave forthwith. I should know I could not do good here. No man ever repented of his sins until he first saw himself to be a sinner, and no man ever saw himself to be a sinner without self-examination. The Spirit of God always carries the mind through that process in producing conviction. What is conviction? I answer, it is your having a clear view of the fact that you are wrong. How can you obtain that? Only by comparing your heart and life with some standard of right. The Spirit of God convicts by carrying the mind through that process. This, in some instances, is done very quick, as the mind can act like lightning.

Now if you turn the eye of your mind from the standard of right, and persevere in doing so, you will not see your sins in a clear light, and of course you will not repent. If you want a thorough revival here, this church must be crushed down in the dust under a sense of her guilt, her *great guilt*. You have been a wicked church. How you have lived here without a revival. Souls all around you have been making fearful strides towards hell, and hardly a warning voice have they heard from this people. How the world has eaten out all your piety. How little you have thought of God and the salvation of men. Do you imagine you can jump right into a revival state, without seeing this great guilt and confessing it? It is impossible. You must see your heart. You must use the *means* to see your heart, if you would prepare God's way. Self-examination is the means. If you will attend to this duty as you ought, God will show you your hearts. He will be thorough with you. He will give you an old-fashioned revival. A revival that will break up the fallow ground of your heart. But in attending to this duty of self-examination you must look to it that you do not set up any false standards by which to try yourself. 1. Do not compare yourself with your creed. That is an uninspired standard and may be imperfect. 2. Do not compare yourselves among yourselves, for Paul says of such, that they are not wise. You may have as much piety as many in the church, and yet be in a very bad state. 3. But take the Bible, that perfect standard, the book by which you are to be judged at the last day, and bring your heart and life in warm contact with its searching truths. Avoid another thing, namely, thinking you are right, because others think you a Christian, and in a good state. Their opinion will not settle the matter for you at the judgment. Then, you must be tested by the Bible. Consequently you should bring your life to that test now.

Begin with the Sermon on the Mount. Read it carefully and prayerfully. Drop on your knees and implore God to show you your sins in the light of its truths. Then read every verse, and put the question home to your heart, as you pass along, " Am I in the state of heart described in this verse?" " Have I done the duty it demands, or have I neglected to do what it requires?" If deficient, mark that down as a sin, and then take the next verse, and the next, until you get through the sermon. Be faithful to yourself. Then take other portions of the Bible in the same way, until your heart is overwhelmed with your guilt. During this process keep this truth distinctly before your mind, that to neglect to do what the Bible requires is sin, or to do what it prohibits is sin. Now will you attend to this duty? Will you do it faithfully? You cannot prepare the way of the Lord and neglect it. Will you set apart a season every day to attend to this work?

Edwards and Payson and other men of God have attended to it. That was what drove them to the mercy-seat in such agony for help. They saw their unworthiness and their sins in the light of God's truth, and flew to Christ for pardon. The Redeemer opened the windows of heaven over their spirits and baptized them with the Holy Ghost. He will do so by us, if we will walk in their footsteps. Doubtless there are multitudes in the church who think they are in the way to heaven, when they are in the way to hell, simply because they never examine their hearts to learn their condition. Oh! what a fearful day it will be to them when they open their eyes in the eternal world and find themselves lost, in consequence of neglecting this duty. How they will then wish they had attended to this matter rigidly.

Will you do it? Will you begin to-day? Will you make personal work of this matter? No one can do this work for you. If you will do it, soon we shall find you on your faces crying for mercy. God's way will be prepared, and the messenger of the covenant will suddenly come to his temple.

4. The next step in order in attending to this work is repentance. To see your sins is one thing, to repent of them is another. John, in connection with my text, pressed the conscience of the Jews with this duty, and cried out to those mere formalists, *Repent*, REPENT, FOR THE KINGDOM OF HEAVEN IS AT HAND. They professed to be God's children and they attended to the outward forms of religion more abundantly than many in the church do now. Notwithstanding all this, John declared they were exposed to the wrath of God. He was a faithful servant of God. He did not flatter men in their sins. Hear him address the Pharisees and Sadducees as they approach him to be baptized. " O generation of vipers, who hath warned you to flee from the wrath to come?" What language! You would exclaim, — severity, vulgarity, and refuse to hear such preaching, if ministers should be half as faithful at this day.

But the church need a John the Baptist to go through the whole land now, to show her her sins and press her to immediate repentance. She has become worldly, proud, and formal in her religion. She does not like the self-denying duties of the Gospel. She will become very restive and uneasy under the plain truths of the Bible, such as John, Christ, and his Apostles preached. She wants a kind of preaching that is more scientific and refined, and better adapted to the age in which we live. This is her plea. This pressing men to repent now, and threatening them with hell if they neglect to do it, is not the kind of preaching she relishes. There is such a want of refinement about it, says one, I cannot endure it.

My dear hearer, stop and think. When you have become so wonderfully refined in your notions and views of things that you cannot love or even bear the plain naked truth of the Gospel, you may know there is a cause for it. Your heart is so in love with sin that you cannot bear the truth. This is the secret of the whole matter. What wonderfully refined beings we have in this age. The naked truth is not refined enough to suit such tastes. They are refined enough for God, or he would have revealed different ones. They are refined enough for angels, for they are desirous to look into them. But for the wise ones of this age they have no charms. What consummate folly! How God will show up *such* wisdom at another day. Have we forgotten that we are indebted to the truths of the Bible for all the refinement there is on earth? Is sin refinement? If so the Devil is much more refined than we are. Sin is debasing, degrading, mean, contemptible, and anything but refining in its tendency. Understanding the great principles and doctrines of the Bible, and conforming the heart and life to them, is refinement such as Heaven loves and adores. It is godlike and noble.

Sanctify them through thy truth, prayed Christ to his Father. That is, refine, ennoble and make them godlike through thy truth, and fit them thus to become the companions of angels. Fit them through the plain truths of the Gospel, to step into the most refined society of the universe. Repentance takes away a want of refinement and brings the soul to the cross of Christ, where it is purified and fitted for heaven. How quick it will make a sober man of the drunkard; convert that licentious man and bring him into a state of purity. It arrested the bloody Saul of Tarsus in the midst of his murderous work, and moulded his heart all over into the very spirit and temper of heaven, and made him a Paul and a herald of salvation to thousands of his race. Let it be exercised by every heart and it would uproot all sin, sweep away every abomination, convert the human race into a state of purity and holiness, and make a heaven of this world.

This repentance God demands at the hands of this church to prepare his way. He cannot consistently come to your help without it.

"Repent ye, therefore," says Peter to the Jews, "and be converted, that your sins may be blotted out, when the times of refreshing shall come from the presence of the Lord."

This church has lived in a cold state for months, while sinners all around you have been in the way to hell. This you know. You know, moreover, that you cannot thus neglect your duty to God and man without *guilt*, — GREAT GUILT. God demands of you to repent of this course of living and return to him with all your heart, and he will return to you, and the times of refreshing shall come from the presence of the Lord. Shall this step now be taken by every heart, or shall it not? You must decide it individually. What say you?

5. Again, if you would prepare the way of the Lord you must advance one step beyond repentance. You must take up the stumbling-blocks you have thrown before the wicked, and your brethren, by a humble broken-hearted confession.

Such is the conduct of professing Christians, in many instances, that their lives become a stumbling-block to impenitent sinners. They are right in the way of their salvation, and their friends, perhaps, are in danger of stumbling into hell over their conduct.

God speaks to such and presses them to this duty. He says, " Take up the stumbling-blocks out of the way of my people." Husband, wife, parent, brother, sister, neighbor, friend, — do you hear God's voice? Go home and take up that stumbling-block. Do it quick, or that relative or neighbor, perhaps, will stumble into eternal ruin, over you.

"But how can I do it?" says one. "Let me know; for I do not wish to stand in the way of others."

I answer, There is but one way to take up a stumbling-block, and that is by a hearty confession. This will be humiliating to you, and there are many in the church too proud to do it. "If I repent," says one, "is not that enough?"

I answer, No, IT IS NOT ENOUGH. Take a case as an illustration of this point. In a place where I was preaching some years since, an old backslider repented one Sabbath evening, and consecrated himself anew to God. The next morning I was in the shop of an impenitent man, and while there, named the circumstance of this man's speaking and praying in meeting the night previous. He exclaimed, "Well, I am glad I was not there to hear him, for had I been present I would have taken my hat and left the house forthwith." I said to him, "Why so? Are you not desirous to have your neighbors repent?" "Repent, Sir," said he, "yes, but I have no confidence in him, and I do not wish to hear him pray." "But perhaps he has repented, and if he is truly penitent, you ought to be willing and even rejoice to hear him pray," said I. "But," said he, "he has abused me wickedly, and I must have some evidence of penitence before I will hear him pray, unless he can run faster than I can."

I left the shop, but business called me back there again before night, when I found this man in a different state of mind altogether. He came to me in tears, and remarked, "Mr. Day, I can hear that man pray now." "Ah!" said I, "what has produced this change in your feelings?" "Oh!" said he, "you had hardly left the shop, when he came in, and in deep emotion took me by the hand, and confessed his wrong and besought me to forgive him. He is honest," said he, "and I most freely forgive all. I wish I was in as good a state of mind as he is. Now," continued he, "I want to hear him pray."

Suppose now this brother had entered the shop and commenced exhorting that sinner to repent. What good would it have done? How quick he would have *felt*, if he had not spoken it out, "Physician, heal thyself." He might have exhorted him until the judgment should sit, and it would have done no good. That sinner would have been perfectly fortified against all his exhortations, however eloquent, and he could not have reached him. But as he stept in and began by putting his finger on his own wrongs, by confession, and thus took that stumbling-block out of the way, how quick it disarmed him, and tore away the breastwork that shielded him, and the way of the Lord is prepared for him to lead that soul to Christ.

Take another case. A professing Christian once went through an entire neighborhood and confessed his unfaithfulness to every family, and a revival followed. Fifteen of the converts dated their first impressions from that man's confessions. He prepared the way of the Lord by taking up the stumbling-blocks. Will you go and do likewise? Let this church be thorough in this matter, if she would have God's way thoroughly prepared; confess to one another, to your families and neighbors, and see how quick God will bless. He will use even your confession to save the wicked, and you shall soon see them flocking to Christ.

6. Purify your church by attending to all cases of discipline.

You have covenanted together to watch over each other. If a brother or a sister wanders from the path of duty, you have engaged to reprove and rebuke, if necessary, such a wanderer, and do all in your power to reclaim him. This is one of the duties of church relationship, and it cannot be neglected without guilt. God demands it at the hands of every church. If a brother trespass, go and tell *him* his fault, is Christ's solemn command. How the churches neglect this duty. If a brother trespass, we tell the fault to everybody else but him, and thus violate our covenant obligations, and the solemn commands of Christ. This is common business in the church, and yet she is amazed that she is not blessed with a revival. Amazed! What church can expect a revival under such circumstances? Why not expect a revival while the church is trampling any other command of God under her feet? The God that commands you to be sober and not get drunk; to be honest and not steal; to be truthful and not lie; commands you to go and tell that trespassing brother his fault betwixt *him and thee alone.*

Now if you neglect this duty you trample Divine authority under your feet as much as if you should lie, steal, or get drunk. It is a sin in the one case as much as in the other. One is a popular sin in consequence of its being common, and the other an unpopular sin. But keep in view, its being *common* does not whiten it into a virtue, nor take away its guilt.

God has a controversy with the churches on this point. How he rebuked some of the churches in Asia for suffering certain characters to remain in their midst. I have somewhat against thee, said God, for neglecting to take steps to reclaim or remove such cases. We should remember that the power of the whole Jewish camp was once paralyzed by harboring in her midst one wicked man. God uttered his voice and declared,—There is an abominable thing in your midst, which is the cause of my forsaking you, and now you cannot stand in the presence of your enemies. They were powerless, and the enemy could vanquish them with infinite ease. But when they sanctified themselves, by putting away their "Achan," how soon they were triumphant. That scrap of history teaches a very important lesson. It teaches the following things: — 1. That the power of the church to reform the world does not depend upon numbers, talent, or wealth, but upon her being *pure*, so as to keep God with her. 2. If she harbors wicked men in her midst, God will forsake her, and then she is shorn of her strength to save the world, and the enemy will triumph. 3. When she will repent and discipline her members, in obedience to Christ's commands, and remove all dead branches, by applying the pruning-knife to those who refuse to be reclaimed, then God will return to the church, and she will be mighty, through Him, in reforming the world. Now if this church is in fault here, will she prepare the way of the Lord by attending to this duty? Go at once and hunt up all your delinquent members, and attend to this matter in the kindness and faithfulness of the Gospel, and see what God will do for you.

7. Put away your party feeling. We have reason to fear that many in the church and ministry have mistaken party or sectarian zeal for true godliness.

Zeal for a party, or to build up a sect, is one thing, and zeal for God and the salvation of the world, is quite another thing. That many have made that fatal mistake is evident from the fact that they feel comparatively no interest in a revival unless it is in their sect, or there is a strong probability that it will give strength to their party. No matter how many souls are converted, nor how much God is honored in their salvation, they feel no interest. Instead of lending a helping hand to advance the work, they can look on with indifference, or stand aloof from it, and perhaps exert an influence *against* it.

All heaven looks on with intense interest, and rejoices if but one sinner is converted, whether it occur among the Baptists, Congregationalists, Methodists, or any other sect, and they do not wait to see where they will join, before they take down their harps to rejoice over their salvation.

This is the spirit of Heaven, and if you are a child of God, your heart will necessarily beat in unison with hearts on high. I very much doubt that man's piety who can be indifferent when he knows souls around him are coming into the kingdom. Such a state of heart among ministers and professed Christians will grieve the Spirit of God, and is in the way of a revival. Paul gives it a correct name in 1 Cor. iii. 4 : " For while one saith, I am of Paul; and another, I am of Apollos; *are ye not carnal?* " It is the spirit of carnality or selfishness, and God abhors it.

Christ prayed that all his disciples might be one, as he and the Father are one. John xvii. 21. This state of harmony among Christians is pleasing to God, and where it exists, God will honor it with his presence and blessing. Let all Christians therefore lay aside their party strife and sectarian prejudice, and come up unitedly to God's help, and we will soon learn that the old maxim is true in religion as well as in other things, "THAT UNION IS STRENGTH." When Christians are of "*one heart and one soul,*" God's way will be prepared.

8. Be willing that God should send by whom he will send. Sometimes church-members and ministers are in a state of heart where they wish to dictate to God in relation to his mode of working. They would like a revival, but they want the privilege of selecting the agents God shall use in carrying on his work. ." Work by *our* church," says one, " for we are the nearest right." " Work by me," says the pastor, " for I cannot have a work here, if it must be carried on by calling in foreign help. If I should call in foreign aid, and God should bless it, my church will think less of me and my preaching." What a state of heart that must be! You had rather sinners would go to hell, than that the people should think less of you. That state of feeling in the ministry is wicked. It is supremely

selfish. God abhors it, and it grieves the Holy Ghost.

Look at this state of heart for a moment. "If God works among my people by some other man, what will become of MY GREAT NAME?" says the minister. When ministers become anxious about their own GREAT NAMES instead of that of God, he will not bless such a ministry to any great extent. When the ministry and church are anxious about GOD's name and glory, and not their own, and when they are willing that their names should be blotted out and forgotten, if the people can be saved, and God honored in their salvation, then God's way will be prepared, and not before. The church and ministry must come into a state where they can offer to God, honestly and from their heart of hearts, this prayer: "*Send, Lord, by* WHOM THOU WILT; *send, only send!*" In that state, God will hear. In that state, God will answer. What would you think of Peter, if he had been in a state of heart which would have prompted him to feel and say, "If Paul should come and preach to this people, they would probably think less of my preaching"? What had Peter to do with that matter, as long as Christ had put Paul into the ministry, as well as himself? Even if Paul could move a class of minds he could not, how thankful he ought to be that God could save those souls by the labors of any man!

If, moreover, the love of souls moved Peter to his

work, as it does every true minister of Christ, that will be true of him. *His name* will be a small matter in his estimation, if *God's name* can be honored, and souls saved. That will be the great moving principle of his heart and life, if he is a Christian.

9. You must put away your opposition to means and measures which God owns to save men, in order to obey the command in this text. You must not undertake to legislate for God about means, any more than you do about men, if you would secure God's blessing. God will not suffer you to dictate. It is not your place to dictate him. God's place is on the throne to direct, and ours is to submit, and take his blessings in any way he may see fit to bestow them, and be thankful to have them in any form. The human heart is always inclined to dictate. That child wants its supper, but it will not eat unless it can have it in its own way. "Very well," says the father, (who sees it necessary to subdue that disposition in his child,) "go to bed without, my child, if you cannot take it in my way." So we dictate to God. We want a revival, but we want it in our own way. We must have God give us a revival by such and such means, or we do not want it. "We must have it by the ordinary means of grace," says one. "We must not depart from our usual form, if the whole town go to hell. We must have it in this way or not at all." "No," says another, "we must have it by extra means; we do not

want it by the ordinary means." Now both are wrong, and God will frown upon them. You must stop dictating to God, and be willing to have it by any means he shall see fit to bless. That kind of dictation is feeling just like an impenitent sinner. He wants to go to heaven, but he wants to go in his own way. He must be willing to go God's way, or not at all. So with us; we must be willing to have a revival in God's way, or not have it. Are you willing God should come in his own way?

10. Finally, if you would obey this text, you must feel your dependence upon the Spirit to bless and make the means effectual, while we use them to save the world.

There are two errors against which the church should be guarded, both of which are fatal to revivals. 1. You teach the church that she is dependent upon God for a revival, and she is strongly inclined to fold up her arms and sit down in a state of idleness, and neglect the means God has appointed to be used to save the world. In that state, you urge her to use means to promote a revival, and how quick she will reply, "I do not believe in getting up a revival. God gives revivals, and our place is to wait God's time." Now, that God gives revivals I have no doubt, but while that is true, he has appointed means to be used by the church and ministry to promote them, and for a church to expect a revival while she lives in neglect of the means which

God has appointed, is wicked and absurd. The excuse that you do not believe in getting up revivals, as you term it, is only an effort to cover up the sin of idleness and keep your conscience still, while you live at ease in Zion and refuse to come up to God's help. You wickedly abuse the doctrine of dependence when you make such use of it. You bring it forward to cover up your wicked neglect of duty, and God will call you to account for such conduct. 2. Another error lies here. If you teach the church she has something to do in promoting a revival, she is strongly inclined to forget her dependence on God, and lean upon the means she is using, instead of leaning upon God.

Both of these states are wrong. An angel could not promote a revival without God's help. It takes God's Holy Spirit to make the means effectual, but the Spirit is not sent to do our duty, nor to work without our using the means, but to bless and make the means effectual when we use them. While therefore we are in the use of all the means God has appointed to save men, we should not lean upon the *means*, but upon *God*, and cry to him by prayer day and night to make the means effectual.

We are workers together with God. You should get up little praying circles all over the place, and cry to God perseveringly for Divine aid. Give him no rest until he establish and make Jerusalem a praise in this community. Remember, a Paul might plant and an Apollos water, but it took God to give the increase. If those holy men could not succeed, without God, what miserable headway we shall make without Divine assistance.

REMARKS.

1. God is ready for a revival. Prepare my way, says God, and I am ready to come. Behold I stand at the door and knock. God is at the door of this church knocking. Will you hear his voice, open the door, and let him in?

2. God waits for the church to get ready, and not the church for God. We frequently talk about waiting for God, as though we were ready, but he not. But the precise opposite is true. God is ready and waiting for us, and will bless us, as soon as we will repent and turn to him. To-day, he says, after so long a time, if ye will hear my voice harden not your hearts. Will you hear his voice to-day? He waits to be gracious. What a long time you have put him off, by refusing to come to your duty. Will you put him off still?

3. God cannot revive his work until the church will repent and come up to his help, without altering his plan. God's plan is to combine human and divine agency in saving the world. That is a work he has appointed for the church and the ministry to

do, and he never will do that for them, nor carry on the work without them. I am not saying what he could do, but what he does not and will not do. He has put the Bible into the hands of the church, and commanded her to give it to the world. That work he never will do for her. She can let the world live without it, but he will hold the church responsible for the neglect. He has commanded her to preach the Gospel to the entire world, and he will not do this work for her. She is to use means to convert men, and promote a general revival throughout the world, but he will not use those means for her. When she will come up to his help and do her part of the work, and look to him for help and to add his blessing, he will do it. This is his plan and he will not change it, nor work in any other way. If this is not his plan, or if he would work without the church, why does he not give revivals to the heathen world, where there is no church and ministry? He does not do it. But let the ministry and church go there with the Bible to preach and pray and exhort them to repent, and God will open the windows of heaven and add his blessing, when they will do their duty and throw themselves upon his almighty arm for help.

This is the Gospel plan. God has seen fit in infinite wisdom to adopt it, and he will not change it. We may neglect our part of the work as we are voluntary agents, but God will hold us accountable.

4. If there is no revival in this place, the church will be responsible for it. I have shown you that God is ready to bless, if you as a church will repent and do your duty. Now what do you intend to do? You cannot throw off this responsibility. It is upon you. God has laid it there, and he will hold you to it, at your last account. This church may neglect her duty and live as she has done, but God will hold you strictly accountable for every soul that would be saved if you should come fully up to his help. Will you repent and take hold of this work, or will you sleep on and go to the judgment covered all over with the blood of the lost; with the blood of that husband, wife, child, or neighbor on your hands and garments? How can you meet them there and meet your judge? What a moment that will be to your soul! Will you go home and get on your knees and tell God what you will do? If you say you will not repent, tell him so. If you are determined to sleep on and go to the judgment, and risk it, tell God so, on your knees. If you say you will repent and come up to his help, tell him so honestly and ask his help. How God is watching around your hearts just now. Watching for your decision. Will you come up to his help? Remember, as you leave this house, God speaks to you in my text and says, "PREPARE YE THE WAY OF THE LORD."

II.

LUKEWARMNESS.

So then because thou art lukewarm, and neither cold nor hot, I will spew thee out of my mouth.—*Rev.* iii. 16.

I. THE THREE STATES OF HEART, VIZ: 1. COLD. 2. HOT. 3. LUKEWARM.

The Bible is a spiritual mirror into which the human family may look and learn the true state of their hearts. A correct knowledge of one's self is vastly important. It is a preparation of heart that is absolutely essential to fit an individual to come to Christ; no one ever comes to Christ without it; and notwithstanding this is true, how few seek or even desire it. So far from seeking it, there are multitudes in the church who will hate, fight, and resist that kind of preaching which is calculated to give them a true knowledge of themselves. They choose self-deception in preference to a correct knowledge of their own hearts. These remarks may look extravagant to some, but a thorough acquaintance with men will convince any individual of their truthfulness. Pause for a moment, my hearer, and think. What an exhibition of the wickedness of the human heart is here presented.

A being created in the image of God; capable of knowing, loving, and adoring him forever, in which case he would be a fit companion of angels and all the holy ones on high, not only deliberately sins and renders his character detestable and loathsome in the sight of all good beings, but then settles down in a state of heart where he is unwilling to know himself, unwilling to look at his own wickedness, and unwilling to see it as it is. He will voluntarily close up every avenue of his soul against all light that is calculated to give him a faithful view of his dark heart and rush on to ruin. What suicidal work! How deliberately such a being fights against his own best interest, and destroys his own happiness! There are many in this congregation, doubtless, who will be ready to exclaim, that is not my case. Take care, my hearer, you may be the very man God is describing in my text. You think because you have not been guilty of this, that, or the other outbreaking sin, and because you do not resist and fight the light on such points, you are about right.

You point to these great sinners, and you think they are loathsome sure enough; such beings ought to be damned, in your estimation. Now, while you are pointing to such sinners, and hating and pouring forth your bitter denunciations of them, you may be harboring in your breast a state of heart far more hateful in the sight of God than all their abominations. The text brings to light a state of heart that God abhors above all others. So he affirms. " I would," says God, " that ye were cold or hot." The men guilty of these outbreaking sins are the cold ones, as we will soon show; and God here affirms that he prefers even that state to the *lukewarm* state. Lukewarm individuals are not guilty of outbreaking sins. They have put away all such things, and are peculiarly bitter against such sins. They are right, in their own estimation, as the connection of my text will show. Let us hear them give a description of their hearts. They may speak for themselves. The very individuals to whom God addressed the language of my text, bear the following testimony in relation to their hearts : " Because thou sayest," says God, " I am rich, and increased with goods, and have need of nothing; and *knowest not that thou art wretched, and miserable, and poor, and blind, and naked."*

This is the testimony of lukewarm hearts concerning their own state, and God has put it on record that they may know themselves, if they will take the pains to look into the perfect law of liberty that exhibits all hearts in their true light. It reflects no false view of man, it is a perfect mirror, and through its teachings we may learn our true state, if we will. But the lukewarm professor is the last being to learn his true state. He is in imminent danger of being spewed out of the mouth of God, and he knows it not. He does not wish to know it. He will not look at the passages which describe his heart; or if he does, he will apply them to some other person. I am rich and increased in goods, is his language. *I* am right, I am doing *my* duty. But those great sinners, how he hates and denounces them. He would hurl them all to hell, if he had it in his power.

Poor, loathsome, self-righteous wretch! How God abhors you, and is on the point of vomiting you up, and you know it not! Sin has strangely blinded your eyes, so that you do not know yourself. Come, you lukewarm church-member, *wake up*, WAKE UP, and look at yourself. Look quick, and upon your knees, repent before your doom overtakes you. The imagery in this text is impressive. Let us turn our attention to it for a moment.

The literal thing referred to is water in three stages: cold, hot, and lukewarm. If you take water into the stomach in a cold state, it will receive it without loathing; so also in a hot state. But if you reduce it to a middle or lukewarm state, the stomach will not receive it without loathing, and perhaps vomiting. Now for the application of this impressive imagery. As your stomach loathes lukewarm water, says God, so my heart loathes and hates a lukewarm professor in the church. As your stomach vomits up or throws off the water, so, says God, I will spew out of my mouth such a church or church-member, unless he repent.

The text brings to light three distinct states of religious feeling, one of which only is pleasing to God. There is a state of feeling described by the term cold, another by the term hot, and another by the term lukewarm. The state of feeling described by the term cold, God hates; that described by the term hot, he loves and admires. This is the temperature of the hearts in heaven; they are in the hot state. Their hearts flow out in supreme love to God, and equal love to each other. But that state of heart described by the term lukewarm, God abhors above all others. This is right. Who would not abhor such a being? Everybody despises a fence-man. God wants beings to take ground somewhere, and every honest man will do it. This striving to strike hands with God and the Devil at the same time, and being on good terms with both, God cannot and will not endure. God has no fellowship with the Devil, and he abhors those who will fellowship him. If you want the Devil, says God, take the Devil, and be open about it. But if you want me, take me; but take me with all your heart. "Choose you whom you will serve. If the Lord be God, serve him; if Baal, serve him."

I will now call your attention to these three distinct states of mind, to help you to ascertain your true position. Will you be honest, look evidence full in the face, and decide correctly? A wrong decision, even under this sermon, may prove fatal to you. How important that you know your whereabouts. God help you, by the Holy Ghost, to see your heart as you will see it at the judgment.

I. WE WILL COMMENCE WITH THE COLD STATE.

Here are two opposite states of heart, or religious feeling, forming a perfect contrast,— the one decidedly for God, the other as decidedly against him. The cold state is that state of heart which leads the individual to take decided ground against the Christian religion. We will notice a few developments of his heart, that we may understand his true position.

1. Then I remark, that the individual in this state of heart hates the Bible. He is not indifferent about the Bible; far from it. He is awake in relation to that book. His whole heart comes out in opposition to it. A single case, as it took place in Vermont, will illustrate this state of mind. An individual who was under conviction, but whose heart was still in open hostility to God, sat reading his Bible in his room one day, and, while thus reading, he became so offended with its truths that he hurled it into the fire, sprang to his feet and exclaimed, " I will not read such a book!" Now the state of heart that man was in, when he hurled the Bible into the fire, was the cold state. This cold state does not always manifest itself in such a violent fit of rage, but the person in this state of heart has a settled opposition to the Bible. He does not like

its doctrines, nor its government. He dislikes the God of the Bible, the Saviour of the Bible, the whole system of salvation as there revealed; and he will manifest that opposition at times, and thus hang out his heart, so that no one can mistake his true position.

2. An individual in this cold state hates also the preaching of the Gospel. He is not indifferent about the preaching of the Gospel, any more than he is about the Bible. When he hears the Gospel he is awake, all awake. He will hate, fight, and abuse the ministry who preach it; perhaps leave the house in a rage when it is faithfully presented, and pour out his hostility and hatred of the Gospel all over town. Nothing stirs up his whole heart like a clear, faithful sermon.

3. A man in this cold state hates revivals. He is not an idle spectator in times of the special outpouring of the Holy Spirit. He is aroused, and bestirs himself, and you will hear from him. He wishes to put down these excitements; he does not believe in them. The people are all going crazy. It is a species of priestcraft, or a mere proselyting course resorted to by the ministry to make converts to their sect. He cries out "excitement," when he is more excited than anybody in the place, perhaps. He will pitch into the ministry and the church, and abuse them in unmeasured terms. Mark such individuals, and write "cold," in relation to religion, all

over them. I could multiply evidences and illustrations of this state of heart; but I forbear, and will only add that they hate all the duties and requirements of religion. The more they see of it, and are brought in contact with it, the more they hate it.

II. WE WILL EXAMINE THAT STATE OF RELIGIOUS FEELING DESCRIBED BY THE TERM HOT.

This state of heart is pleasing to God, as we have already remarked. All that is necessary to understand this state of feeling, is to take the precise opposite of the one we have examined.

1. The man in the cold state, I remarked, hates the Bible; the one in the hot state loves it. It is dearer to him than all other books on earth. He can honestly exclaim, in the language of the Psalmist, "Oh, how love I thy law! Sweeter also than honey and the honeycomb." He loves its doctrines and he loves its duties. He loves its promises and he loves its threatenings, because he believes them just and right; necessary to guard and protect God's authority and the rights of the universe. He loves the God it describes and the Saviour it reveals. Its system of mercy captivates and fires up his whole soul; and, as he contemplates its beauties, he is ready to join with the angels who sung over the plains of Bethlehem, and cry "GLORY TO GOD IN THE HIGHEST, AMEN AND AMEN!" He does not receive the New Testament as of Divine authority, and reject the Old, nor select this, that, or

the other portion as Divinely inspired, and reject other portions of it as not Divinely inspired. He is no such an inconsistent, half-way, absurd infidel, for such infidels are the most inconsistent on earth. The Old and New Testaments are so linked together that you cannot receive the one, and reject the other, as every thinking man who has investigated that question very well knows. They mutually prove each other, and must stand or fall together.

The truth is, you must receive or reject the Bible *as a whole,* and the man in the state of heart I am now considering, receives it as a whole. He has no wish to dispense with any part of it, not even with one of its doctrines. He binds it to his heart as God Almighty's lamp, put into his hands to guide his feet through this dark world to heaven, and he would suffer the loss of all things earthly, sooner than be deprived of it.

2. The individual in this state of heart loves the preaching of the Gospel. He, too, is not an indifferent hearer of the Gospel? He is moved by it. He is all ear, all awake when he listens to the faithful unfolding of this grand system of salvation. I have frequently heard men in this state of mind exclaim, " Oh, how I was delighted with that sermon! I could have sat there all night, and heard that man preach." It was not a captivating manner that delighted him, but it was the bringing out, expound-

ing and unfolding the great but simple truths of the Gospel, in a clear and forcible manner. This it was that fired up his soul, and made it glow and burn like the heart of an angel, for the time being. Do such beings want the theatre, or some wonderful scientific lecture to amuse them? Give them the Gospel, and they are captivated with it. It is food to their souls. Give them the Gospel, and they can dwell upon its truths endlessly.

All the theatres and scientific lectures on earth cannot charm and delight them like the Gospel. They love its duties. They love its terms, and have no wish to alter them. They love it because it is God's Gospel. It is his plan to save men. They love it because it is right, and because it unfolds in a striking light God's great heart of love and compassion for this fallen world.

3. The individual in this state of mind loves revivals.

Revivals are the result of the outpouring of God's Spirit, applying and making the Gospel effectual upon the hearts of men. The Spirit convinces men of sin, and leads them to cry out in bitterness of soul, as on the day of Pentecost, "What must I do to be saved?" Under this convincing, moving, melting influence, the sinner flies to Christ for pardon and salvation, and the Spirit renews and fits the soul for heaven, and fills it with joy unutterable, in many instances. This is the crowning work of the Gospel. There is joy in heaven at such times. Angels and saints above rejoice. Our Saviour informs us that " there is joy in heaven over one sinner that repenteth." The true saints on earth rejoice. " Wilt thou not revive us again," says the Psalmist, "that thy people may rejoice in thee?" Hearts in this hot state beat in unison with hearts on high. In heaven they praise God when sinners are converted. Professed Christians on earth, who have the spirit and temper of Heaven, will do the same. Let them but learn that God is converting sinners around them, and their souls are on fire, at once. They would gladly unite with the angels in giving glory to God for this grand exhibition of divine love. They are moved at such times, but they move in harmony with God and his angels. They are moved by just the opposite spirit that moves the hearts of those in a cold state. Cold hearts are moved to hate, denounce and do all in their power to put down revivals, while individuals in the hot state are moved to love, rejoice in and do all they can to help forward revivals. In a word, hearts in this state love all the duties of the Christian religion, and are deeply enlisted in the work of bringing the world to Christ.

III. WE COME NOW TO CONSIDER THE LUKEWARM STATE.

There are multitudes at this day, in our churches, who are in this state of mind. They know it not because they will not examine their hearts and be faithful to themselves. They are cases difficult to be reached. They are in a dangerous state. They will be damned unless they can be aroused. God will spew them out of his mouth into hell, unless they repent. They will wake up amid its burning embers, and feel the pangs of the second death, while the smoke of their torment will ascend up on high. You who are before me at this hour, and whose ear I am addressing at this moment, and who fill seats in this sanctuary from Sabbath to Sabbath, may be the individuals whom God is addressing in this part of my subject. Unless you can be awakened speedily, you may know, by sad experience, the fearful import of these words, " I WILL SPEW THEE OUT OF MY MOUTH." Pause, my hearer, for this once; be candid for a season, and put the question home to your heart, *Is this my state?* Look close, weigh the evidence I will now present of the lukewarm state, and decide your case in the light of truth, and decide for eternity.

1. Then, I remark, one of the first steps into this state of mind is a stationary, or stand-still state. The very first step is, coming to a dead-stand in religious growth. To help you to understand what I mean by this language, a few remarks in explanation will be necessary.

The view the Bible gives of the living, faithful child of God, who lives in the daily discharge of his duty is this. He is always taking advanced ground in piety. You do not find him to-day where he was yesterday, nor this week where he was last, but advancing on the heavenly road. If he does his whole duty, he will be rising higher and higher in piety every hour. Take a few Bible illustrations on this point. Prov. iv. 18: "But the path of the just is as the shining light, that shineth more and more unto the perfect day." Let us dwell on this passage for a moment. What is the literal thing referred to? It is the sun rising in the morning. Most or all of you present, have been out in the morning before daylight. As the sun was about to make its appearance on this part of the earth, where we reside, the first visible indication of the fact was a little glimmering of light in the eastern portion of the heavens. As you watched, you noticed that that light increased and spread over the whole heavens until the sun was fully visible, and even then the light increased in power until it passed on to the meridian. This is the literal thing, or the shining light referred to. Now the path of the just resembles this shining light. Where is the man when he is first converted? The light in his soul is like that little glimmering of light in the eastern horizon, compared with what it will be, if he will live so as not to grieve the Spirit, and drive God away from his heart. His light will increase and increase as he travels the whole length of the heavenly road, until he is caught up to the third heavens, and stands basking under the full blaze of the light of the Sun of Righteousness, around the throne of God and the Lamb.

But let us take another view of this passage, which perhaps will make this matter a little more clear. "THE PATH OF THE JUST." Let me suppose for a moment that the broad aisle before me is *the path of the just.* On either side is midnight darkness, while the broad aisle itself is illuminated. At this end, however, the light is dim compared with the other. From this to the other, over every inch of ground you pass, the light increases as you advance. Now let a man start at this end where the light is dim, and keep advancing with good eyes, wide open, what will be the necessary result? He will find the light increasing as he advances.

Suppose he complains that he has no more light now than he had a few moments ago. What is his position? Why he is in the stand-still state.

You next hear him complaining that the light is diminishing. Where is he now? He is sliding back; or, to use the Bible term, backsliding.

At length he exclaims, "I am all in midnight darkness." Where is he now? He has wandered entirely out of the path, on either side of which is midnight. Now, my hearer, in the light of this imagery, where are you? Can you look up to God and say without hypocrisy, my light has been constantly increasing ever since I was first converted? If you should speak the honest truth would you not be constrained to say, I have no more light and love to God's cause than I had a month, a year, or two years ago? Or is your case still worse and more alarming? If you own the whole truth, perhaps you would exclaim, Oh! that I loved God, the Sabbath, the Bible, the prayer-meeting, and the souls of men as well as I did when I was first converted. Now stop, my hearer, and be honest for a moment. Is not this last position precisely yours? Look up to God solemnly and deny it if you can. You dare not do it. Oh, STOP, STOP, you are the man! "*I will spew thee out of my mouth*," says God. Think of these awful words. They are not fulfilled yet. God is merciful and long-suffering, which is the reason we are not consumed. Use this moment to confess this awful state of heart which God hates, and fly to Christ for forgiveness at once.

2. Another evidence of a lukewarm state is this. You keep up the form of prayer, but get no answer. It is possible that there are some before me who neglect even the form. That such are in this fearful state of mind no sane man can doubt. They may be so stupid that no sermon can reach them; but remember, my precious friend, the agonies of the second death will arouse you; — but we will not stop with such here. The class I am now describing keep up the form of prayer,

and satisfy themselves with the form. They receive no answer and do not expect it. They would be amazed if God should answer their prayers. They have lived for months and even years, perhaps, without an answer to prayer. Now I affirm that it is the privilege of the living Christian, not only to pray, but to pray so as to have God hear and answer his supplications. This is his daily privilege, if he will live so as not to grieve the Spirit. If an answer is withheld, and we do not get access to God so as to be refreshed while we pray, the fault is ours and not God's. The language of God to all in a right state is this: "Every one that asketh receiveth, and he that seeketh findeth. Whatsoever things ye desire when ye pray, believe that ye receive them and ye shall have them." These passages, the living, spiritual child of God, believes. He looks for and expects an answer, and is grieved and distressed if it is withheld. If we have no access to God, and an answer is withheld, the fault is ours as I have remarked above. So God affirms: "Mine arm is not shortened that I cannot save, neither is mine ear heavy that I cannot hear," but "your iniquity has separated between you and your God." Individuals in this loathsome, lukewarm state grieve the Spirit, and God withdraws from them. He will not hear the prayer offered by a heart while in this state. It is a mere form of words with no unction, no soul in them. It is a drawing nigh to God with the lips while the heart is far from him. Now, my brother or sister, how is it with you on this point? Is this evidence against you? Look God in the face now and answer this question honestly. He is here looking into your heart. What do you say to your Maker; are you guilty or not guilty? When did you get an answer to prayer? When was your last refreshing from the presence of the Lord, — in that closet, at that family altar, or in the prayer-meeting? Are the heavens brass over your head? Is that soul full of darkness, barrenness and leanness? If so, that settles the question. Your lukewarmness has separated between you and your God. Will you be honest and own all to God, and repent?

3. A third evidence of a lukewarm state is found in a class of individuals who satisfy their consciences by barely praying for a revival, or for the conversion of the world. They seldom speak to a sinner personally about his salvation. Now a heart that prevails with God in prayer, and is deeply in earnest for the salvation of men, will not be satisfied with simply praying for sinners. His feeling will be so intense that he will wish to lay hold of them and pull them out of the fire. He will feel he must open his mouth for God, and speak to the sinner and reason with

and try to prevail upon him by argument and entreaty to flee from the wrath to come. Sinners expect this, if we believe them in danger, and they have a right to expect it. Said a young lady to me, where I was laboring in a revival, "I cannot believe my father is a Christian, although he stands high in this church." I replied, "Madam, what makes you doubt your father's piety, we have great confidence in him as a child of God." She returned this answer at once: — " If my father was a Christian, would he not speak to me about my soul's salvation, and show me the way of life? I have been anxious for weeks, and have longed for some one to speak to me and teach me how to become a Christian."

In another place a prominent sinner was converted, and almost the first prayer he offered for the church, he besought of the Lord to cure the church in that place of the lockjaw. "Lord," said he, in addressing the Deity, "this church have the lockjaw so that they cannot speak to us poor sinners and invite us to Christ." What a prayer! How impressive, when we look at the state of things in our churches!

Now when Christians are awake and full of compassion for souls, they will not only pray in earnest for the salvation of men but they will speak to them, and urge them to repent and turn to God. You cannot keep them still. The apostles and primitive

Christians *would* speak, and you could not silence them until you hushed their voices in death. All the prisons on earth could not seal up their lips.

Now point me to a man who lives and associates with sinners for months together, without a word for Christ, and I will point you to a lukewarm man.

4. Another evidence of lukewarmness is a man who is all talk but prays but little. Give such an one a chance to talk and he is on his feet. He loves to talk. He thinks he is wise and full of eloquence, and he loves to give the world an exhibition of it. Give him a chance to make a speech and he is ready. But when his speech is ended his duty is done, in his estimation. Now that is a lukewarm man, and he knows it not. If he was not lukewarm he would follow up his talk with agonizing prayer, and he would be in distress until the talk was made effectual by the accompanying influences of the Spirit.

5. Another evidence of lukewarmness is want of interest in revivals. The heart in this state will not openly oppose a revival perhaps, for it does not feel interest enough about them for that, neither does it feel interest enough to do much to promote them. Such an individual may attend meeting when that will not interfere too much with his worldly speculations and business plans. He may be willing to see the work go on, if it can be carried on by others. But

you call upon him to deny himself, break his heart and enter fully into the work himself, and you will soon see he has no heart for it. In his business matters he is awake and full of interest. He will go through any self-denial and hardship to accomplish his ends in money-matters, but has no heart to labor to save sinners. Our churches are filled up with such worldlings. God has a controversy with them for this want of interest in his cause, and he will make short work with them, unless they repent. I might multiply evidences of this state of heart yet for another lengthy sermon, but I must not weary your patience longer. I have already said enough to convict many of you, if you have made a self-application of truth. If not, the sermon is lost to you and the responsibility is on your soul and you must meet it soon.

REMARKS.

1. This text represents God as hating the lukewarm state even worse than that state of heart which is denominated cold, as we have already shown. Now there are good and sufficient reasons on the part of God for this feeling. God is a benevolent being and is seeking the highest good of his creatures. Whatever stands in the way of his securing that end he must hate. He would not be a good being if he did

not. That state of heart or course of conduct on the part of man, which throws the greatest obstacle in his way of securing this end, he must hate above all others.

Now the only obstacles that can lie in the way of God's securing the highest good of all is their sins. He cannot secure their highest good unless he can secure their holiness. When there is sin in the heart, that sin must be removed, or the good of that individual must be sacrificed. There is but one way to remove sin. The individual must be led to see and repent, and fly to Christ for its removal. That state of heart therefore, which renders it the most difficult to show an individual his sins and lead him to Christ, is the worst possible state a person can be in to endanger his highest good, and God must hate it above all others. Now let us see if this is not true of the lukewarm state. This state of heart is peculiarly a delusive state, as we have already seen. The individual in this state is resting on a false hope. To save a man who is resting on a false hope, you must tear away that hope, every vestige of it, or you cannot save him. This is very difficult, if he is in the state of heart we are now examining. He is very confident he is right now. I am rich, he says, and increased in goods. I am doing my duty. I am in the way to heaven. In this he is very confident. He is deceived in relation to his state of heart. He is also deceived in relation to his future prospects, and he knows it not. He is wrong and still he thinks he is right. He is in the way to hell, while he thinks he is in the way to heaven. What state of heart can be more alarming. How very, *very* difficult it is to reach such cases. Reached however they must be and their delusion broken up, or they cannot be saved. If they were guilty of some outbreaking sin which they detest and abhor, they could not maintain a hope for an hour. They are in a state of heart still more alarming, and which God abhors even more than the cold state, and yet they will cling to a hope which will be their ruin, and dream on in their delusion, doubtless, until the flames of hell flash in their faces, and the fires of the pit break up their dreams of heaven, and scatter them to the winds, when it will be too late to repent. Now what state of heart could be worse? Why should not God and every good being hate it above all others?

Again, this state of heart stupefies the soul and renders it unfeeling. The most interesting truth and the most solemn appeals will not move such hearts. They can sit in God's sanctuary, when the Gospel is breaking upon their ears, and doze away such precious moments; or, if awake, they can, while Mercy is speaking through the minister's lips and calling them to repentance, be revolving over in their minds their worldly speculations, and laying their plans for the week, before the minister has closed another message for them to meet at God's bar, and then pass from the place of worship without a conscience to reprove, and hearts as unfeeling as marble. Such stupidity, such death, is always alarming. That man who is aroused by truth, even if he fights it, shows that he has some sensibility left, and there is hope in his case. But this dead, unfeeling state, where the truth cannot arouse up any feeling of any kind, is the worst of all. This is the state about which God is complaining in the text, — neither *cold* nor *hot*. No feeling, no sensibility left. Can't be moved. Why should not God abhor such a state, if he loves the good of his creatures?

Again, the influence and example of such individuals lead more to hell than any other class. Fifty sinners will fall into the wake of one such churchmember, sooner, in my estimation, than one will be led astray by the example of an openly wicked man. Such an example is just what the wicked would demand. There are two antagonistic principles in the breast of every sinner. The sinner has a conscience that demands that he should have some kind of religion. You cannot satisfy the demands of his nature without it. He also has a heart that hates true godliness. Now he wants a religion that will compromise the matter between these two contending principles of his nature. Give him that and he will go in for it. Offer that kind to the impenitent world and how quick there will be a rush to embrace it. Now the example of the lukewarm man is just the thing the sinner wants. He has a form of godliness without the power. The form partially satisfies his conscience while in health, and the power of godliness that offends his heart is left off. There, says the sinner, is the Christian to suit me. He is a member of the church, is a moral man, and doubtless is in the way to heaven. If I imitate him, and do not join the church, I shall be saved. Joining the church is a mere form that does not amount to anything. That man is not a fanatic. He keeps his religion to himself. He is not always urging it upon others, and troubling them with it. Let the church be filled up with such men and we will not object to such a religion.

Now multitudes will walk in the footsteps of such church-members, indulging at the same time a secret hope that they shall reach heaven by so doing. You will frequently hear them exclaim, "After all, we do not see as there is much difference between the church and the world." Of course there is not much difference between such church-members and the world. They are all travelling one road and that is the road to hell. The main difference is this,— the church-members are taking the lead, and, by their example, leading the rest down to perdition.

Now remember, you lukewarm man in this church, you are just in a position that gives you an influence to lead men to destruction, and every moment you live in this state of mind you are using it for that end, whether you design it or not. This forms another reason why God abhors your state of heart. It is doing such immense mischief to others, as well as yourself, he must abhor it. What an account you will have to render when these sinners, who are walking in your footsteps, meet you at God's great tribunal. Now will you persist in this state of mind and meet this fearful responsibility?

Finally, let me remark, and draw this lengthy sermon to a close, any individual in this congregation, who is in this state of heart to-day, must repent or be damned.

To hope for heaven in this state of mind is the height of presumption. The liar, the thief, the drunkard's prospects for heaven are just as good as yours. The very language of the text settles that question. The individual in this state of heart is so loathsome that God cannot endure him in the church on earth. Think you he will spew him out of his mouth, and then take this loathsome being right into the church triumphant, and give him a place among the holy ones on high, to be an eternal loathing to them? The very thought is the height of absurdity. What could he do there? It would be no heaven to him. The fire, the zeal, the burning, glowing love of those hearts on high, would annoy and make him all but infinitely wretched.

There is no harmony between his state of heart

and the state of things in that heavenly world. God, angels, and the saints on high would all loathe him. He would be a nuisance in heaven. He would loathe himself amid its eternal flashes of light, that would reveal to him the abominations of his heart. He would long to leap from its lofty battlements into the burning gulf of hell, and hide himself away amid the smoke of the pit, rather than meet the gaze and scorn of those holy ones, who would utterly detest and hiss him from their presence.

Now, my brother, or sister, in the light of this sermon, what say you? Are you in this state of mind? Have you been honest in trying yourself by these evidences? Do they convict you? If so, remember your hope of heaven is a delusion, unless you repent.

I will repent *some time?* Ah! remember that resolution has ruined thousands. Before *sometime* comes you may be dead and damned. God does not command you to repent sometime. He commands you to repent NOW. Will you do it? God help you to do it at once. Do you say I will, I will. AMEN.

III.

IDLENESS.

Why stand ye here all the day idle? — *Matt.* xx. 6.

1. DEFINITION OF TERMS IN THE TEXT. 2. IDLENESS INCONSISTENT WITH DUTY, AND FRAUGHT WITH GUILT. 3. WHY WE ARE IDLE. 4. CHRIST DEMANDS A REASON FOR SUCH CONDUCT.

These words are taken from one of the parables of our Saviour, all of which are designed to convey some practical instruction to the mind. In discoursing from this portion of divine truth, it will be my object to draw out the practical lesson it is designed to communicate. The state of things condemned and rebuked by this question is the idle or do-nothing state. There are many in our churches in this state, and still they maintain a comfortable hope of heaven. They do nothing to save men, and they never expect to. Many of them never led a soul to Christ in their lives. They think that work belongs mainly to ministers. They love to see the work go on, they say; but call upon them to break their hearts and go out and weep on the pathway of the sinner, and try and win him over to God, and they have no heart for such work.

Christ puts this question directly to the consciences of such individuals: — "Why stand ye here all the day idle?" Why? says Christ; what reason have you to offer for such neglect of your duty? I converted you and sent you into this vineyard to work. You sit down in idleness and neglect my work. Why, your Redeemer demands, do I find this field, committed to your charge, uncultivated? I appointed you to attend to this business. Now look, says he, at this rank growth of the weeds of sin and error springing up all around you, and not an effort on your part to subdue and uproot them. Why do you thus betray your trust and the confidence reposed in you? What is your excuse for this neglect? Have you any? If so, let us hear it. Are you dumb with silence? Does your conscience thunder "guilty"? Are you covered with shame? Then repent, — confess the past, — up and at the work. Redeem the time, — work while the day lasts. Gird on your armor, and fight the good fight until called home to your reward.

In considering this truth further, let me, I. Define one or two of the terms in the text. II. Show that this idleness is inconsistent, and deeply fraught with guilt. III. Call attention to the question WHY we are idle. IV. Christ demands a *reason* for such conduct.

I. THEN I AM TO DEFINE TWO OF THE TERMS IN

THIS TEXT. 1. The term day. What are we to understand by this term when we take its spiritual application to us? I remark, we are not to understand by it the term of twenty-four hours. That is not its spiritual, practical meaning here. By the term day, we are to understand the day of our probation. Each man has a probationary day. The Bible uses the term in this sense in some instances. Take a case from John ix. 4: "I must work the works of him that sent me while it is day; the night cometh when no man can work." The meaning is this: I must do up the work of him that sent me during my lifetime or probationary day, for the night cometh; the night of death will overtake me, when no man can work. No man can do the work that was assigned him to do during his probation day when death comes. The work of time must be done in time, or not at all. Why, says Christ, let all your probationary day run to waste? There is a work to be done during this day that is as weighty and important as eternity. Your happiness for the endless future that lies before you is suspended upon your faithful performance of this work. Why, then, idle it away? Its moments are precious and rapidly flying. Its last one will soon come. Death stands before the door. Wake up, shake off this idleness, and improve these precious hours as they pass.

2. What are we to understand by the term idle,

when we take the spiritual application of this text to us? 1. We are not to understand by it that an individual is destitute of a worldly employment. A man may have a worldly avocation, and pursue it with great diligence three hundred and sixty-five days in the year, and still be an idler in the sense this term is used here, when we take its spiritual meaning. Wicked men generally have their business plans and modes of making money, and they pursue them with great zeal; but still they are idlers, all idlers. The work which this text demands they have uniformly neglected. God has invited and urged them to it from their childhood up, but they have closed their ears against all his entreaties, and persistently pursued their own chosen way. They are determined to do their own work first, no matter what becomes of God's; and as to his demands, they are determined to have their own way, let the consequence be what it will. 2. By an individual being idle, then, we are to understand this: Whenever you find a person, either in the church or out of it, doing nothing, directly or indirectly, to save his own soul or that of his fellow-man, he is an idler. One word upon the thought directly or indirectly, so that you will understand my meaning. That merchant behind his counter, that farmer following his plough, or that mechanic in his shop, may be laboring indirectly to convert the world to God. In pursuing their daily employments, it is the purpose of their hearts to accumulate means to support their families, and train them up for God, and, over and above that, to support the Gospel at home and abroad, and help forward the great benevolent movements of the day, which have for their object the subduing of the world to Christ, and filling it with the knowledge of salvation. A brother at the West, who is now dead and gone to heaven, remarked to me, when living, " I do business not to accumulate wealth to lay up for my family, but to secure means to spread the Gospel. I cannot preach myself, but I will preach the Gospel by proxy as extensively as possible. Its truths are precious to me," said he, "and I wish I could give them to the whole world." *He* labored *indirectly* to save men. To labor *directly* to save men is to come in direct contact with the sinner's mind; to sit down and instruct him about Christ and the way of salvation ; to prevail upon him, if possible, by argument and entreaty, to turn to God and live. You now have the meaning of this term. If there is an individual in this church who is doing nothing, directly or indirectly, to save his own soul or the souls of his fellow-men, he is an *idler*. God speaks from his throne to such, and says, " Why stand ye here *all the day* IDLE ? " Do you hear him, my brother? Hark! Oh, how he thunders this question upon your guilty soul! You idler, what have you done the past year to lead men home to God?

Sinners all around are sinking to hell, and to whom have you raised a warning voice? What soul have you led to Christ? What soul have you tried to lead to Christ? Not one, do you reply? IDLER, IDLER! wake up and listen, while I proceed to show you your guilt.

II. I AM TO SHOW THE GUILT AND INCONSISTENCY OF THIS IDLENESS.

The guilt of doing nothing, or of inaction, is not trifling but great. When you take upon yourself the responsibility of refusing to act under certain circumstances, you assume a responsibility that is high and fearful. There is a neighbor's house wrapped in flames. He and his family are in the chambers asleep, and know not their danger. By lifting up your warning voice and flying to their relief, you can arouse and save them. But you deliberately fold your arms in the street, look on, see the building fall in over their heads and consume them. You do nothing. You are idle. You just refuse to act, that's all. Is there any guilt connected with your conduct? Can you plead innocence? Is not your guilt fearful? You are a murderer. The blood of that family is on your hands, and God and every good being will hold you strictly accountable for their death. You could have saved them, but refused to do it. You are a wicked *wretch*. You say, I did not know positively I could save them. What has that to do with the matter? Did you *try?* No. Then the responsibility is upon you, and you cannot shake it off. There is an assassin yonder who has assaulted a man and is beating him to death. Another stands by and sees him do up that bloody work. He could take him off and save the man's life, but he refused to do it. He looks on and sees his fellow-being murdered without a warning or an effort to save. What would you say concerning him? What would the community say? What would the law say? The law puts its hand upon him at once and arraigns him as accessary to the murder before the fact. Did *he* kill the man? No, he did nothing, he refused to act, he was an idler. His guilt under such circumstances is great. It is as visible as the light. The church seems to think that the guilt of inaction or idleness is trifling. But it is fearfully great. You are in this merciful world where sinners all around you are deciding the question whether they will be saved or damned. That question they decide here. You can do much, God helping you, towards prevailing upon them to decide that question right. Their happiness for a long eternity hangs upon their coming to a right decision. Now to be idle and refuse to act under such circumstances is wicked, supremely so.

Why stand ye here *idle,* says God, in this merciful world? These sinners at your side will soon be gnashing their teeth in hell, unless they repent. Why not speak and be in earnest? Work, says

God, while the day lasts. Can you refuse to work under such circumstances without guilt?

But let us look at this guilt a little more in detail. It is important that you have a clear view of it, or you never will repent of this idleness as you should.

1. Then, I remark, your guilt is apparent from the fact, that your time, which you are wasting, was purchased by the death of the cross. To make you see the full force of this remark, let me have your attention for a moment to the law under which our first parents were placed, immediately after their creation. God placed them in the garden of Eden, under the following law. Gen. ii. 16, 17: "And the Lord God commanded the man, saying, Of every tree of the garden thou mayest freely eat; but of the tree of knowledge of good and evil, thou shalt not eat of it; for in the day that thou eatest thereof, thou shalt surely die."

Please observe the language of this law. It does not say, if you eat of that prohibited fruit to-day, you shall die next week or next year, or a thousand years hence; "*but in the* DAY *thou eatest thereof thou shalt surely die.*" Here the question arises, What is meant by the death spoken of in this text? Was it the death of the body? I think not. The first you hear of the death of the body, was after the promise of a Saviour. It is in this language. Gen. iii. 19: "Dust thou art, and unto dust shalt thou return."

Death of the body was not introduced until after the merciful dispensation was introduced. It is a part of that dispensation, as I could show if I had time. It was introduced with that dispensation and will continue while it continues. Men, all men, come to the grave under this dispensation, and will, while it continues. When it closes up at the end of time, then comes the resurrection, which counteracts this death, and restores to each individual his body.

One thought settles the question with me, that the death of the body was not a part of the penalty of the moral law. The atonement of Christ opens the way for the penalty of the moral law to be set aside toward all who repent and comply with its terms. If the death of the body was a part of the penalty of the moral law, all who repent would be pardoned, and in that case the penalty of the law would not be executed, and their bodies would not die. Now we know that a man may repent, and still his body must go to the grave. The bodies of the penitent as well as the impenitent must die, which settles the question that it is not the penalty *for* sin, or the moral law. Was the death threatened upon our first parents spiritual death? I think not, for this reason: To make it spiritual death is to confound the act of transgression and the penalty *for* transgression, and make it one and the same thing. What is it to die spiritually? It is to die to holiness. The act of transgression was dying to holiness, or dying spiritually. God's threatening, according to that notion, is this.

If you transgress my law, and thus die spiritually, says God, you *shall* die spiritually. Or, it would be like this Government saying to the murderer, if you transgress the law and become a murderer, you shall be a murderer. Such nonsense is too glaring to be embraced by any thinking mind. The death threatened in the law under consideration, is a death to be inflicted *for* dying spiritually. Man had no *right* to die spiritually, and God threatens him with another kind of death, if he does die spiritually.

The question now returns, what is this death? I reply, it is the death of *soul and body* in hell, or eternal death. Had God executed the penalty of the law upon our first parents in the garden, he would have sent them soul and body to hell, from that hour. He would not have sent their bodies to the grave, and their souls to hell. He would have thundered the whole man to hell, soul and body. The whole man was engaged in the transgression, and the whole man would have suffered the penalty of the law. So it will be at the judgment, when he executes the penalty of the moral law upon the finally impenitent. He will not send the body to the grave and the soul to hell. He will send the soul and body, united, to hell, which will be the second death. Now this would have been true if God had executed the penalty of the moral law upon our first parents the day they sinned, according to its threatenings. Here let it be distinctly understood, that, at that hour, there was no posterity. Had the law been executed then, there would have been none. It is wholly inconsistent to suppose that the original pair would have been permitted to propagate their kind in the world of woe. In that case, Adam and Eve would have been the beginning, middle, and end of the human race. We should have had no existence. But the penalty *was not executed,* IT WAS LAID OVER, for the time being, to introduce Mercy's dispensation, to save rebellious man. Christ lays it over by his death, and he places man on a new probationary state under grace, where he regains the privilege of propagating his species, which he had lost by the fall, so that we get our very being through Christ. We are indebted to him therefore for our existence. Every moment we have on earth was purchased by his death. Now can we take these moments which were bought with blood, — the precious blood of the Son of God, — and waste them in idleness, without guilt? The moments we spend here to-day, and every moment of our lives, were purchased for us by the agony of the cross. To spend and waste them in idleness is to trifle with the blood of the Son of God. How can we do it without guilt as high as heaven! Think of it, you idlers in this church,— when you take your time to do your own work instead of God's, you are trifling with Christ's death. He bought your time with his blood, and he demands of you to use it for him.

2. This idleness is inconsistent in the member of a church, from the fact that, if he has ever been converted, he has had a glimpse of the worth of a soul. When you were under conviction, when the commandment came home and sin revived, and you saw yourself dead by the law, how infinitely valuable your soul seemed! Had you been sole proprietor of the globe, you would have given it all for the assurance from your Maker, that your soul should be finally saved. Now when you saw the worth of your own soul, you saw the worth of the soul of every man living. The soul of your neighbor is equally valuable with your own, which forms the reason why God commands us to love our neighbor as ourselves. To sit down in idleness after we have seen the worth of the soul, while we are in a world where there are souls to be saved, is conduct deeply inconsistent. This the sinner believes. Impenitent men have often declared to me, "If I believed what you professing Christians profess to believe, I would not rest, nor give my neighbors rest until they were in the kingdom."

3. Such conduct is inconsistent, from the fact that we have declared publicly that we love God's ser-

vice; and that it is dearer to us than anything of an earthly nature. After making such a declaration, to sit down in idleness is to give our professions the lie. " Actions speak louder than words." Our words proclaim one thing and our actions contradict it. The wicked look on and are confounded. They know not what to believe. I hate to call in question the sincerity and honesty of that church-member, says the sinner, but he certainly manifests more interest and zeal in almost anything else than in the subject of religion, which he *says* lays so near his heart. What shall I think, what must be my conclusion, if I judge him by his fruits? Such conduct on the part of church-members staggered me beyond measure when I was an impenitent sinner. It led me to doubt, very much, the reality of experimental religion. I felt that the religion of the church was a religion of the head and not of the heart. Such conduct on the part of the church is making infidels by thousands. All sceptical men refer to it, and stumble at this stumbling-stone. The things which the church professes to believe, says the infidel, if true, are calculated to stir the soul to its very depth, but where is the corresponding zeal and action? If I could see them as zealous and as much in earnest in religion as they are in politics or in making money, I should think them sincere. But go into their meetings, says he; how few there,— how cold and formal in their worship.

Is this the subject that is dearer to their hearts than anything else? Who can believe such hypocritical nonsense? This idleness in the household of faith places the church in just this unfavorable attitude before the world. It is making sceptics by the wholesale. It leads the world to doubt and call in question the sincerity of the church,—cripples and cuts off her influence for good over others, and is doing immense evil. How such conduct dishonors Christ! How can we meet our account for it? If we persist in such idleness, we shall come up to the final judgment covered all over with guilt and shame.

4. Your guilt is seen again, from the fact that you violate your own solemn pledges when you sit down in idleness. My brother, what did you promise God when you became a Christian? Did you not consecrate your whole being to him? Can a man become a child of God without? It is impossible. God never accepts any half-way consecration. You promised to give yourself away,—*wholly* away to him. But what does giving yourself away imply? What did you mean by that act? Did you mean by it that you gave yourself away to be an idler? Did you give yourself away to do your own work, and neglect his? God commands you to go into *his* vineyard, and work,—*not yours*. You promised to do it. Now if you are an idler, you have violated your own pledge.

Have you no regard for your word? What would you think of a fellow-being who would promise you over and over again he would work for you, and never redeem his pledge? You would say he is a man of no principle. He is not to be relied on. A worthless fellow. I want nothing to do with him. Now pause and think how many times you have promised God, secretly in your hearts, that you would wake up and be faithful! You promised him on your knees in prayer, and these pledges have all been broken, if you are an idler. Can you thus forfeit your own word, and take back your own consecration without guilt! But look again at your covenant when you joined the church. That was a public act,— a solemn agreement made with your Maker in the presence of witnesses. Please read over that written agreement on your knees when you get home. You stood up in God's house and gave your assent to it, and bound yourself in the most solemn manner to devote your whole being to God. What did you say to God? Read, my brother, and think. What *did* you say? "I do, now, in the presence of this assembly, avouch the Lord Jehovah to be my God." What does that mean? To take God as your God, is to take him as your king and lawgiver; and you take your place as a subject of his government, and fully commit yourself to do all his will. That is as it should be; that was taking your right position. What more did you promise God? You promised, moreover, to walk *in all his commandments and ordinances blameless*, until death. What can be more binding and solemn than such a public consecration of yourself to God? How have you kept that pledge; that written agreement with God? Are you an idler? If so, you have broken your covenant with your Maker, and your guilt has gone up on high. You covenanted with God not to be an idler, but to enter his vineyard, and labor and toil for him faithfully until death removed you to your seat above. What guilt there must be here! Your word forfeited, your written agreement violated, and you hastening to the judgment to settle up your account with God for this idleness! How can you meet him? Before you step up to that great reckoning-day, please read carefully Deut. xxviii. and see what God says about covenant-breakers; then cast your eye into old Jerusalem and see him carrying those threatenings into execution against that covenant-breaking nation. Now if God thus hates covenant-breaking, how can you escape his wrath unless you repent? If the guilt of the Jew was great, can yours be less, with all the increase of light the Gospel has shed upon your pathway? Think, you idlers in this church. This sin is upon you. You cannot deny it. Go into your closet, drop on your knees, raise your eyes to heaven, look God in the face and say to him, if you can, that you are not a covenant-breaker. You cannot do it. Your conscience thunders GUILTY, GUILTY.

5. Our guilt is manifest again from the fact that we are in a land of liberty. When I say we are in a land of liberty, do not misunderstand me. I am not ignorant of the fact that the Governments of the slave States are despotic; their liberty was dead and buried years ago. One essential thing that goes to make up liberty is the liberty of speech and the press. Whatever may be my honest convictions of truth, Liberty gives me the privilege of advocating those convictions with the tongue and pen, and also protects me, in doing it, from violence, imprisonment, and death.

She stands by and says, the only weapons that shall assail you shall be argument to meet argument, speech to meet speech. Let intellect grapple with intellect, truth with error, and if truth or error cannot stand such a conflict, such fair play, let them be vanquished and driven out of the community. Now despotism and error do not like such fair play for this intellectual warfare. When her arguments are exhausted she wants to resort to the fist, the pistol, the knife, the mob, the prison, and even death, if the tongue cannot be silenced without.

But, says one, you can go to the South and talk, if you will talk to suit the South. I can go to Rome and talk upon such conditions, and to any other despotic government under the whole heavens. Despots love to have you talk, if you talk to please them. They like your service of course. That is just the liberty of the South, no more and no less.

When that is the fact, Liberty is dead and buried, and mourners go about the streets. While this is true in a portion of this nation, there are other portions of it where we can preach, pray, print papers, tracts, and other documents, and circulate them broadcast through the community, with none to molest or make us afraid. What would the primitive ministry and church have accomplished, with the privileges we enjoy? They exposed themselves to torture and imprisonment, to persecution of the most malignant kind, and death in its most horrid forms, in spreading the Gospel and laboring to convert the world to God. If this idleness could be excusable under any circumstances, it would be under those in which they were placed. But had the church and ministry become idle, even under those circumstances, it would have been at the expense of their piety. What! Paul fold up his hands and become an idler? He would have become a wretched backslider and forfeited the smile and approbation of God by so doing. Hear him exclaim, "*Woe is unto me if I preach not the Gospel.*" Now if they would have been guilty and lost the favor of God, to have sat down in idleness, situated as they were, what must be our guilt, situated as we are? We can preach and hold meetings over a vast tract of country, in this land, with none to harm us. To leave this field uncultivated, to sit down in idleness under such circumstances, our guilt and sin must be extremely aggravating in the sight of God. It is not surprising that he hides his face while this sin is unrepented of.

6. The guilt of this idleness is great from the fact that our means and advantages for doing good are great.

God holds men accountable according to the means put into their hands for doing good. With this thought before the mind, let us look at a few things. 1. Our conveniences for travelling from place to place, to get access to the people, to give them the Gospel. The Apostles, if they wished to visit different cities and places by land, would start off on foot and make their way over the country as best they could. But how is it with us? A minister can preach in Cincinnati, Ohio, one evening, Columbus the next, Cleveland the next, Buffalo, N. Y., the next, Albany the next, New York City the next, then on successive evenings in Boston, Mass., Rutland and Burlington, Vt., and Montreal, Canada. Thus we can almost fly through the midst of heaven, having the everlasting Gospel to preach. If the efforts now making to navigate the atmosphere should prove successful, how that passage in Revelation will be almost literally fulfilled! 2. Look at your telegraphic facilities. A sermon may be preached in Boston to-day, and it will be in your next morning prints all over the country, and be read by thousands and even millions in a few hours. So with prayer. Our lips may utter a petition at the throne of the Infinite One, and the lightning wing and the press communicate it to a million of hearts in a few hours, so that thousands of amens, added to that petition, may come pouring into the ear of God from all parts of the land. In a short time it doubtless will be true that sermons delivered in this country on the Sabbath, can be read in London or Paris the next day. What a day is this! What opportunities to spread light and say to the world, " BEHOLD THE LAMB OF GOD." 3. But look again at your printing presses and your mails. Your presses can issue, daily, tons of sermons, tracts, religious papers, and other matter, which the mails can scatter through this whole land, and, in a very brief period, across the rolling ocean to other lands, and to the islands of the seas. Thus you can speak to the nations, and make your influence felt in the remotest corner of the earth, in a short time. Put the zeal and piety of Paul into the ministry and church, with such means of doing good in their hands, and how long do you think there would be a spot on earth destitute of the Gospel? How God is opening doors in all parts of the world for this mighty work. 4. There is wealth enough in the church to fill the world with the knowledge of eternal life, if she will only consecrate it to that end. With all this means of doing good in our possession, what must be the guilt of this idleness in the church, which lets a great share of the world lie in darkness, without being reached by the Gospel! What responsibility there is here! What guilt to meet the professed Church of Christ at the great reckoning-day!

7. Such idleness is guilty from the fact that death is dropping our friends by our side into eternity, and what we do to bring them to Christ, we must do quickly.

When we look around and behold the inroads death is making in our own family connections, how God in his providence is stirring us up to work! A few years since, I shook a father's hand, and left him in health. I have not seen him since. He has gone to his long home. I bade a brother good-by, — he is no more. Three brothers-in-law, — they are gone. Two sisters sleep in the grave. I saw a niece married on Thursday, and went to her death-bed on the following Thursday. I left a blessed, sainted wife on the Sabbath, comparatively well, though not able to attend church, and in the midst of my prayer, was called from the sacred desk to the death-bed scene, only in season to behold the clay tenement from which the spirit had just taken its flight. Now I put the question to myself: What does God mean by all this? WORK, WORK. He speaks by these providences. Work while the day lasts. If you have a word to say to that relative, utter it now.

If you have a prayer to offer for them, offer it soon. If you have a tear to shed upon their impenitent pathway, shed it at once, ere they are dead and lost.

Now, my hearers, let me request that you look into that family circle of yours. Are its ranks broken? Where is that father, mother, brother, sister, relative, friend? Are they missing? What does God mean by these providences? "Why stand ye here all the day idle," in this dying world? Your turn will come soon. Speak while you can. Labor while you have an opportunity. Death is doing up its work all around us. Labor for the salvation of the dying ones before they die.

III. I AM TO CALL YOUR ATTENTION TO THE QUESTION IN THE TEXT.

"*Why?*" says Christ. He here demands a *reason* for this conduct, an explanation, an excuse if you have any to offer.

When he puts a question like this, he expects an answer. To treat his questions with indifference, or silence, is an insult. You set your servant about a piece of work of vast importance to himself as well as to you, and you rely upon his attending to it. He wastes his time in idleness, or in attending to his own business when his time is lawfully yours, and you call him to an account. You put the question directly home to him. Why is this work of mine neglected? Is there any reasonable excuse for it? you demand. If there is, let us know it. He passes along and treats the question with indifference. He gives you no answer, no satisfaction whatever. How would you view his conduct? You would unhesitatingly pronounce it insulting in the highest degree. You would say, such treatment is unendurable. I will dismiss him from my employment forthwith.

Now, here is a question from your Saviour. It is put directly to you, and you must be cautious how you treat it. He has sent you into his vineyard to work. The work he requires you to perform is of vast importance to yourself, to the interests of his kingdom on earth. You have wasted your time in idleness, and neglected this work. In this question he demands a reason for this conduct. Why? says he; what have you to offer as an excuse? Now will you treat this question with indifference? Will you thus add to the sin of idleness the sin of insulting your Redeemer? What do you say? Bring on your strong reasons, if you have any. Christ is ready to listen to any reasonable explanation.

1. I will now mention some things that you cannot offer as reasons why you are idle.

2. I will then turn your attention to some things which are the causes of this idleness, and urge you to remove them, that Christ may no longer be grieved by this state of things in this church.

1. What you cannot offer as consistent reasons. You are not idle because there is no work to be

done. You begin to press up to duty a class of individuals in the church, and how quickly they will turn upon you with the question, What can I do? I lament this state of things about us, but I do not see as there is anything *I* can do to remedy it. So you pretend to be idle because, you say, there is nothing for you to do. Nothing for you to do? Stop, my brother or sister, and let me put a few questions directly to your conscience. If you will be candid and thoughtful, I am confident you will come to the conclusion that there is work enough for you to do. Let us begin with your heart. Is the work all done up there? Have you repented and put away every sin? Have you cultivated diligently every Christian grace in that soul? Do not deceive yourself. Look close here. That wicked heart will hide from your eye those sins, if you are not on your guard. Remember you cannot hide them from God's eye, and he will not forget or overlook them at the judgment. Unless you repent, they must come out there. Lift up your heart to God now, and plead for the illuminating influences of the Holy Spirit, to pour light into all the dark corners of your soul, and help you to see it as it is. Search now; is there no sin there, no selfishness, no pride, no self-conceit, no deception, no envy nor jealousy, no love of the world nor dishonesty, no disposition to draw money out of your neighbors without rendering an honest equivalent, no want of truthfulness, no peevishness nor irritability there, no want of interest in reading the Bible, and prayer? Is the soul in full sympathy with Christ in his great work of saving men? Are you more anxious to save men than to make money? In a word, is that soul of yours all ripe for heaven? Are you ready to die just as you are, without a moment to repent of the past? If not, there is work to be done in your own heart,— work that must be done, or you are lost, — work that no being can do for you. Do you ask what can I do? Do up the work in *your* heart, and then I will point you to something further.

But let us suppose for a moment that the work is all done up with you, and you are ready for heaven; could you then say, I am idle because there is nothing to be done? How is it with your family? are they all ready for heaven? How many of them, think you, would sing in glory, if God should take them all to eternity, just as they are? If one flash of lightning should kill them all now, how many of them would you expect to meet on high? Do not let your desire that they should be saved deceive you here, and lead you to indulge a hope for them when there is no ground for it. Look at the matter soberly; are they ready for heaven? If not, there is work at your own hearthstone,—work that you should not neglect. There may be some stumbling-blocks you ought to remove before you or any other being can lead that family to Christ. Have you prayed with, and exhorted them to come to the Saviour? Have you lived before them as you should? If not, that may be the reason why your minister here cannot lead them into the kingdom. Will you go home and begin that work? Do not ask, what can I do? while there is work in your own house that you are neglecting. But if all the work were done up in your house, could you then say, I am idle because there is no work to be done?

Look through your neighborhood, and over the community where you reside. Is there no work here? Are they all ready for heaven? What portion of them even profess to have hopes in Christ? What portion of that number have any just grounds to hope? The great mass here are in the road to hell, and if ushered by an earthquake into God's presence in twenty-four hours, how few would be saved! Look at the want of reverence for God and his Gospel, and the general stupidity on the subject of religion! How few think of God and their eternal interests! Surrounded by such a state of things, and idle because there is no work to be done! Here is work which would interest an angel, and call forth his whole heart to bring this people to Christ.

But we will suppose for a moment that this whole community is safe; that they are all sealed by the Holy Spirit of promise and on their way to heaven; could you say even then, I am idle because there is no work to be done? Glance your eye through this county, state, and nation, what do you behold? Mark the Sabbath-breaking, the profanity, the drunkenness, licentiousness, rowdyism, theft, murders, forgetfulness of God and everything of a serious nature. See how atheism, infidelity, and error in all its manifold forms, is lifting up its head and stalking abroad to poison and destroy the souls of men. Look at the slavery in our land; open your ear and listen to the groans of four millions of human beings who are robbed and spoiled evermore, and who are literally heathenized by this professed Christian nation. They call for your sympathy and help to deliver them from this house of bondage.

Look at your public men; see how they grasp at the reins of government in this land. What unrighteous means they will resort to, to secure the high places in the nation. With a very large share of them the question is not what is truth, what is just, what will secure the highest good of all classes in the nation; but what sentiments, if advocated, will best please the North and South so as to secure for me the greatest number of votes for president, senator, representative, governor, or judge; or advance me to some other station of power, where I can be honored and get my hand into the public purse and secure to myself a fat salary. How such men show themselves utterly destitute of all principle, and debase themselves to secure an office! This office-worship in our land at the present time is enough to disgust even the Devil. We have a class of individuals at the present day who will sell soul and body, with the interest of the whole nation, for office. How amazingly patriotic such men will pretend to be! how ready to serve their country! Ready to serve their country? They are ready to serve themselves, and make the whole country serve them if they can. A man who is honestly anxious to serve his country, simply for his country's good, will wait until his country calls for his services. He will not be eternally pushing himself into public notice, and electioneering all through the land to secure an office. This whole brood of office-seekers, who are constantly electioneering for themselves, should be utterly discarded and rejected by the community as wholly unfit for office. Their object is to serve themselves and not their country. Selfishness is at the bottom, and a selfish man is not fit for a public station. A man to be fit for a public station should be self-sacrificing, with an enlarged soul; who at heart seeks the highest good of all classes in the nation. None other is fit for office. This lesson the nation should learn, or it will be ruined by such men. But look again, and see how such men will stand up in the halls of the nation and defy God and his authority. How they ridicule the idea that a higher law can be binding upon the subjects of this government. In their estimation, the authority of congress is the supreme authority in the universe, or particularly of this people. They claim that their authority is higher than that of God, for they demand that the laws *they* enact *must* be obeyed, even if in opposition to the express command of God. What an important body congress has become! From what source, it would be well to inquire, did this body derive such supreme authority? Do you say, from the people? And from whence did the people derive it? This, I suppose, you call Protestantism; and if this is so, will you tell me what Romanism is? What more abominable doctrine did Rome ever hold, than this? Let some of your wise congressmen, who are so ready to instruct us ministers, give us a little light on this question if they can. Let them show the distinction between such a doctrine and Antichrist. Men holding such doctrines should go over to Rome at once. Go over to Rome, did I say? They are already there, only they are hypocritical, and are deceiving the nation by *pretending* to be Protestants.

With all these abominations staring us in the face,—not only in this land, but a great share of the world yet unconverted,—can you affirm that you are idle because there is no work to be done? Such an excuse you will never present at the bar of God. Why, then, present it here? Why ease off your conscience by such a falsehood? The fact is, every family, neighborhood, town, county, state, and nation, under the whole heavens, is full of work.

The sins and errors of all kinds, among high and low, rich and poor, throughout the world, demand our attention. Christ has commissioned the ministry and the church to set all these things right, and there will be work to do as long as there is sin and error in one solitary soul on earth. Men who are ignorant of our high calling may think we are out of our place when we meddle with this, that, or the other sin and error; but they only expose their own narrow, contracted views of the work assigned the church to perform. She is to war with sin, *all* sin, — sin in the church and out of it; sins of public men and private men; organic sins, whether of legislative or other bodies. She is to labor and toil to overthrow all iniquity, and bring the entire world home to God; and there is work enough for all until this grand end is secured.

2. You are not idle because the work Christ demands at your hands is not right and honorable.

Some men refuse to enlist in certain enterprises, because, they say, the employment itself is unjust, and would involve them in guilt. But you cannot make this excuse in relation to Christ's work. The thing which he demands is so completely righteous that all your unrighteousness consists in neglecting it. As to its being honorable, what employment can be more so? This work has called forth the admiration of all good men on earth. It is the work in which the good of every age have enlisted with all

their souls. It enlists, moreover, the sympathy, the
coöperation, and admiration of all heaven. Nay
more, it is the work in which God himself is engaged; it is God's work! God's work not honorable! Can God have a dishonorable thought, or
require a dishonorable thing of one of his creatures?
To harbor such a thought of your Maker would be
a vile slander upon the pure and holy One. When
you take hold of this work, you enlist with God in
helping forward one of the grandest schemes of benevolence ever devised by the Infinite Mind.

3. You are not idle because there is a want of
ability to do the work which God requires.

I am aware that some men make this an excuse;
but this is the only world where they will ever offer
it. They will not go up to the judgment with this
excuse upon their lips. God's commands are not
grievous. But a commandment requiring an impos-
sibility would be grievous in the extreme, and most
tyrannical, if you were to be sent to hell for not
obeying such a command. Again, Christ says,
" My yoke is easy and my burden is light." That
could not be true if Christ required an impossi-
bility.

The duties which God requires of his creatures
are always graduated by their ability to perform
them. How strikingly this appears in the distribu-
tion of the talents! " And he gave to every man
according to their several ability." To the man who

was capable of improving only one talent, did he give five? or to the man who was capable of improving five, did he give only one? Nothing of this kind. To the one who was capable of improving five, he gave five; and so to the one who was capable of improving only one, he gave one. Then, in the reckoning, did he require of the man to whom he had given but one to account for five? Not at all. He only required him to give an account for what he had received, and a just improvement upon that. How that parable of Christ perfectly annihilates the doctrine of inability! It is amazing to me that any man could ever plead or believe such a doctrine, who had ever read that parable. No, my brother; God's work which he requires is reasonable, for it requires no impossibilities. He requires of you to use all the ability he has given you for him at all times, and under all circumstances,— no more and no less.

4. You are not idle because Christ has failed to place before you inducements to prevail upon you to enlist in this work.

What inducement do you want? The very work itself ought to move any heart that has any regard for right. Christ calls upon you to enlist in the noble work of promoting the holiness and happiness of the human race, by prevailing upon them to love God and one another, and travel together up to the New Jerusalem. Such a work ought to be motive enough. To have the privilege to engage in such a work ought to captivate and delight all your hearts. But he has not left the matter here. Christ steps upon the battlements of heaven, and waves before the inhabitants of earth a crown of righteousness that fadeth not away. "They that turn many to righteousness," he proclaims, "shall shine as stars in the kingdom of God forever." What higher inducements do you want? What higher inducements can a God give? A heaven of unspeakable bliss and joy, a seat in the heavenly world among the glorified ones, is to be the reward of the faithful in his service.

IV. I AM NOW TO TURN YOUR ATTENTION TO SOME THINGS WHICH CONSTITUTE REASONS WHY YOU ARE IDLE.

1. Then, I remark, one reason is this: You do not take time to look at the work,— its extent, its importance, and its rewards. You are so absorbed with What shall I eat? what shall I drink? wherewithal shall I be clothed? and how shall I make money and become rich? that you will not take time to think. If you would take one half hour each day, sit down and think seriously and intelligently upon the infinite value of one soul, then look around and see the multitudes who are in the way to death, you would awake, if you are a Christian. You would act, your tongue would be unloosed, your voice would be heard pleading for Christ and

the souls that are ready to perish. But now you rush through one day and then another in pursuit of earth and earthly things, without taking time to look into eternity and dwell upon what lies beyond the tomb; and of course you have no feeling, no heart that yearns over dying men. Truth will not produce an effect upon the heart only as the mind dwells upon it, and views it in all its solemn realities. Topics upon which the mind dwells will call forth corresponding feeling. If your thoughts are mainly absorbed with the riches, pleasures, and honors of earth, you will feel and act upon these subjects. But let the mind contemplate God, heaven, hell, the judgment, eternity, the value of the soul, the beauty and claims of the divine government, the great evil of sin and the value of holiness, the great system of reform God has instituted to save men, and a multitude of other great moving considerations such as you find in the Bible, and how quick the soul of the Christian is aroused, his stupidity is broken up, his idleness is at once abandoned, he girds himself afresh for the fight, he sees distinctly and truly that the fields are all ripe, ready for the harvest, and he hastens into them without delay to gather souls to Christ. Do you doubt in relation to the correctness of this position, go and test it by experience, and then you will be qualified to judge.

2. Another reason why you are idle is, because you lose sight of the fact that, if you neglect your

part of the work it will remain undone forever. But, says one, if I neglect my part of the work, will not God send some other being to do it? No, NEVER! There is no other being that can do it. Every other being in the universe has all the work assigned him to do that he is capable of performing, let him work with his might through all the coming ages of eternity. To turn aside to do your work, if it were possible for him to do it, would be to neglect his own and become a transgressor. He can only do his own, if he does his best. But, says another, if I neglect to warn and labor for the conversion of that sinner, cannot God send some other one to warn him? Doubtless he can; but when that other man warns him, he is doing his own work, not yours. God has now sent him to warn, and he is doing his own duty, in obedience to God's command. Your duty still remains neglected and undone. Please sit down and contemplate this truth and keep it before the mind. If I neglect my duty, no other being can do it for me. It will remain a neglected duty forever, and the responsibility is on me. I cannot shake it off, and do my duty by proxy. It must meet me at another day.

3. Another reason still is, because you lose sight of the fact that you cannot do the work of the present hour in the next. Present duty must be done in present time, or not at all. Neglect it to-day, and there is no point in all the future when you can

attend to it. But, says an objector, if I neglect to warn that sinner to-day, and we both live until to-morrow, can I not warn him then? No doubt you can; but when you warn him, are you doing the work of yesterday or to-day? You are doing the work of the present moment, and not of any preceding one. The duty you neglected yesterday is neglected still, and will be when you die and go to the judgment, and never can be done through all the coming future. Each moment as it comes is loaded down with all the duty you can do, if you do your best; so that you cannot go back and take up a duty you neglected yesterday. You have all you can possibly do which belongs to the present. Consequently, when your duty is once neglected, you can never afterwards make any amends or atonement for it. If atonement is made, it must be made by some other person or being, and not by you. Now keep this truth before the mind, and if you have any piety it will move your heart. Think, when you are about to neglect present duty, if you neglect it now it can never be done, and will forever remain a neglected duty.

4. You forget or do not realize another truth which is a reason why you are idle. That truth is this, You will be held strictly accountable for all the good you *can* do, whether you do it or not.

Who has any realizing sense of this truth? What multitudes in the church who hardly think of their usefulness to others! Do they inquire, Can I do good to-day, and if so, how? If I engage in this, that, or the other business, will it contribute to my usefulness to the world? How and in what employment can I best promote God's glory and the highest good of man? These are questions that have but little influence over great multitudes in the church. Now remember, that the life which leaves usefulness out of the account, or makes it a secondary matter, is an impenitent life. The sinner lives neither for the glory of God nor the good of man, but for himself. When a professing Christian does the same, he is an impenitent sinner, and not a Christian. To lose sight of your usefulness is to lose sight of the great end for which you were created. God created you to glorify him and communicate good to others. He reigns to secure the highest amount of good that can be secured to the universe over which he presides. He demands of all his creatures to coöperate with him, and labor for the same great object. A true Christian will do it. When he gave himself up to God, he gave himself up to glorify his Maker and do good to others the rest of his life. In the light of this truth, have you ever been a true Christian? If so, have you backslidden from that work, and become an idler? Have you forgotten that God will hold you accountable at the judgment for all the good you can do, whether you do it or not? Not only for the good you *do,* but for all the good you are *capable* of doing. What immense good this church could do, if each member would give himself fully up to this work to-day, and make it the great end for which he lives, the remainder of his life. If you would fly to God for the Holy Spirit to fill your hearts, study and pray over your Bibles, cultivate your intellectual powers, store your minds with useful knowledge, and then communicate that knowledge to the world. What an influence you would exert over this community! Again, remember for every soul you could lead to Christ, and for all the influence you could exert for good over your families and others, you are to be held solemnly accountable at God's bar.

If you would keep this truth constantly before the mind, how could you be idle and be a Christian? Idle you would not be. You would be awake, all awake. You would work with your might, and the whole region would be aroused. Sinners would look on and say, that looks like it. There is a church that believes what she professes. God is with them, and it is time for us to prepare for eternity.

5. Another reason why some are idle in the church, is because they do not love the work God requires at their hands.

They love wealth, and long to be rich. They are full of zeal in every money-making scheme. They love the honors of earth and will seek them. They love to have their names before the world, and be called of men, " Rabbi, Rabbi." They love earthly pleasures and will pursue them. Their hearts are in such things; but God's work they do not love. Now such beings may be in the church, but they are not in the way to heaven. Such beings may vainly think they are Christians, and pretend they are leading a godly life; and some of their neighbors may think them so, but God knows better. What! be a Christian and not love God's work! What does the Devil himself do more than hate God's work? The very thing which makes him the Devil is because he does not love God's work. And can you be in the same state of heart and be a Christian? It is utterly impossible! A person who hopes he is a Christian in such a state of heart, is resting upon a false hope that will fail him in the day of trial. He is in the way to hell, and will lie down in sorrow at last, being dragged down to the pit under the delusive idea that he is in the way to heaven. No, my precious friend, if you are in the church and do not love God's work, give up your hope, it will be your ruin. Go home and repent; get a good hope, and then you will love God's work. It will be dearer to you than anything else. It will break up your idleness effectually, and you will become an active, laborious child of Jesus Christ.

6. Another class in the church are idle, because they are not willing to meet the self-denial which the work demands.

"If any man will come after me," says Christ, "let him deny himself and take up his cross and follow me." Christ's whole life was one of self-denial. He left heaven with all its joys, and came to this wicked world to labor and toil, suffer and die for man. What an example he has set us in this particular. He proclaims to all the world, if *any man* will come after me, let him deny himself. This implies that no man can come after him without self-denial. The life of the Christian is a life of self-denial. The man who thinks he can live a Christian life without it, is laboring under a grand mistake. It is impossible! To be a Christian you must seek not your own honor, but Christ's! Not your ease, but the highest good of the world, and be willing to wear yourself out to secure that end! Not your pleasure, but God's will, which is to govern and control your life. How many in the church falter here? They are not willing to meet this self-denial, and consequently sit down in idleness. They want their own way, and to attend to their own business to the neglect of that of God. Consequently, they are idlers so far as God's work is concerned, and are hastening to the judgment in this state of mind.

REMARKS.

1. God never created any being to be idle. All the intelligent beings he ever formed he created to

be active, do good, and coöperate with him in promoting the highest good of the universe. But, says one, were not our first parents idle before the fall? Not at all. God had no sooner created them, than he put them at once into active life. He put Adam into the Garden of Eden, and commanded him to dress and keep it. He called upon him to name the beasts of the field, and the fowls of the air. Such scraps of history show that Adam was not idle in the state of holiness. He was active in doing God's will and not his own. But, says another, if we ever reach heaven, we shall have nothing to do but sit down and enjoy it. Idle in heaven! Heaven is one of the most active places in God's universe. How he keeps his angels on the wing to do his bidding. Look yonder, there are four standing on the four corners of the earth with the winds of heaven under their control. There is another ascending from the East with the seal of the living God in his hand, and he cries out to the four angels and demands of them not to hurt the earth until he has sealed the servants of God. There are seven others having seven trumpets to sound. Here are seven more with the seven last plagues to pour out upon the earth. There is another on the wing with the everlasting Gospel to preach, and still another flying through the heavens crying "Woe, woe, woe, to the inhabiters of the earth!" Yonder comes another with a rainbow about his head, and he puts one foot upon the earth and the other upon the sea, and raises his hand to heaven and closes up time. How these descriptions show that heaven is awake, and all activity! The angels on high coöperate with God in the affairs of earth, and in carrying out his great designs in relation to this world. If you expect or wish to go to an idle heaven, you must go to some other than the one God has provided.

2. I remark, the true way to be happy is to work not for self but for God. As man was created for activity, and not for idleness, he cannot find happiness in idleness. A man in this state not only fails to answer the great end for which he was created, but he fails to meet the demands of his nature. His nature demands a useful station that will call forth his intellectual and physical power and give them employment. His moral nature demands that that employment shall be calculated to secure good to himself and others, and be honorable to his Maker who conferred upon him these powers of usefulness. To live therefore with no useful end in view, or waste your time in idleness, cannot and will not satisfy the mind. The soul is uneasy and unhappy.

The most unhappy beings on earth are the idle loungers who are living with no good end in view. The happiest men the world ever saw, are those who have labored and worn themselves out for God. Their peace has been like a river. They could speak of a fulness of joy. How they have triumphed in death and left the earth with a soul full of Heaven! Your own experience, doubtless, has taught you this lesson if you have watched your own heart. Let a Christian go into the field and labor and toil to save men, how quick his heart is full! Let him sit down in idleness and live for other purposes and not to do good, how quick his heart is lean! If you would be happy then, my brother or sister, give your life up to be useful to mankind.

3. You can see the cause of all the leanness of heart among professing Christians. You are idle; that is your trouble.

4. A religion which does not make an active Christian, is a delusion. Religion made Christ active, the apostles active, and the primitive church, Luther, Wesley, Whitfield, Edwards, and all men in every age of the world, who have truly had it in their hearts. You cannot keep a man from acting for God and the good of man, whose soul is alive with religion. The primitive church whose hearts were fired up with this holy religion would die by the thousand, rather than sit down in idleness. Now remember, my brother, if you are an idler you are not a Christian. If you are a Christian you will act and labor and toil for the good of man and for the honor of your Maker. Why dream about being a Christian, when you are destitute of the feeling and life of a Christian?

5. Sinners in this congregation should hear God's voice in this text, for it is addressed to them as well as to us. "Why," says Christ to these sinners before me, "stand ye here all the day idle?" Your soul is neglected. Not a step have you taken yet to prepare to meet your God. You are wasting your life. You can do good if you repent. You may lead others to Christ. God wants you in his vineyard, and will judge you for all the good you can do. You are capable of doing good, and were created to do good and not evil. You are now doing evil, immense evil. Why, says Christ, persist in your evil course? Young man, he addresses you, do you hear him speak? He wants your life given to him. Now is your time to commence a career of usefulness. Why, why throw away that useful life? Will you not come to him now and consecrate your whole being to his service? How honorable, how noble to give yourself up to do good to the world. Young lady, he calls you also; open your ear and hear. In your station what good you can do! You can mould others for heaven. Christ wants your affectionate heart consecrated to him and his service. Shall he have it, or will you throw away that life, and lift up your eyes in despair in another world and lament your folly? No, no; come to Christ to-day and live for him and all is safe.

IV.

THE TITHES.

Bring ye all the tithes into the storehouse, that there may be meat in mine house, and prove me now herewith, saith the Lord of Hosts, if I will not open you the windows of heaven, and pour you out a blessing, that there shall not be room enough to receive it.—*Mal.* iii. 10.

1. THE DUTY TAUGHT IN THE TEXT. 2. THE STRENGTH AND MAGNITUDE OF THE PROMISE.

WHAT a text! What a God, who is the author of such a rich portion of truth! How this text unfolds his heart, his *great* heart, his boundless benevolence! How he loves to do for his creatures! He is never satisfied with doing, he cannot do enough! Can such a heart be satisfied with bestowing small blessings? No, *never*, NEVER. It wishes to do great things. Its treasures of Grace and Mercy are inexhaustible; and does it wish to hoard them up like a selfish, covetous soul? Nought of that mean, niggardly disposition. Benevolence is an eternal stranger to selfishness. She has no communion or fellowship with such a state of heart. Her happiness consists in doing, not in receiving. She loves to distribute and scatter abroad; to fill a world with bliss; to roll a tide of glory over all heaven and make angels shout with joy inexpressible; to send out her light and her love to the uttermost corner of the universe, and fill it with infinite delight, so that every heart shall be full and still then not room enough to receive it. Such is God's great heart. Such are his infinite desires. With such a text on record, why is it that there is a sinner found unconverted where the Bible is read? Why are they not all saved, and their hearts full and overflowing with God's boundless love and mercy? The fault cannot be with God. This he affirms in many parts of the Bible. He is ready and willing to save, and waits the opportunity. If he possesses the heart and disposition which this text unfolds and ascribes to him, this must be true; it cannot be otherwise. If he is so desirous to bless, says an objector, why not bless? Why not open the windows on high and let the blessing come, until there is not room enough to receive it? There is one thing in the way. That thing is with man, and man must remove it out of the way or the blessing cannot be given.

You should remember, God is acting in the capacity of a public lawgiver, and not in that of a private individual. In dispensing his blessings he must do it so as not to indorse iniquity or set his seal of approbation to crime. His own character and the good of the universe require that God should be guarded and particular on this point. He must make a distinction between right and wrong. He should bestow his mercies so as to encourage the one and discourage the other. To treat the rebellious and obedient subjects of his government precisely alike, would be to say by a public act of his, that he looked upon rebellion as meritorious as obedience, or sin as deserving of his smile as holiness. Such conduct on the part of God would not only tarnish his character, but would do immense mischief to the universe.

What would be the effect, if this Commonwealth should treat the murderer the same as it treats the man who has a sacred regard for human life, or the thief the same as it treats the honest, upright citizen? Such a course would break down all the safeguards thrown around society to protect it, and open wide the floodgates of iniquity. It would break down all government, all order, and the State would be ruined. The life and property of every man would be in jeopardy. Who would wish to live amid the state of things that would soon follow.

So in God's kingdom, if he, by his public acts should encourage sin, or cease to discourage it, who could tell the result to the universe? With all the discouragements to sin which an infinite God has hung out in his government, sin has entered the universe. It has ruined a large class of angels, it has invaded our world and spread over the whole human race. What other worlds it would destroy, and what would be the limits to its ravages, if God should cease to discourage it, no mind but the Infinite one can foresee. For aught we know the whole universe might be ultimately ruined. How important, therefore, that God in dispensing his blessings, should do it so as not in the least to encourage sin. He is particular here, for he has a most sacred regard for right, and he would sooner let the whole world go to hell than indorse their iniquity to save them. For this reason he requires of all individuals, before he will bless, to come into a right state of heart. Then he is ready; then the windows will be opened and the blessing come. How clear this truth stands out in my text. Here is a great and rich promise; a strong motive presented to encourage us to come out and seek for great blessings. But here is a duty presented in the front rank, and the promise lies in the rear of the duty. "Bring in your tithes," says God; that is the duty. Then "I will open the windows," &c.; that is the promise. How many will try to reach their hand around the duty to get hold of the promise, if possible! Your arm is too short, my brother. There is no way of access to this promise but to march up like an honest man and take up the duty. The duty lies between you and the promise; and the duty must be met, or the promise is not yours.

How wicked hearts wish to reverse the order of things here, and bring God to abandon his ground and bless them on other terms! Let God first open the windows of heaven, says such a heart, and pour out a blessing until there is not room enough to receive it, and then we will bring in the tithes. Wonderful! Let God bless you in a wrong and wicked state of heart, and thus indorse your unrighteousness, and *then,—then* what? Oh, then we will do our duty. No, you would not. That is false. You would say, Well, I have obtained the blessing; that is all I wanted. God would not have blessed if we were not about right, and we will live as we have done. God will do no such thing; he understands your deceptive heart too well, and he will not be misled by it. He has taken his position; that position is right, and he will not come over an inch, and he ought not. Bring in your tithes, says God, *all your tithes*, and then the blessing is yours; but on no other conditions can you have it.

Do you, as individuals, as a church, desire this great blessing on these terms? Do you say yes? Stop, my brother. Look again at these terms. *Look close.* Bring *all* your tithes. One half, nine tenths, ninety-nine one hundredths will not answer here. That is not *all.* ALL YOUR TITHES. You will desire to get off with a part. God will make no compromise with you. You must meet these terms *exactly,*—with a willing, cheerful heart, and lay *all* on his table; and when *everything* is consecrated, then the windows will be thrown wide open, and the blessing will come.

Now then, do you wish the blessing upon such terms? Do I hear you respond *yes*? Very well, then let me have your undivided attention while I undertake to expound these terms in the text.

I. I will show what this duty implies.

II. Call your attention to the promise,— its strength,— its greatness.

I. I AM TO SHOW WHAT THE DUTY IN THIS TEXT IMPLIES.

The word tithes meant this, under the Jewish dispensation: They were required to give one tenth of all they possessed to God, to support the Jewish religion. One tenth of their sheep, one tenth of their oxen, one tenth of their grain, one tenth of all they had was to be brought to God and presented to him. Another thing, in bringing this offering to God, they must bring the *best* they had. God would not accept the lame and sickly of the flock. They must select the hale, the robust, the best of the flock, or he would spurn their offering. No selfishness was to be allowed in this matter; he would not tolerate a little, niggardly spirit. He wanted an offering made in righteousness, one that came from a cheerful heart, a whole-souled offering.

But we are not under the Jewish dispensation, says one. I admit it. But all these Jewish customs teach, and were designed to teach, lessons of importance to us. What does bringing in the tithes under the Christian dispensation imply? I answer, to meet God in his claims, *all* his claims, and submit to do them cheerfully. This was the spirit of the passage in its application to the Jews. God demanded one tenth. To meet God in that demand, and obey him, was bringing in the tithes.

To bring in our tithes, *all our tithes*, is to meet God in every claim he lays upon us, and submit in obedience to those claims, cheerfully and with a full heart. Under this general idea let me specify a few things to make this duty simple and clear to all.

1. Then God says, son, daughter, give me thine *heart*. This is God's first, this is among his most important claims. This neglected and all is a failure. No other duty can be acceptable to God, if the heart is withheld. "If I give my goods to feed the poor, and my body to be burned," says Paul. "and have not charity or love, I am nothing." All is unacceptable without the heart. *Give me thine heart*, says God. Do you hear him? Bring in your tithes. Will you obey God in this first demand? Or do you wish to back out from the position that you wish this great blessing upon the terms propounded in the text? Some one inquires, perhaps, what is it to give the heart to God? Do you make that inquiry because you wish to give God your heart, or as a mere matter of speculation? If you wish to give up your heart and comply with this demand, I will explain this duty so that all may understand. Now mark the definition.

The soul's heart is the mind's choice of an end for which it lives. If it select a right end, and consecrates its whole being to secure that end, it has a right or a good heart. If it selects a wrong end, and consecrates its powers to secure *that* end, it has a wicked or impenitent heart. Giving the heart to God, then, is always an act of the will. It is the mind's choice. It is the mind's choice of an end, — the mind's choice of a right end. It is the mind's choice of an end, to promote which she consecrates all her powers. What, then, is the end which the mind selects in giving the heart to God? I answer, *it is God's will.* It selects *God's will* as the *end* for which it lives; and to secure which, consecrates its whole being. That is giving the heart to God. That is something you can understand. That is something you can do.

Will you do it? Will you meet this first claim of God now? Will you now say to God, whose all-pervading spirit surrounds you, Here, Lord, is my heart. I now, henceforth and forever, give up my whole being to do thy will. Not my will but THINE be done? Bring in your tithes; you must not fail here; if you do, you fail of the blessing.

2. The second claim God levys upon you is upon your bodies.

Says Paul: " I beseech of you by the mercies of God, that ye present your bodies a living sacrifice, holy, acceptable to God, which is your reasonable service." Present your bodies to whom ? To God. Present them a *living* sacrifice, not a dead one. Present them *holy*, not sinful. This will be acceptable to God. It is a reasonable service or demand, says the Apostle. Thus God sets up a claim to your body, as well as your heart. He demands that you give it to him, and use it for him in his service. God has a just and righteous claim upon your body as well as upon your soul. He created the body; it is the workmanship of his hands; it is his lawful property, and he demands that you use it for him. He claims the right to dictate in relation to its use. He legislates as much over the body as he does over the soul. He tells you how you shall use it, and how you shall not. We get up a controversy with God, about the use of the body. We say we will use it as *we* please. No, says God, you must use it as *I* please. Now while you keep up this controversy he will not bless. You must stop it and submit to his will, and let him dictate about the body, and you obey. There is that hand, says God. It is my hand, I created it. Use it for me and not my adversary, the Devil. If the Devil created it, use it for him. But the Devil did not create it. I created it, use it therefore for me. How can you use it for the Devil? If you wish to use it to please the Devil instead of God, use it to knock your neighbor down, to stab or shoot him, or harm him in some form. But if you wish to use it for God, use it to do your neighbor good. If he has fallen yonder in the street, and needs help, use it to lift him up, and administer to his wants. If he is hungry, use it to feed him. If he is sick, use it to administer to his relief. If you must use it to defend your neighbor, use it to defend the wronged party, and not the party which is inflicting the wrong. Use it to defend liberty and justice, not oppression and sin. If the slaves at the South rise and undertake to fight in defence of their inalienable rights, as our fathers did, and you are sent there to put down the insurrection, when you use your hands to handle your musket, be sure and not aim at the head of the *oppressed* party. What! fight in defence of oppression! No, sooner die than do it. If you must fight at all, fight for liberty and justice, and not for oppression and wrong.

Never take sides with a party that is inflicting a wrong, but take your position with the wronged party; and if you have any defence to make, make it for him. I am aware that slaveholders and their sympathizers, will cry out that such a doctrine is horrible. But why horrible? I answer, simply because they want you and the nation to defend them in their deviltry. That has always been the cry of tyrants. It is horrible, in their estimation, to fight for liberty and justice; but patriotic and noble to stand ready to fight to put down liberty, and in favor of oppression. Such men think they are heroes, and that we ought to make presidents of them while they live, and raise monuments over their graves when they die. Now understand, I am not saying it is your duty to fight in any case. That is not a question for me to discuss here. I do say, however, you have no right to use your hands to put down liberty and defend oppression. That is not using them for God, but for the Devil. You should use them to bless the human race.

Then there is the tongue, another member of the human body. God demands that you use it for him, and not for the Devil. It is a little member, but you can do immense evil or immense good with it. If you wish to use it for the Devil instead of God, use it to backbite and slander your neighbor; use it to swear away his liberty, his property, his reputation, his life; use it for profanity and to blaspheme God; use it to ridicule and sneer at sacred things; use it to keep your neighbor from repenting and turning to God; use it to defend error, sin, and wrong-doing; use it to cheat and deceive your neighbor, so as to draw money out of him, without rendering an honest equivalent, and in a thousand other ways we have not time to name. But if you wish to use it for God, use it to pray to him, and bless his holy name; use it to preach his Gospel, and defend his truth; use it to prevail upon men to turn to God, to repent, to be good, holy at heart, and upright in all things; use it to plead for the poor, the oppressed and down-trodden; use it to rebuke sin in all its forms, and in all men.

Thus give your tongue to God. This he demands. He claims the right to dictate about the use of the tongue. He legislates over it, and you must give it up to be controlled by him, if you would give your body to God. God legislates over your ears also, and tells you how to use them; over the appetites and propensities of your bodies, and tells when and how you may indulge them, and how not. These were all placed in your bodies for good ends, but they can all be abused, and turned to bad account. God tells you how to use them, and you are to submit to his dictation, if you would give the body to him. Paul understood it, and you must follow his example. "I keep under my body," says the Apostle, "and bring it in subjection, lest after I have preached to others, I myself should be a castaway." Bring it in subjection to what? To God's will, to God's dictation. Now we must do as the Apostle did, and thus give the body to God. Bring in your tithes. Bring your bodies and present them to God. Will you do it? Do you do it? Now, God looks on, and knows whether you do it or not. Will you meet God in this claim he makes upon your bodies? If not, you are not bringing in all your tithes; you are keeping back part of the price, and will fail of the blessing.

3. The next thing God demands is your time.

This also belongs to God the author, who measures it out to you moment by moment. From whom do you derive it? It is God who imparts it. That he claims it as his, is evident from the fact that he makes you sick and well as he sees fit. He numbers your days here on earth, without consulting you or your wishes, and he cuts short your time by death, when he sees fit; all of which would be wrong in God if your time were not lawfully and rightfully his. That time is valuable. With a right use of it you can do good, or with a wrong use of it you can do evil, great evil. How one rash act of one man, perpetrated in a few moments, may plunge a whole nation into war, and sacrifice thousands of human lives, sending mourning and lamentation into a million of hearts perhaps! Oh, how it sends those wretches unbidden into the presence of a righteous God, amid their blasphemies and their blood! What an awful moment to them! How ill-prepared for such a meeting!

On the other hand, a moment's time, rightly used, may turn the scale with that sinner, and bring him over to Christ, who, after a career of usefulness on earth, may be exalted to heaven to tread her most lofty heights of bliss, and drink of her river of life through all the coming ages of a boundless eternity. What consequences hang upon the right use of time! How many sinners have been saved by listening to one sermon, one prayer, or from receiving one invitation to come to Christ! As I came out of church in Boston, a gentleman approached me, and remarked, that some twenty years ago, in Ohio, he was invited to hear me preach one sermon. That sermon, said he, arrested my attention, led me to Christ, and I hope I am now on the way to heaven. How many instances I have known in my ministry, where five minutes' talk has brought a sinner over! The nail was fastened in a sure place and clenched, and the soul sealed for heaven. Oh, those moments, my brother, my sister, how precious, how precious! God wants them, Christ purchased them with his blood. Will you give them to him? Will you now lay that time on God's altar, and give it to God to do good to the world? Bring in *all your tithes.* Do not have a controversy with God about your time here, if you want this rich blessing. If you give it to God, you will inquire of him how you can use it to the best advantage to build up his kingdom on earth, and glorify his great name. How much time you have wasted! Repent of that. How you have undervalued your time, and used it for yourself, instead of God! Put away all that iniquity. Redeem the time for the future, and seek forgiveness for the past.

Dear sinner, God will put you at a future day where you will see the worth of time. When you lie down to die and look over into eternity, then how precious time will look! Said a dying queen, as she was going into eternity, " Millions of money for a moment's time!" Now you have time measured out to you by your Maker. Improve it as it passes, so that you can meet your account joyfully at another day.

4. In bringing in your tithes, God also demands your influence. Are you ready to reply, " I have no influence?" Individuals frequently make that remark, but it is not true of any person living. Every one has an influence, and all are exerting it for good or for evil every day of their lives. You are not aware of the amount, nor the constant influence you exert over others. You hardly move, speak, or give a look in the presence of others without exerting an influence over them. You may change the whole purpose of a man's soul, ruin him, and blot out his happiness endlessly by a look. In a congregation where I was preaching, and where there was a very interesting state of things, one evening, at the close of a sermon, I requested all who would give their hearts to God to kneel in the last prayer. Many dropped down before God to do up this important work. One man, in the very act of kneeling, caught the eye of an old scoffing companion, whose scornful look changed his purpose, and he resumed his seat, where he remained till the close of the exercises, as unmoved as a marble statue. The judgment will probably reveal the fact that that look ruined that soul and sent it to hell. A lady in my presence was

about to close a trade with a man, when a friend caught her eye and gave her a meaning look. She changed her purpose in an instant, and concluded to take a little more time for consideration. That look did up the work. I name these instances to show what can be done by a look. You may kill the influence of that good minister over the minds of your children, and prevent his leading them to Christ, by a very few remarks. " Father," says the child, " how did you like that man to-day?" " Oh," says the father, " what he *said* was well enough, but his *manner* — I dislike his *manner*." That child henceforth goes to church to watch the minister's *manner*. It loses sight of all the *truth* he utters, and goes home to imitate the father in criticizing the *manner* of the minister. There may be rich, weighty, and vastly important truths in the sermon, which, if reduced to practice, would save the soul. But the child goes down to hell criticizing the *manner* of the ministers, in imitation of the father. If the father had called the attention of the child to those rich and weighty truths, and said to the child, " Reduce that truth to practice, and you are safe," what a different influence he would have exerted over the child. These wonderfully wise ones, however, who are always criticizing the manner of ministers, are not always the best judges of manner. That manner which produces the strongest and most lasting effect upon an audience; which chains and fixes attention; absorbs the congregation in the subject discussed, so as to make time seem half its length — that is the manner God approves, and let those condemn it who dare. The minister who possesses it has uncommon power over his hearers, and sends his congregation home with the truth all cleared up and fixed in the memory. That is the manner which will produce a lasting effect. The hearer will refer to that sermon in after years, and say "how clear and conclusive that subject was handled. It settled the question in my mind forever." But you should be cautious how you turn off your own attention, and the attention of your children and others, to the manner, and thus divert the mind from the truth. It is the truth that will save, and not the manner, any further than the manner enforces the truth.

Again, the influence you exert by example will be good or bad. You can give it to God or against him. To show what example will do, take one case out of many I might name. In a church where I was holding a meeting, one of the members, a praying lady, had an impenitent husband She became very anxious that he should attend the meeting and hear the preaching. After much persuasion, she finally prevailed upon him to come one afternoon. They started; but just before they reached the place of worship, he looked over into the field and saw one of the leading members of the church at work on his farm. He stopped his team instantly, and, putting the reins into the hands of his son, said, "If that church-member can stay at home to work, so can I, for his business is no more important than mine." He went back to his farm, and his wife could never start him out again. The influence of that example may have been fatal to that sinner. Take care my brother how you step. The eyes of the world are upon you, your example may ruin them. There is a question of reform before the community; truth and righteousness on the one side, and error and sin on the other. Perhaps error and sin are popular. The mass of the people are in their favor, and you want to be on the popular side, so you go against the reform. Pause now, for you are giving your influence against God. God is on the side of truth, and he wants you there. Bring in your tithes, says God, I want your influence for truth. Here you hesitate; you say, if I take that stand, it will hurt my influence; it will affect my business. But stop, my brother; that is the devil's reasoning. Your inquiry should be, on which side are truth and righteousness? The answer to that question should settle the question of duty. God takes his stand for truth and right. He wants all his people to do the same. You cannot bring in all your tithes without giving your influence where God gives his. You say, then, I will take *neutral* ground. That will not answer. That will not be bringing in *all* the tithes. There is an influence you could exert for truth and the right, but you withhold it. That is withholding the tithes, and not bringing them in as the text demands. How quick the church could kill out all the abolitionism there is in the land, if she would throw all her influence against the system! Let every member, in every visible church in the nation, take his stand to put down this evil, and be as immovable as the hills, and abolitionism could not live in the nation ten years. Let every pulpit in the land thunder against this awful crime, and let the church walk up in a solid column to the ballot-box, north and south, and deposit their votes against this "spawn of the devil," and, together with the influence they would thus exert over others, they would kill abolitionism dead, and bury it so deep that it would never have a resurrection until the last trumpet should call it up to the final account. Now God wants this influence of his church brought into his storehouse, and he would open the windows of heaven and deluge the nation with his mercy. What say you, my brother? Shall your influence from this hour be given to God? Will you now dedicate it, and let it be henceforth sanctified and consecrated to the great work of promoting truth and righteousness, and the highest good of man?

5. In bringing in your tithes, God wants you to bring your children, and give them up to him.

He not only wishes to save you, but he wants

them saved. He desires not only your influence for good, but theirs. He wants you to give them *to* him, then instruct and train them up *for* him. Come into a state of heart where you will be more anxious that they should be useful, than to accumulate wealth; to suffer privation and hardship in God's cause, than to be honored by man. How many pretend to give their children to God, when it is not heart-work. God, in after years, may wish to convert and put them into the ministry, or send them to the heathen, to lead them to Christ; but how quick their hearts object and rise up in opposition. Why object, if you have truly given them to Christ, and are willing he should use them to the best advantage to build up his kingdom? Are they his or yours? If they are his, it is his place to dictate, and yours to submit and acquiesce. Ungodly men will give up their children to fight and sacrifice their lives in honor and defence of their country, while you, a Christian, are unwilling to give up yours to fight the good fight of faith, and lead souls up to heaven. God wants them. He has a work for them to do. Will you bring them today and give them all up, and let him send them where he pleases? Will you pledge yourself that you will do the best you can to train them up for him? Do you hesitate here? Then God may take them by death; or suffer them to pursue the road to destruction; to grow up to be a disgrace to themselves and those who gave them birth, and lie down in sorrow at last. Will you bring in these tithes?

6. In bringing in your tithes, God claims your property.

Hear him assert his rights on this point, for a moment. "The silver is *mine*, and the gold is *mine*, saith the Lord of hosts." Hag. ii. 8. "Every beast of the forest is mine, and the cattle upon a thousand hills. The world is mine and the fulness thereof. Psalms l. 10, 12."

In these passages, and in many other places in the Bible, God lays claim to all the riches and wealth of earth. He declares it is his, and he claims the right to dictate to the world in relation to its use. He legislates over your property as much as he does over your soul or body. Look at his right for a moment. It is a most sacred one. He created you, and the earth on which you reside, with all its gold and silver, the beasts of the field, and the fowls of the mountains. "The earth and the fulness thereof," which includes everything. This he affirms, and upon this act of creation, he bases his claim to the whole, and his right to control the whole.

The right of property which grows out of the act of creation, is the highest possible right. It is the original or foundation right. No other right can annul or set it aside. Here God sets up his claim, and what court in the universe can set it aside? It can and will be maintained against all other claims, by whomsoever set up. God is a righteous being, and would not claim this property if it were not lawfully his own. But he knows it is; he knows his rights and how to maintain them at a future day. God demands of you to take his property in your possession, and dedicate it to him, to whom it belongs. It belongs to God. Dedicate it to him. Use it according to his wishes and dictation. Bring in your tithes, says God. Under this command, you will, perhaps, grow uneasy. Some of you may turn away as sorrowful as the rich young man, who turned away from Christ, when he told him to sell all he possessed and give to the poor, and then follow him. Riches were his idol, and he was unwilling to have Christ dictate on that point. There are men in the church, whose property is their God. If you touch the one, you certainly will the other. They do not feel that even God himself has a right to dictate in relation to their property. My property is my own, they affirm, and I have a right to use it as I please. That property is not yours, it is God's. So he affirms, and you are under obligation to use it as *he* pleases, and not as you please, unless you agree with him. Take care how you get up a contention with God on this point, if you want a blessing. This was the point of difference between God and the Jews. They undertook to use God's property as they pleased, and not as he pleased. God demanded one tenth of their property to be given up to the support of the Jewish religion, or rather his religion among the Jews.

They refused to be dictated to by God, and withheld this property from him, who charged them with being a set of robbers. Says God in Mal. iii. 9: "Ye have robbed me, even this whole nation. Ye are cursed with a curse." As a consequence, God withheld his blessing from them, because they would not bring and dedicate to him their property, according to his direction. Will you fail of a blessing on the same ground? You get up a controversy with God here.

Think now, does this touch your idol? Do you say, This is carrying the matter too far; we cannot stand that; I do wish you ministers would let that matter alone? I presume you do. But we are not at liberty to do so. If you have any fault to find here, find it with God, for he commands us to cry aloud and spare not, and your controversy is with him and not with us. We are only showing you his claims and not ours. We are bound to press all the claims we find in the Bible. We are commanded to do it " whether men will hear or forbear." The Bible's claims are God's claims. This is a Bible claim as here shown you, and if you wish to feel uneasy under this claim, and contend with your Maker, and shut this blessing from your heart, you can do so. God demands that you dedicate that property, which he says is his, to him, and use it for his glory. You can refuse to do it, and he will withhold the blessing, as he did from the Jews. Now what will you do? He waits for your answer. Will you write holiness to the Lord on everything you have, give up all to him, and take this great blessing on those terms. Or does your heart rebel, and do you say this is requiring too much? What say you? Decide, and God will decide.

II. I AM TO CALL YOUR ATTENTION TO THE PROMISE, — ITS STRENGTH, — ITS GREATNESS.

1. I remark it is a strong one; one of the strongest promises that can be couched in human language. The promise is much stronger than it would have been if God had said, bring in your tithes and I will open the windows and pour you out a blessing. God here challenges you to put him to the proof. After such a challenge, do you think he will fail on his part, if you test him?

You have dealt with that neighbor for years. In all instances you have fulfilled your part of all contracts to the very letter. You are now about entering into another agreement with him. You say I will do *so*, if you will do *so*. He looks you in the face and replies, If I thought you sincere in that proposition, — if I could believe you would do as you promise, I would do it. Indeed, you reply, have I not dealt with you many years? Have I ever failed in one instance? Put me to the proof before you call in question my word. What a challenge! How it expresses the strongest possible determination to fulfil, on your part, if brought to the test!

God, in the text, challenges you to bring in your tithes and put him to the proof. He could not give you a stronger promise. He could not express his determination to fulfil, on his part, in stronger language. Test me, he says, by bringing in all your tithes, and see what I will do.

2. I remark this is a great promise.

There is everything embodied here that is necessary to save a world. God will pour out a blessing, and fill up your cup to overflowing, which will flow to the next heart, and then to the next, and the next, until the town, county, state, nation, and world is deluged with his mercy, and then there shall not be room enough to receive it. God's resources and blessings are infinite, and never can be exhausted. What a rich promise, enough for each and all forevermore. Let all the world bring in their tithes, and the whole earth shall know by happy experience the richness and extent of this promise.

REMARKS.

1. From this subject we learn why they had so great a revival on the day of Pentecost. In that upper chamber the hundred and twenty brought in

all their tithes, and we learn how God opened the windows of heaven, and sent down that power from on high, the Holy Ghost, to fill all their hearts. Then how the work spread like fire through the city! What multitudes were gathered into the kingdom. Hard hearts were melted. Individuals who, a few weeks previous, had been ready to join in the cry, away with him, crucify him, crucify him, were now found calling for mercy, and submitting to his peaceful reign. Three thousand were gathered into the church the first day! Five thousand were converted soon after. What a triumphant work! How the city moved in the face of the most bitter opposition, and thousands on thousands were added unto the Lord.

2. We see why revivals are greater in some places than in others.

In some places only a few bring in their tithes. God opens the windows and gives them a few mercy-drops. In another place the church generally come up to the work, then how God shakes the place! How he subdues and converts some of the most abandoned in it! He makes his power known until there is not a dog to move his tongue in opposition.

3. We see why revivals stop. At the commencement the church came up heartily to the work, and laid themselves on God's altar for a season with a cheerful spirit. God's mercy came in great power.

After a season she became weary of giving all to God, and began to take from his table a part of her offering. Then he began to shut the windows down. At length one retires to his farm and another to his merchandise, and there is a general declension. God hides his face in consequence of their backsliding and iniquity; withdraws his mercy; curses them with barrenness and leanness of soul; and leaves them to contend and strive and bury themselves up in the world more deeply, perhaps, than ever.

When a people have had a great blessing and great light, and backslide from that light, what a great curse will follow! Look out for a fearful state of things in that place. I will be with you while you will be with me, says God; but if you depart from me I will depart from you. The church always forsake God first, then he is under the necessity of withdrawing his blessing, lest he should indorse their iniquity.

4. I have now shown you how you can have a revival; how you can have a great revival. Will you have it on these terms? That question I want you to settle now, before you leave this place. My brother, my sister, will you do it? I must test you here. Think now, God looks into your heart. You cannot deceive him. He will know if you keep back part of the price. All in this congregation, both saint and sinner, who will now consecrate

everything to God, and bring in all their tithes, I want to stand in the last prayer, and give yourselves up anew to God. Give *all*, ALL to him. Think, my brother, before prayer is offered. Do you give up ALL? God help you! *Amen.*

V.

PRAYER.

Ask, and it shall be given you; seek, and ye shall find; knock, and it shall be opened unto you. — *Matt.* vii. 7.

1. PRAYER A DUTY. 2. AN IMPORTANT DUTY. 3. A HIGH PRIVILEGE. 4. ASK, SEEK, AND KNOCK. 5. HOW TO PREVAIL IN PRAYER.

WHAT promises, coming from such a high source! How absolute these assurances! No *perhaps* it shall be given here. " IT SHALL BE GIVEN," is the solemn pledge! Then the connection, making it still more forcible and striking. Adding to this the weight of God's moral character, his holiness and truthfulness, and who can doubt for a moment these absolute assurances? What encouragement to seek him; to knock loud at heaven's gate; to come to such a God with all our wants, and to plead earnestly and confidently to have them all supplied! Nothing more delights the infinite heart of our Maker than to have us fly to his arms for help, and lean upon his Almighty strength to do for us more than we can ask or think. We are dependent creatures; dependent upon him for all temporal and spiritual blessings to supply our present and future wants. Every good and perfect gift comes down from the Father of Lights. Our bodies and our souls are the workmanship of his hand; and if their wants are supplied, they are supplied from his great storehouse. How befitting that such dependent creatures should pray! Prayer is the language of dependence. It is a frank and full acknowledgment to God of our true state. Such frankness is pleasing to him, as he wishes all beings to see and acknowledge their condition as it is. He can do for us all that we need. He can supply our every want. In the text, he manifests his willingness, and gives us the assurance that he stands ready to do, upon the simple condition of our asking. What easy and reasonable terms! If our wants are not supplied under such circumstances who is to blame? If we are too proud and haughty to ask for help, we ought to suffer. If we perish, the fault lies at our own door, and our Maker is clear. Under the guidance of this truth, I will proceed to show, —

I. That prayer is a duty binding upon all men.

II. That it is a very important duty.

III. That it is a high privilege.

IV. I will then examine the three terms in the text separately, — ask, seek, and knock.

V. I will answer the question, What is it to pray as the Bible directs, or how can we offer prevailing prayer?

I. I AM TO SHOW THAT PRAYER IS A DUTY BINDING UPON ALL MEN.

Look at our condition and the relations that exist between us and our Maker, and reason will teach us that it is the duty of all men to pray. We are not ignorant of the fact that sceptical men often affirm that they can see no consistency in this duty. It is, however, amazing that a thinking, reasoning man, who has any enlightened or intelligent views of the state of things that exist between us and God, could come to such a conclusion. Prayer is one of the most reasonable duties that can be performed by the human heart. A prayerless life is a most unreasonable one. I do not believe that the *reason* of any man ever led him to the conclusion that it was not his duty to pray. It is a wicked *heart* that hates prayer, and has forced him to such a conclusion, and not reason's voice. That heart which is deceitful above all things and desperately wicked has palmed off its own wishes for reason's voice, and made him believe it. If his heart loved prayer, how differently he would view this whole matter. But let us hear reason speak for a moment upon this vital question. Reason affirms that two things are due from a being who is receiving blessings from the hand of another: 1. That he should cultivate a spirit of gratitude towards his benefactor. 2. He should express his grateful acknowledgment in a becoming manner, for favors conferred, to the being who is the author of the blessings. This is a plain dictate of reason. How natural to man to say "thank you, sir," or "much obliged," when others confer favors upon him. It is so natural that they do it without stopping to think or to reason upon the point at all. It is the spontaneous outgushing of human nature.

Take an instance as an illustration of this feeling. When multitudes were dying with starvation in Ireland, some years since, and America stretched out her hand of relief and saved a large class from an awful death, was it necessary to introduce an argument to prove to those who were snatched from an untimely grave, that they should feel and express their gratitude to those who had sent them relief in this hour of peril and distress? Argument? Nature would not wait for argument. The Irish heart poured forth its gratitude in every form in which human nature was capable of expression. Their tears of joy, their shouts of thanksgiving to God and the strangers who had sent them relief, and their prayers to the Infinite One for a thousand blessings upon the heads of the Americans, was but a faint expression of what the heart felt within. This is reason's voice in the soul. It is her utterance of what is right and befitting under such circumstances. One other thing is a dictate of reason, namely, that the gratitude and thanksgiving should be in proportion to the blessings received. Now, are we correct in the above sentiments? Probably no one will call in question their correctness. If, therefore, the above positions be correct, they settle the whole question of the reasonableness, consistency, and duty of prayer. They decide the fact that it is the duty of all men to pray. There is not a being on earth who is not receiving great and constant blessings from the hand of his Maker, — greater, higher, and more numerous by far than he receives from any and all other beings in the universe. If, therefore, man is under obligation to feel grateful for favors conferred, and express that gratitude·to his benefactor, then he is under obligation to pray. Thanksgiving is one of the important branches of prayer. Consequently, he should approach his Maker in prayer, and pour forth his grateful acknowledgment for the thousand mercies which have been scattered in his pathway· from the morning of his being. Thus reason decides.

Now let us turn our attention to the Bible, and listen to its teachings in relation to this duty. In looking into that sacred volume we shall find this duty urged in a variety of forms.

1. The fact that God has given promises to prayer settles the question of duty. Promises to prayer are designed to encourage men to pray. But will God encourage men to do what it is not their duty to do? To harbor such a thought of God is insulting and wicked. You would do well to look into the Bible carefully, and search out its promises. The Bible is

full of promises to encourage men to pray. Look at my text, " Ask, and it shall be given." Again, " Whosoever calleth upon the name of the Lord shall be saved." Again, " Whatsoever things ye desire when ye pray, believe that ye receive them, and ye shall have them." We could greatly multiply promises under this head, but it is not necessary.

2. The duty of prayer is made manifest from such passages as the following, — Prov. xv. 8: " The prayer of the upright is his delight." When we learn that a given course of conduct is pleasing to our Maker, that settles the question of duty. Whatever is pleasing to God must be right, and the opposite must be wrong. The Bible makes it the duty of all men to please God and to avoid all things that will displease him. The text under consideration, affirms that the prayer of the upright is *his delight.* That is, it is highly pleasing to God.

From this text two things are manifest.

1. All men should have upright hearts. Why? Because it is pleasing to God.

2. They should pour forth such upright hearts in prayer to their Maker, as that is in harmony with his wishes.

Now such passages as the above, teach the duty of prayer as explicitly as a solemn command. They fully reveal God's will. God's will decides the duty to all.

3. But God commands men to pray. Pray always

with all prayer. Pray with all prayer; what does that mean? Pray with all kinds of prayer. Pray in your closet. If you have families, pray with them. Build up that altar never to go down until you go down into the dark valley. Pray in the social meeting and in the public sanctuary. Pray when about your business or on a journey. Pray always. Do not begin a praying life and then give it up. PRAY ALWAYS.

Again, pray without ceasing, is God's command. Live so as to have a spirit of prayer at all times and under all circumstances. Always be in a praying state of heart. Secure the divine influence to make intercession in your heart, which always begets a spirit of prayer. Never grieve it away. For no man can maintain a spirit of prayer who grieves away the Spirit. He may keep up the form, but it will be a mere form with no God in it. *Pray.* Not say your prayers, but *pray.* Live so that the soul will take hold of God and his promises at all times *without ceasing.*

Again, I would that men should pray everywhere, lifting up holy hands without wrath and doubting. Everywhere. That is, wherever there is a man let him pray,— in any house, town, city, state, nation, or island of the sea. Anywhere on this wide earth where there is a man, let him pray. That is my command. That is my will, says God. What! All sorts of men pray? All sorts of men, from the emperor on his throne, down to the most forlorn beggar. The liar, thief, profane man pray? "*I would that* ALL, ALL MEN SHOULD PRAY." So this text affirms. Would you have the liar pray? Most certainly. What! and continue his lying? Certainly not. The lying part I would have him stop, and become a truthful man, and pray for forgiveness for the past. And the profane man,—would you have him pray? I most certainly would. And continue to swear? No. I would have him stop at once the swearing part, and use his tongue to pray instead of profaning God's name. Let him seek forgiveness in prayer for the manner in which he has used his ungodly tongue. But would you have men pray with a wicked heart? No. I would have men give up their wicked hearts immediately, and pray with right hearts. What business have you to have a wicked heart? God never gave you the right to have a wicked heart. He demands of you to have a right heart. To plead your wicked heart as an excuse for neglecting this duty, is to plead your sin as an excuse for remaining sinful. It is like the liar pleading his want of truthfulness as an excuse for remaining a liar. Or like the drunkard pleading his drunkenness as an excuse for remaining a drunkard. Again, I demand what right have you to have a prayerless, wicked heart? God would have every man on his knees giving up his wicked heart, in his first prayer, as the publican did, and crying, "God be merciful to me a sinner." No, sinner; this command is upon you as much as it is upon Christians. God does not say I would that *Christians* should pray everywhere; but I would that *men*, ALL MEN, should pray everywhere. You are a man, and God speaks to you, and this command is binding upon you, and you cannot shake it off. How many feel that because they are not Christians, they are not under obligations to do the duty of Christians. God's Bible does not give a set of rules to govern Christians simply. It legislates over *men*. It lays down a set of rules to govern *men*, ALL MEN. It demands of all to be Christians, and to attend to all the duties of Christians. Your wickedness consists in not being Christians, and in neglecting the duties that are binding upon all men. Now remember this text demands of *all men* to pray. You cannot flee from this responsibility. You will have to meet it in future. Every hour you neglect this duty you violate this solemn command of God. Will you pray? If you never have prayed, will you begin now? I think I have now sufficiently settled the question, that it is the duty of all men to pray.

II. I AM TO SHOW THAT PRAYER IS A VERY IMPORTANT DUTY.

For wise reasons God has seen fit to offer certain blessings to man, and make the reception of those blessings depend upon the condition of their praying for them. Why God has adopted this course we know not. He has not given us all the reasons why, but the *fact* is revealed. It is manifestly a part of the economy of grace. So the good book teaches, and in this matter we are wholly dependent upon its light to guide us. Blot out the light we derive from that quarter, and there is not a philosopher on earth, that could ever decide whether God would positively hear prayer or not. Much less could he determine upon what condition he would hear it. Why does such a man as Theodore Parker pray? What evidence has he that God will hear prayer? He has no light on that subject, except what he has borrowed from the very book he has rejected as an unsafe guide.

Will God hear a set of rebels against his government pray? Will he answer their petitions? If so, upon what conditions? Such questions can only be answered by a direct revelation from God. That revelation such men reject, and of course must be all afloat, and wholly in the dark upon such points. But to the Christian, the Bible is God Almighty's lamp to guide his footsteps to a throne of grace. It reveals the great truth, that God is a prayer-hearing God, — that he will hear those pray who have sinned and broken his laws, — that there is mercy and pardon for such. The condition upon which he can be pardoned and saved, and his prayers find acceptance on high, are here all made known.

Why should not the Christian love such a book?

He does. He would sooner part with all things earthly, than be deprived of the light it imparts upon this and kindred subjects. But let us return from this little digression to the point under consideration.

In the Bible, prayer is presented as a very important duty, for the following reasons: —

1. It is made the condition upon which God will bestow certain spiritual blessings upon man. Take an instance from Ezekiel xxxvi. 25–37: "Then will I sprinkle clean water upon you, and ye shall be clean; from all your filthiness, and from all your idols, will I cleanse you. A new heart also will I give you, and a new spirit will I put within you: and I will take away the stony heart out of your flesh, and I will give you an heart of flesh. And I will put my spirit within you, and cause you to walk in my statutes, and ye shall keep my judgments, and do them. And ye shall dwell in the land that I gave to your fathers; and ye shall be my people, and I will be your God. I will also save you from all your uncleannesses: and I will call for the corn, and will increase it, and lay no famine upon you. And I will multiply the fruit of the tree, and the increase of the field, that ye shall receive no more reproach of famine among the heathen. Then shall ye remember your own evil ways, and your doings that were not good, and shall loathe yourselves in your own sight for your iniquities and for

your abominations. Not for your sakes do I this, saith the Lord God, be it known unto you: be ashamed and confounded for your own ways, O house of Israel. Thus saith the Lord God; In the day that I shall have cleansed you from all your iniquities I will also cause you to dwell in the cities, and the wastes shall be builded. And the desolate land shall be tilled, whereas it lay desolate in the sight of all that passed by. And they shall say, This land that was desolate is become like the Garden of Eden; and the waste and desolate and ruined cities are become fenced, and are inhabited. Then the heathen that are left round about you shall know that I the Lord build the ruined places, and plant that that was desolate: I the Lord have spoken it, and I will do it. Thus saith the Lord God; I will yet for this be inquired of by the house of Israel, to do it for them; I will increase them with men like a flock." 1. Notice in relation to this passage. Here are great blessings promised to God's wandering people. 2. These blessings, however, are not to be received unless they inquire of the Lord to do these things for them. " Thus saith the Lord; I will yet for this be inquired of by the house of Israel, to do it for them." These great blessings, promised in the above passages, were absolutely essential to fit God's ancient people for heaven. They could not enter heaven without this same preparation of heart promised in this portion of truth.

Still the fulfilment of the promise hangs upon the condition of their inquiring or praying to the Lord to do these things for them. How important a duty upon which such weighty consequences hang.

2. Take another case where salvation is offered to man, suspended upon the duty of prayer. Acts ii. 21 : " It shall come to pass, that whosoever shall call on the name of the Lord shall be saved." Here, so far as man is concerned, salvation hangs upon the right performance of this duty. Call on the name of the Lord and you *shall be saved.* Sinner, life or death, heaven or hell hangs upon your calling upon the name of the Lord as you should. Will you refuse to pray ? Drop upon your knees and cry out to God with every breath for salvation, and give him no rest until you are saved. Do you ask, how shall I pray ? I answer, pray as the publican did. Follow his example in earnest, and you will find God's ear will be open to hear, and your soul will be safe. How important a duty upon which such eternal things hang!

3. The gift of the Spirit is represented as being given in answer to prayer. Luke xi. 13 : " If ye then, being evil, know how to give good gifts unto your children ; how much more shall your heavenly Father give the Holy Spirit to them that ask him ? " The gift of the Spirit is absolutely essential to make the Gospel effectual in saving the world. It is necessary to convince of sin ; to convert the soul ; to make

intercession for the saints; to help understand truth; to assist in hearing and preaching the Gospel, and to finish up the great work of leading and helping the soul on to heaven. It is the crowning work of the system of grace. It is the Almighty Agent that nerves up the ministry and the church, and makes the weapons of their warfare mighty to the pulling down the stronghold of sin. In this great gift is embodied our only hope of success.

Now this great blessing, this blessing that is of infinite worth, is given in answer to prayer. He is more willing to give the Spirit to those *who ask him.* He will give it, then, if we ask. Who will refuse to pray for such a great gift; a blessing of such infinite moment? A man deserves to be damned who will haughtily turn away, and refuse to pray under such circumstances. And shall we, who profess to be Christians, be indifferent about, and neglect a duty upon which such great things hang? No. Let us cry out to God for this great gift until the whole region moves under its power.

4. And finally, the Gospel always produces effect in any place, just in proportion as it is accompanied by the prayer of faith. I have marked that, in my labors in revivals, for years. When Christians begin to have a deep spirit of prayer, that draws out the whole heart to God. When they begin to pray in the Holy Ghost, the Gospel will begin to cut its way. Then sinners begin to tremble. Then they

begin to cry for mercy, and the slain of the Lord will be many. I never knew it to fail, when there was a deep, solemn, agonizing spirit of prayer, but that salvation would come.

This being the fact, how important this duty! What responsibility is resting upon the church! God is ready to give the spirit in answer to prayer. Are you living without a spirit of prayer, so essential to bring salvation to the people? How long have you lived in that state? Sinners all around you are in the way to hell, and you with no spirit of prayer? Think of it, what a state of heart that must be! Will you not repent at once, and fly to God for the outpouring of his Spirit, and give him no rest until you see displays of his power all over this region? Look up for great things. He loves to do great things.

III. I AM TO SHOW THAT PRAYER IS A HIGH PRIVILEGE.

What a strange state of mind the human family are in! How blind! How infinitely blind to their own best interest! How their lives demonstrate the truth of the assertion in the good Book, — Ecc. ix. 3: "Madness is in their heart while they live." They act more like deranged beings than like rational, accountable creatures. The things that are calculated to promote their highest good for time and eternity, are the things which they hate, despise, and neglect. The things that are calculated to destroy their peace and happiness both for this and a future world, are the things to which they cling with all the tenacity of human demons.

Take the subject under consideration as an illustration of their folly and inconsistency. Prayer. How few view prayer as a privilege! The great mass of men view a praying life as the most gloomy, unhappy life a man can live. To them prayer is anything but a privilege. It may be a duty, but talk about its being a privilege, that is wholly out of the question. Still it is true that prayer is one of the highest privileges ever bestowed upon man. To come to God with the assurance from him, that he is both able and willing to supply all our wants; to commune with the Infinite One; to hold converse with the most exalted being in the universe; to have the privilege of access to that being before whom the master intellects that burn in heaven bow with profound reverence, and cast their crowns at his feet, and cry, Holy, Holy is the Lord God Almighty; to have access to such a being is a privilege so high and noble, that the grovelling heart of man cannot estimate it. Men as a general thing are so wedded to earth and earthly things, the mere trifles of a day, that they have no relish for the high and holy work of communing with God.

How sin has blinded their minds! How it has led them to view evil as good and good as evil! But, poor sinner, you who hate prayer to-day, you who would consider yourself disgraced to bow the knee in this house and call on the name of the Lord, the day is approaching when you would give all the world if you had it at your command, if you could have the privilege of offering up one prayer and have it heard on high. You may see that moment before you step down into the dark valley. You may, however, rush into eternity before you awake to view this matter as it is. But mark! Awake you will. View it in its true light you must. If the Bible and the means of grace cannot arouse you, and bring you upon your knees to cry for help, the agonies of hell and the pangs of the second death will do it.

What think you the rich man, who lifted up his eyes and called for water to cool his tongue, would have given to have had the privilege of offering one prayer and had it favorably heard and answered? He prayed, and you would do well to read his prayer and ponder it long. What a prayer! Hear him for a moment! Hark! "Father Abraham, have mercy on me, and send Lazarus that he may dip the tip of his finger in water, and cool my tongue; for I am tormented in this flame." Look at this prayer. Did he ask to be delivered from hell? No; he knew doubtless that such a prayer would be fruitless. Did he pray, send Lazarus with a bucket of water? No; note its language,—" That he may dip the tip of his finger in water, and cool my tongue." That tongue which had been profane and abusive on earth, perhaps. What anguish now! Only a drop of water hanging to the tip of the finger would be some relief. But no, no. No prayer coming up from hell can be heard. In that world they may call, but I will not answer. Sinner, in hell you will see the value of prayer, if you cannot be led to see it here and fly to Christ. But why rush into the flames of the pit to learn it? Why not learn it in Mercy's world where there is a Mediator between God and man, and where your prayers can be heard and answered? Why wait until you are forced by sad experience to learn the full import of those dread words: "Then shall they call upon me, but I will not answer; they shall seek me early, but they shall not find me: for that they hated knowledge, and did not choose the fear of the Lord?" To illustrate this high privilege let us suppose a case:

Here is a man of immense wealth. His treasures, we will suppose, are inexhaustible. He sends abroad to the wide world this promise and pledge: If any man, from any part of the globe, will come and ask for it, he shall have all the gold he desires. One man comes and asks for a thousand dollars; he hands it over. Another ten thousand; his wants are supplied. Another ten millions; the more the better, is the reply; giving does not impoverish me; it is my delight to give. Not a man approaches, but his wants are all supplied. What a privilege to pray under such circumstances! Men would rush from every part of our land and the wide world to pray to such a being. I am not mistaken on this point. When the news was fully confirmed that gold could be washed from the sands, and dug from the mountains, in California, what a rush from almost every part of the earth! Men sold their property to procure means to reach the land of promise. They left their families, and were ready to brave all manner of dangers and hardships, and even look death in the face, to obtain riches. They were not sure when they reached there, that they should obtain the desired object. They only had high hopes they should find a vast treasure. Now let it be settled and fully believed, that all that was necessary was for men to come to the city of Boston and ask for all the gold they wished, and they would certainly receive it, and what a rush there would be to the old Bay State! Every vessel, steamboat, and railroad car would be freighted with applicants.

Now mark! God, the Infinite God, who cannot lie, and who is both able and ready to redeem his pledge, looks down from heaven and proclaims to the world, to all the inhabitants of earth : " Ask and it shall be given." What shall be given ? gold ? No ; something far more valuable than all the material universe, if it were all one solid mass of gold, shall be given. Eternal life shall be given. The forgiveness of all your sins shall be given. "An inheritance incorruptible and undefiled, and that fadeth not away, reserved in heaven for you," shall be given. Here is something substantial; something that is lasting and valuable as heaven, shall be given; something that will stand by when the sun is blown out, and when earth and all the gold and wealth shall be consumed with one breath of the Almighty. Now what a privilege to pray if these are the blessings,—if these are the rewards of prayer! Who can refuse to pray with such promises breaking upon his ear, and with such a God to back them up? If they will slight such promises, they ought to die.

DIVISION NO. II.

We have already shown, 1. Prayer a duty; 2. An important duty; 3. A high privilege; and now,

IV. I AM TO EXAMINE THE THREE LEADING TERMS IN THE TEXT SEPARATELY: ASK. SEEK. KNOCK.

1. ASK. We have had many labored definitions of prayer, perhaps too labored in some instances to be easily understood. The most simple and literal definitions, as a general thing, are the best; always literal, unless the connection of the text shows that it will not bear a literal construction. The first definition that Mr. Webster gives to the word *pray*, is, the first word in my text, ask. To pray, accord-

ing to this definition, is, to ask. Prayer supposes that there are blessings in the hand of another being that we need, and we come to that being and ask for them. One of the first lessons we ever learned on earth was to pray. Understand, now, I do not affirm that the first lesson we learned on earth was to pray to God. We pray to other beings besides God. We pray to one another. Children pray to parents. They are dependent upon their parents, very dependent in the early stage of their history, and they come and ask for things they need. That is, they pray to them for such things. Children pray before their infant tongues can pronounce a word. How often I have seen such little fellows ask. And there was an eloquence about their petitions that would move a mother's or a father's heart. The reaching up of that little hand for help, accompanied by that wishful, imploring look, which expressed its whole heart; or that cry of distress,— how it would go through a parent's soul, and move him to grant at once, the relief or blessing sought! If this definition of prayer be correct, it fully disposes of the position taken by some, that prayer consists simply in having good desires. A man who thinks he is a praying man, because he has good desires, is deluded and deceived. Good desires are not prayer. We admit there is no prayer without good desires. But the good desires are one thing, and prayer is another. Prayer consists in having good desires, and offering up those desires to God in the name of Christ, and asking that they may be granted. Having the desire in the heart, and leaving off the *asking* part, is not prayer. Why? Simply because prayer is asking for things we need. But, says an objector, God knows my desires; he looks into my heart, and knows my heart fully. Grant all that; but his knowing your desires does not take away your duty of asking, nor perform it for you. He has made it your duty to ask, and he will not bestow the blessing unless you ask. He has made that the condition of your receiving the blessing, and he will not alter it. Now why deceive yourself, and cheat your soul out of the blessing you might receive, by such cavils? Why undertake to dodge this plain duty? Why not meet it like a man? The terms are simple and most reasonable, and your undertaking to define, so as to dodge this duty, shows a state of heart of which you ought to be ashamed, and over which you ought to weep and repent.

But, says the objector again, do you pretend we cannot pray without using the tongue? No, certainly not. In communing with God, the mind frequently dispenses with the use of the tongue. But that does not settle the question that desire is prayer. Far from it. In all such cases the desire in the heart is one thing, and the mind's offering up those desires to God, and asking that the desires may be granted is another and distinct thing. The mind asks and urges her suit before God, and does it effectually in multitudes of instances, even when the tongue is silent.

2. SEEK. To illustrate this word let me suppose a case. Here is an individual who steps into the congregation and assures you that in a certain field in this vicinity, which he describes, there is an immense treasure deposited. He does not know precisely where in the field it is to be found, but the fact that it is within the limits of that field, he does know, and he makes every one believe it. The treasure, when found, is enough to supply all your wants; and now he assures you, if you will but go and seek for it, you will find an abundance. In that case you would understand the word *seek*. You would go and hunt after it diligently and earnestly. You would go there for months and seek, if you knew for a certainty you could make yourself independently rich by so doing. You would look in every corner, turn over every stone, tear up by the roots every stump, and dig up the earth ten feet deep, before you would fail of finding the treasure. Now when you will search for God and his salvation, as you search for hidden treasures, he will be found of you.

Prov. ii. 3–6 : " Yea, if thou criest after knowledge, and liftest up thy voice for understanding; if thou seekest her as silver, and searchest for her as for hid treasures; then shalt thou understand the fear of the Lord, and find the knowledge of God." Look at this promise for a moment. "If thou criest after knowledge." What knowledge? Knowledge of God and his salvation. If you cry out to God for it, be in earnest about it. If you lift up your voice for understanding, to understand God, to understand his government, his great system of grace, the way of life and salvation, lift up your voice for this understanding, seek it of God; seek it as you would silver, with all the zeal, earnestness, and perseverance that you hunt for hidden treasures; search for this important knowledge in the Bible and in the use of all other religious means within your reach, and when thus in earnest, you shall soon find the knowledge of the Lord. Seek thus and you shall find.

3. Knock, and it shall be opened. To help you to understand this part of the text let me resort to a little more imagery. I will suppose, then, that an individual, living in the country some three or four miles, comes in this evening to hear the sermon. After the meeting closes, he drives home and enters his residence, when his wife thus addresses him. "Husband, is the horse unhitched from the carriage?" "Yes," he replies; "but what led you to ask that question?" as he discovers an anxious look upon her countenance. "Because I wish you to go for the doctor immediately. Our little son is very ill, and I am fearful he will die before a phy-

sician can reach here. He is very stupid, and is evidently sinking very fast." "What!" says he, "Charley sick! What is the matter?" Picking up the light from the stand, he steps to the bed and looks at the little fellow as he lies there pale and emaciated, wholly insensible at what is passing. "Sure enough," says the husband, "he is sick; and I am fearful we shall lose him. How long since was he taken thus ill, and what have you done for him?" Now I will suppose that, while they are consulting in relation to what shall be done, an angel makes his appearance at that bedside to communicate an important fact to them in relation to the child. I will suppose that the revelation comes from an angel, so that it can be relied on. He informs them that there is a physician residing in this city, on such a street, at such a number, who can save the life of the child, if they will procure his services before morning. He is the only man who can save him, and unless they secure him before morning the child must die. Now, with such a revelation, what will be done? Done? The father rushes to the barn, and is soon in his carriage, and on his way to the city. In a short time his carriage wheels make the city ring as he drives, Jehu-like, through one street after another, until he arrives at the door of the physician. How does he manage now? Does he step to the door and knock once very cautiously, and if he gets no answer turn away discouraged, to let his child die? Not he. His soul is in earnest. His heart palpitates, and he is in agony. He knocks once, and if he gets no answer he knocks again, and again. His anxiety increases every time he knocks. Delay only increases his earnestness; and he thunders away at the door until the doctor is aroused, in his carriage, and both hastening with all possible despatch to the bedside of his sick child, to save his life.

Now says Christ, " Knock, and it shall be opened." Knock where? At heaven's gate. Knock how? By prayer, by earnest prayer. But, says one, do you intend, by your imagery, to represent Jesus Christ as being indifferent to our prayers? Not at all. But I intend, by this synonyme, to represent Christ just as the Bible does. But, continues the objector, do you intend to teach that we must pray very loud, and make a great bluster about it? Nothing of the kind; for there can be a great deal of noise and bluster when there is but little praying. Prayer does not consist in making a noise. It consists in having the heart enlisted, deeply enlisted, and in having it drawn out to God in solemn earnestness for the blessings we need. Let us turn to the Bible on this point. " The effectual fervent prayer of a righteous man availeth much." 1. It must be the prayer of a *righteous* man. 2. A fervent prayer; not a cold, heartless, formal prayer. God will not hear such. But a *fervent* prayer, one that enlists and calls out the whole heart, God will hear. When the whole soul knocks at heaven's gate, it shall be opened. Take another case. Luke xviii. 1-8. Christ illustrates and enforces, by his striking imagery, the very point now under consideration. Hear him: " And he spake a parable unto them to this end, that men ought always to pray, and not to faint; saying, There was in a city a judge, which feared not God, neither regarded man. And there was a widow in that city; and she came unto him, saying, Avenge me of mine adversary. And he would not for a while: but afterward he said within himself, Though I fear not God, nor regard man; yet because this widow troubleth me, I will avenge her, lest by her continual coming she weary me. And the Lord said, Hear what the unjust judge saith. And shall not God avenge his own elect, which cry day and night unto him, though he bear long with them? I tell you that he will avenge them speedily. Nevertheless, when the Son of man cometh, shall he find faith on the earth?"

From this parable please notice the following things: 1. It teaches that men should always pray. 2. That they should persevere in prayer, and hold on until the object sought is obtained; that they should not faint if the blessing is not obtained the first time asking, but importune at the throne of grace. 3. That God will answer the prayer of his own elect who cry unto him day and night. Who are his own elect? His own dear children who have been born of the Spirit, and are faithful in his work. Notice the terms the Saviour uses. They express earnestness, deep earnestness. 1. They cry unto him. This term expresses deep and intense feeling. The soul cries out to God for help, from the living God. 2. They cry to him *day and night.* The heart is so enlisted that it cannot and will not let go until the blessing comes. It pleads day and night. Such passages teach conclusively that, when we knock at heaven's gate, we must be in earnest if we would be heard. As much so or more, if possible, than the man would be supposed to be at the door of the doctor, under the circumstances I have described. Then God will hear.

But, you reply, your imagery supposes danger, imminent danger, and of course a man would be in earnest under such circumstances. But pause for a moment. Is not your child sick unto death? Is it a sinner? If so, it has a disease far more fatal than any that can be inflicted upon the body. The disease is certain death unless it is removed speedily. And then *the death,* it is the death of the soul! ENDLESS DEATH! Now remember there is but one Physician who can heal and save it. He thunders upon your dull ear to-day. Knock and it shall be opened. Knock now. Why, your child may be dead and damned in a few hours! Knock in earnest. Here, heaven and eternal life are at stake.

Wake up and knock! Christ says, knock. Do you hear him? Fly to heaven's gate by prayer, and knock there until deliverance comes.

V. I AM TO ANSWER THE QUESTION, WHAT IS IT TO PRAY AS THE BIBLE DIRECTS, OR HOW CAN WE OFFER PREVAILING PRAYER?

This question is of infinite moment to every man. One object of praying is to secure an answer, — to secure the blessing we need. Moreover, we cannot be saved unless we can come to God, so that he will hear and answer us.

God save a man whose prayers he cannot answer! He never will. There are beings pointed out in the Bible who call upon God, and he will not answer; such are impenitent, and in the way to hell. We must come into a state, therefore, in which we can approach God, and have him hear us, or we cannot be saved.

The Bible teaches, that some ask and receive not, because they ask amiss. They do not ask aright; consequently, God will not hear. There is a right and a wrong way to pray.

The question now to come under consideration, is, which is the right way? The Bible is the book that teaches us the way. How can we pray according to its teachings so as to have God hear us?

In reply to this question I remark: —

1. If we would offer prevailing prayer, we must have correct views of the character of the God to

whom we pray. We must see to it that we do not pray to a false God. We must be sure that we pray to the God of the Bible. If you were to pray to the sun as your God, you would not expect an answer to prayer. Why? Because in that case you would not pray to the God of the Bible, but to a false God. It is not necessary to hew out a God and bow down to that to be guilty of idolatry. We can set up a false God in our imagination, and pray to such a God, and be as guilty as we would be to pray to an idol that we could see, or that our own hands had formed. I believe there are many such idolaters in this land at the present time. They do not like the God of the Bible, and they have formed a God in their imaginations to suit themselves. Some men have set reason to work to frame for them a God. They want a God they can comprehend. Very well. If you have a God you can comprehend, you will have a false God. The infinite God is not to be comprehended by any creature he ever formed. He is infinitely above the comprehension of all creatures. What? A finite mind comprehend an infinite? It is a glaring contradiction. Now the God to whom you are to pray is an infinite God. You must approach such a God, if you would secure an answer to prayer. Some men pray to a God, they say, who will save all. That is not the God of the Bible, for he declares he will not save all men. He affirms that he shall damn a class of men endlessly. Such a God, says one, I do not like. I presume you don't. But that is no new thing under the sun. The wicked have always disliked the true God. The good Book informs us that they do not like to retain him in their knowledge. Well, says the objector, I will not love and worship such a God. I presume you will not. You can hate and reject him, and take the consequences of such a course. You can take as a consequence the very damnation you affirm never will come. But, after all, the God that will punish some men endlessly is the God who answers prayer. He is the Bible God, and you must pray to him or get no answer.

Once more. Some men want a God that is all love, and no wrath in him. Such an one is not the true God, or the Bible God. The Bible presents us with a God of love; at the same time it informs us that he has wrath in reserve for the wicked. Rom. i. 18: "The wrath of God is revealed from heaven against all ungodliness," &c. The wrath of God revealed, when God has no wrath? That is impossible. Eph. v. 6: "Because of these things *cometh the wrath of God* upon the children of disobedience." How can the *wrath* of God come upon the children of disobedience if God has no wrath? In fact the Bible says almost as much about the wrath of God as it does about his love.

There is a holy indignation and wrath, which is

right and just in God, and he would not be a perfect being if he were destitute of it. And if you pray to a God who has no wrath, you are not praying to the true or Bible God. You must banish from your mind all such Gods, and pray to the God the Bible reveals. One great object of the Bible is to reveal to us the true God. He knows himself, and can give to man a correct revelation of himself. That revelation he has given in the Bible. Now, if you would offer prevailing prayer, you must come to the God the Bible reveals. He is the hearer and answerer of prayer. You must not be deceived or misled here. If you are, it will be fatal.

Let me now name four things concerning God, which you should have deeply impressed on your mind, if you would secure a blessing when you pray.

1. You should remember that God is everywhere. Psalms, cxxxix. 7–10: "Whither shall I go from thy Spirit, or whither shall I flee from thy presence? If I ascend up into heaven, thou art there. If I make my bed in hell, behold, thou art there. If I take the wings of the morning, and dwell in the uttermost parts of the sea; even there shall thy hand lead me, and thy right hand shall hold me."

What a view of God is here presented! How wonderful! If you could fly into any corner of this vast universe, you would be surrounded with God. What a thought! How can we grapple with such an immense idea? Pause before you pray, and dwell upon it. I am surrounded with this great Being. He is searching my inmost heart. Not a sin can be concealed from him, and now I am about to address this great Being. Open your mouth, and pray to him as a present God. Say not in your heart, who shall ascend into heaven to bring him down. He is here. He puts his ear down to your very lips to listen to the first breath of prayer. How many feel, when they pray, that God is away up in heaven, so far from them that they can hardly send up a petition to his throne. Now such are not praying to the *true* God. They are praying to a *false* God as much as if they were praying to the sun. They are praying to a God shut up in a local place, no nearer to them than the heaven of heavens. That is not the true God. He is here as well as in heaven. His presence fills the immensity of space. Now, you never offer prevailing prayer in that state of mind. Why? Because you are not praying to the true God. Repent of that state of heart, and pray to a present God. When a man prevails with God in prayer, he always feels that God is near him, and he can talk with him as did Moses, face to face. Realizing that you are surrounded with this great and awful God, that his holy eye is upon your heart, and that you cannot deceive him, will have a tendency to fill you with that religious awe and holy reverence, which is befitting as you attempt to spread your wants before this Infinite Being. In such a state of heart approach his mercy-seat, and plead with him for the blessing you need. To bring this truth of a present God home to your mind, let me suppose that you are gathered around your family altar, and after reading a portion of truth from the Bible, you and your family have just fallen upon your knees to make known your morning request. Just at this important moment Christ steps into your midst, and spreads his holy hands over your heads, and addresses you in the language of my text: "Ask, and it shall be given you; seek, and ye shall find; knock, and it shall be opened unto you." Now, it is truly Christ in your midst. You look up into his holy face, — you see the prints of the nails in his hands, — you hear his voice, you listen to his promise. How would you feel under such circumstances? Could you not pray in earnest? Would you not confess to him all your sins? Would you not lay before him all your wants, and the wants of your entire family? Would you not take hold of his promises, just fallen upon your ear, and plead them with great confidence and earnestness until you had obtained the blessing that you and your family need? How could you be turned away, or let Christ depart, until you had received the blessing? You would feel, now is the time, and we cannot be denied. Yes, says one, if I could only *see* Christ, how I would order my speech before him. Now attach this attribute to Christ, and you have him with you. He is everywhere. " Where two or three are gathered together in my name, there am I."

This could not be true of him if he were not everywhere. He is in heaven interceding, but he is here also to hear us pray. Think then, when you pray, Christ is here. You cannot see him, but he is present to listen to your every desire, and to answer your every prayer offered in faith.

2. Another thing in relation to God should be distinctly before the mind when we pray, namely, that our God is unchangeable. " He is the same yesterday, to-day, and forever." " He is in one mind, and who can turn him?" This attribute of the Deity lays the foundation for confidence in the promises of the Bible. Take the promise in my text as an illustration of the thought I wish to communicate. Here is a promise that fell from the lips of Christ more than eighteen hundred years ago. If Christ is changeable, who knows but he has changed his mind since the promise was given? He said, eighteen hundred years ago, " Ask and it shall be given you;" but, perhaps, he feels differently now. The promise was good then, but how can I know that it is good for me to-day? If he is a changeable Christ, he may have changed his mind in relation to this promise, and in relation to prayers generally. Perhaps he will not hear prayer, now, at all. Moreover,

if this be true in relation to this promise, the same mode of reasoning will apply to all the promises in the Bible, and would undermine our confidence in the whole of them. Under such circumstances we never could know whether any of these promises were good for us to-day, without a new revelation direct from his throne at the present time. But, attach the attribute under consideration to God, and it makes this and other promises in the Bible just as good as if God should speak from heaven now, in an audible voice, and thunder these promises in our ears, while we are here together. He said to men on probationary ground, eighteen hundred years ago, " Ask, and it shall be given you;" and he is in the same mind to-day. This attribute is God's fresh indorsement of these promises. They were designed for men, *all* men in mercy's world. They are part of the Gospel system, and are good to men here on the shores of time until the Gospel dispensation is closed up and removed. The same unchangeable God is on the throne that caused these promises to be proclaimed originally, and the same unchangeable Mediator is yet before the throne to make intercession for the transgressor. Consequently, we may come with confidence to him to-day, and take hold of these promises as ours; and if we plead them by faith we shall know by happy experience that he is the same yesterday, to-day, and forever. What a glorious attribute this is to the saint and to angels!

They can look up to his throne, and behold it filled with a Being who is unchangeable in his purposes, and all his great plans, and all the minute parts that go to make up his great plans. He sees the end from the beginning. There can be no new or unforeseen event spring up to produce a change in his infinite mind. They know that he loves holiness to-day, and he will love it forever. They understand that he arranges all things to promote and perfect the happiness of the obedient subject of his government now, and he will pursue the same unchanging plan forever. Into the hands of such a Being they can commit their cause with confidence, and hang upon and plead his promises with unwavering faith.

3. Another attribute of God, which we should ever have before the mind, when we pray, is this: Our God is an Almighty God. Losing sight of this attribute may prevent our prevailing in prayer. If we come to God feeling that he is a weak being, something like ourselves, such a state of heart would prevent our receiving the blessing. Taking such a view of God is dishonorable to him, as it is a false view, and would grieve the Spirit. Then, again, if we think he is not able to do much, we shall not ask for much; we shall not have faith. How could we have faith in such a being? We want a God who is able to do. Thank Heaven! we have a God who is able to do; and we must not dishonor him by

having low and contracted views of his ability, if we would receive a blessing, a *great* blessing.

Let us see how God has connected this attribute of ability directly with the subject of asking. Hear Paul for a moment, in Eph. iii. 20: " Now unto him that is *able to do exceeding abundantly above* all that we ask or think." How Paul connected the ability of God directly with the subject we have under consideration! Is he able to do as much as we ask, as much as we think? More than that! How much more? a little more? " EXCEEDING abundantly above all that we ask or think." Not only a little above, but *abundantly above*, EXCEEDING ABUNDANTLY ABOVE! It would seem as though the Spirit labored to throw terms together, here, to get out this great thought upon our minds, and impress us with this idea as we approach the mercy-seat. Now, here is where I believe Christians fail, in multitudes of instances. They do not, at *heart*, believe God is able to do much. Remember, I am not now talking about what the tongue affirms. I am talking about the utterances of the heart. God looks into your hearts to see what is there.

I doubt not there are angels in heaven who have more physical power than many in the church believe, *at heart*, God has. Take one or two Bible specimens of the power of angels; 2 Kings xix. 35: " And it came to pass that night, that the angel of the Lord went out, and smote in the camp of the

Assyrians an hundred four score and five thousand." What messengers of death God has at his command! Look at it. One angel, *in one night*, walks through the camp of the Assyrians, and 185,000 are dead in the morning. He looks at them, and they are pale in death. If God wished to vanquish all the armies of earth, he would have to commission and direct only one angel into the field, and he would be more than a match for all the armies this world could muster. What could all the nations of the earth do in the presence of one angel? Take one specimen more: After Christ's death, the Jews came to Pilate with a request. They remarked, that this deceiver predicted, before his death, that on the third day he should rise again; and they request that the sepulchre be made sure until after the third day, lest his disciples should steal the body during the night, and then report that he had risen from the dead; and the delusion, as they termed it, would break out afresh. Pilate replied, " You have a watch; go and make it sure as you can." With this permission from the governor, they went and rolled a large stone upon the door of the sepulchre, sealed it, and stationed a strong guard of soldiers to watch it until after the specified day. On the third day God sent down an angel to attend to that matter. He just rolls back the stone, takes his seat upon it, barely casts a look upon these armed fellows, and they fall like-dead men at his feet. Did he put his hand upon them? No; he barely turned an angel's countenance upon them, and they are powerless in an instant. What power! Who can resist it? But this is only the power of an angel; and if angels have such immense power, what must be the power of the God of angels, to whom we are to pray? When you pray, you should try to have the mind impressed with this great truth. You should dwell upon it until the soul is full and overwhelmed with it. Look at the displays of power all around. Ponder this great mass of matter on which we live and ride in its career through the depths of space. Go back to its creation, and hear our God speak and call it into being. Did he exert all his power, and then just be able to perform this mighty work? Mark with what ease it is done. A purpose of his will, a word of command, and it is done! Hear him thunder, " *Let there be light!* " and how quick all is illuminated! Hear him again: " *Let the waters under the heaven be gathered together unto one place, and let the dry land appear!* " How quick the mountains rear their heads, the vales are depressed, and the ocean begins to roll her mighty billows in her appointed bed. All, all is done with infinite ease, with a simple word of command. Then, once more, one impulse from his mighty hand at that moment, and this great mass of matter has pursued its journey around the sun at the rate of 68,000 miles an hour, from that moment to the present time. But what is this earth compared with the great universe in which we reside? Look abroad into the heavens and behold the thousands of systems of worlds that have been called into being by this same Almighty hand, and mark how he upholds and governs them all in harmony with his will and wishes. Now remember, that it is to this Almighty God that we pray. We may come with all our wants. He is able to meet and supply every demand of the soul. We may bring our families, and he can do for them also. We may come and lay this city at his feet, and he can rock it to its very centre under his awful treading. We may come with our wayward and wicked land, and he can cause salvation, like an overflowing flood, to roll a wave of mercy over every part of it, sweeping away, in its power, all its abominations. Nay, more. We may take this wicked world in the arms of our faith, and fly to the mercy-seat, and he can open the windows of heaven and pour out a blessing until there is not room to receive it, and then he has blessings enough in reserve to supply the wants of ten thousand such worlds. Such is our God; and why not let us open our mouths wide, and look up for great things, and expect great things?

If the world is ever converted, this limiting God with our wicked unbelief must cease, and we must take the world in the arms of our faith and rush to Christ with it, and expect he will subdue it by the power of his Gospel. Will you come to this Almighty God to-day? Will you spread your wants and the wants of this people before him, and press your suit until you see great exhibitions of his power in saving men?

4. One thing more in relation to God, and then I will leave this branch of our subject. When we pray, we should have our minds deeply impressed with the fact that God is infinite in his benevolence. We should feel that God's willingness to hear prayer is equal to his ability. He is infinitely able, and he is also infinitely willing when we approach him as he directs. We lose sight of his willingness when we pray, or our hearts call it in question, which shuts out the blessing. God loves to hear and answer prayer, if we are only in a right state of heart to be blessed. He must not dispense his blessings so as to sanction our wickedness, and he will not, if we all go to hell. But when we take a right position, then he is ready. God's willingness is expressed in his promises. Every promise to prayer in the Bible is absolute demonstration of his willingness to hear. God was voluntary in giving his promises; he was under no compulsion when he gave them. They were not extorted from him, nor drawn out of him by some other being. They are a full and free expression of his own choice. If he is not willing to hear, why give them, or encourage prayer at all? But he has given them, and given

multitudes of them. The Bible is full of them, and they forever settle the matter of his willingness. To present his willingness in the clearest possible light before our minds, God has appealed to one feeling in the human heart that is stronger than all others. He has appealed to parental love, parental care and anxiety for children, parental willingness to do for their offspring. Those in this congregation who are not parents cannot understand me on this point, but parents can. I was a stranger to this feeling until I became a father. Since that time, I can understand a thousand things that were said to me by my parents, as I could not understand them before. My mother's anxiety, — what a mystery it was! It was expressed in her every look, her every movement. She would caution me about this thing, and express anxiety about that; and I thought it so unnecessary. I would frequently say to my mother, "Mother, why so anxious about me? I can take care of myself. Do not make yourself unhappy about me." Still she would have a mother's care and a mother's anxiety; it was as natural as her breath. Then her willingness to do in sickness and in health was manifest all through her life. That kind of feeling I did not understand until I was a parent. Now I can see why my parents felt thus. My anxiety for my children is constant; and to say no, when they come with a request for me to grant, is one of the most unpleasant things of my life. I love to do for them;

it is the delight of my heart to benefit them. Now it is to this parental love that God makes his strong appeal, to show his willingness to hear prayer. He is more willing to give good things to them that ask him, than we are to give good things to our children. Hear him on this point: "If ye, then, being evil, know how to give good gifts unto your children, how much more shall your father which is in heaven give good things to them that ask him?" Now, what stronger appeal could God make to show his willingness to hear and answer prayer? To enforce this point, let me relate a little incident that took place a few years since, west of this. I had this account for a fact; but whether it was all literally true or not makes no difference, as it is a good illustration of the point under consideration.

In one of our western villages were parents who had a lovely little boy, whose name we will call Willie. He was a bright little fellow, an only child, and the idol of his father's heart. His father was a mechanic, whose shop was some little distance from the house. Frequently when he became weary, he would throw down his tools, run to the house, catch up Willie, play with him a season, and then put him down with the remark, " Now, my dearest, I must go back to my work." The boy was old enough to play about the house and yard, and occasionally he would wander down to the shop to his father. One day the father came running in, and looked for his little pet, as he called him, but did not find him. He finally turned to his wife, and said, "My dear, where is Willie?" "I know not," she replied; "I have not seen him for some time; I supposed he was at the shop with you." "No," said he, "he has not been there." "Not been there?" she asked; "then he must be looked up." Accordingly they searched the house, yard, barn, and patch of woods near by, calling to Willie, but could get no answer. They ran to the neighbors and inquired, but could obtain no tidings of the lost child. It was growing late in the day; night was coming on, and their anxiety increased every moment. They rallied the neighbors, and searched and inquired; but night closed in upon them, and the lost child was not found.

The next day many of the neighbors turned out, searched the whole village and vicinity for nearly three days before he was found. On the third day, a party of men, returning from a long search, discovered the little fellow upon a ledge of rocks, one of whom caught him up in his arms, and exclaimed, "*I have found him!* I HAVE FOUND HIM!" With cheerful and joyous hearts, they all hurried to the house, to convey the glad tidings to the broken-hearted parents. The parents, with a few sympathizing friends, were in the parlor when they entered with the famishing child. The father, as he beheld his lost pet, leaped from his seat and clasped him to his bosom, weeping for joy. Recovering a little from the first shock, the little fellow finding himself once more in his father's arms, looked up imploringly in his face, " Pa, I want a piece of bread." What father's heart could refuse such a request under such circumstances? With what delight he would feed that famishing child! Now is God as willing to feed our starving, dying souls, as that father was to feed his starving child? " He is more willing." Can it be possible? So he affirms. How much more willing? As much more as he is more holy and benevolent than an earthly parent can be. Our benevolence is but finite, his is infinite. But your case is too strong, says one. Not at all, I reply; you cannot get one too strong. There was danger, the child was starving. So are we in danger. Our souls are starving for the bread of life, — the true bread of life. " But the child would have died." So shall we die eternally, unless we have help from heaven, and our heavenly Father knows it. He is not insensible to our danger, if we are, ourselves. Let us believe what God says. He is more willing to bless us than we are to feed and bless our children. What stronger appeal could God make to convince us of his willingness to hear prayer? But our hearts are unbelieving, hence we do not believe God is willing to hear us. This unbelief shuts out the blessing. These important things in relation to God should be deeply engraven upon our hearts.

The soul should dwell upon them until they become living realities. Then, under a realizing sense of this truth, we should approach the mercy-seat with all our wants to be supplied.

2. To offer prevailing prayer, we must have a correct view of ourselves. A correct knowledge of one's self, is almost as essential as a correct knowledge of God. You will not come to God for the things you need unless you know yourself. There may be sins which separate between you and God, and if you are unacquainted with your own heart, those sins will not be confessed and put away, consequently God will not hear.

There are difficulties attending this part of the matter. The heart is deceitful, and it will mislead you here unless you are rigid with yourself. We love to think well of ourselves, and we want others to think well of us. It is painful to take such a view of our lives as to loathe and detest them. To avoid this unpleasant view, we will neglect to search our hearts by God's truth. This state of things will shut God away from our souls, and he will not hear us. Keep in view, then, a most thorough, honest course of self-examination is absolutely essential to secure a spirit of prayer, or to maintain it. A person who neglects it will not offer prevailing prayer.

DIVISION NO. III.

In the first division of this discourse we considered the subject of prayer, 1. as a duty; 2. as an important duty; 3. as a high privilege. In the second division we examined the terms, Ask, Seek, and Knock, and then proceeded to answer the question under the fifth head, How to offer prevailing prayer. We now continue the subject, and remark —

3. A spirit of forgiveness towards those who have injured us in any form, is another thing that must not be overlooked if we would offer prevailing prayer.

The Bible is very clear and decided on this point. Mark xi. 25, 26: "And when ye stand praying, forgive, if ye have aught against any; that your Father also which is in heaven may forgive you your trespasses. But if ye do not forgive, neither will your Father which is in heaven forgive your trespasses."

Please notice how this passage connects forgiveness with the subject we now have in hand. "When ye stand *praying*, forgive." At the very time you are praying and seeking forgiveness from God, forgive those who have injured you. "That is a hard lesson to learn," says one. "I *cannot* forgive certain individuals." Very well, if that is true your doom is fixed for eternity. You are lost, in that case, irrecoverably lost. God declares he will not forgive, unless you forgive others, and of course you must go to hell. "But how can I forgive that wrong, it was so very aggravating?" Does that form a sufficient reason why you should not forgive? says God. If so, then I cannot forgive any of your wrongs, for they have all been very aggravating. They were committed against the best Being in the universe; the Being who has sought your highest good for time and eternity; against a perfect government, that if obeyed by all, was calculated to secure the highest good of the universe; against an infinite Redeemer who gave up his life to save you; against an all-sufficient Holy Ghost who is sent here to sanctify and fit you for heaven; and they have been repeated so many times, that if very aggravating wrongs form *the* reason why they should not be forgiven, then I cannot forgive you, says God, and you must go to hell. Do you wish God to let you stand or fall by your own theory? No, no, says one; I want forgiveness at the hand of my Maker. Very well, says God; when ye stand praying, *forgive them*, and then I will forgive you.

But that was not an imaginary, but a real wrong, and a very great one. Of course it was a real wrong, for if it had only been an imaginary one, it would need only an imaginary forgiveness. The very idea of forgiveness supposes you have been wronged. If you had not been wronged there would be no ground of forgiveness. Well, says one, I think I can forgive all the members of our church. Does God say, forgive all the members of your church and I will forgive? The passage does not read thus. That does not meet the conditions of the text; for you might forgive all the members of your own church, and feel very wicked towards the members of other churches, and particularly churches of other denominations. God will not forgive while there is any hardness in your heart towards any Christian on earth. Well, I can forgive all the Christians, but that sinner, that slanderous sinner, or that hypocrite. Stop, stop, my brother; let us look at this text critically, for eternal life hangs upon complying with its conditions. Does it read, if ye forgive all Christians I will forgive you? "When ye stand praying, forgive, if ye have *aught against any.*" Now turn to Matt. vi. 14, 15, and that explains the term *any*: "For if ye forgive *men* their trespasses, your heavenly Father will also forgive you. But if ye forgive not *men* their trespasses, neither will your Father forgive your trespasses." This settles the whole matter. If you would be forgiven and offer prevailing prayer, when you pray you must forgive *men*, ALL MEN who have injured you. Now remember, if you have an old grudge in your heart towards any man living, when you pray and do not forgive, God will not hear you. You may as well stop praying as to pray. God's ear is closed to all such prayers. Forgive, says

God, if you want I should hear, and I will forgive. You say, I cannot forgive. Very well, God will not forgive. Bring no more vain oblations, your prayers are a smoke in my nostrils, says God; I will not hear until you forgive. But what shall I do? says one; I cannot give up praying, and I cannot forgive. You may as well give up praying as to pray. God will not hear you, and he will not save you unless you forgive. Some seem to think they can bring God over by teasing him for a season. My brother, you mistake your Maker. His terms are like himself, unchangeable. He would sooner let the whole world go to hell, than change them in the least. They are right as they are, and they demand the state of heart, and the only state in which you can be saved. God understands this and he will not change. Now you must make up your mind to come to these terms, and then you can pray and God will come into your heart sweetly. Will you forgive? Settle that question here, and bury that hatchet now, and then offer your petition, and the answer is yours.

As this subject is important, let me detain you with one other remark before I leave it. In the little model prayer which Christ has left on record to teach us how to approach our Maker, he puts this petition into our lips: After this *manner* pray ye, he says, "Forgive us our debts *as* we forgive our debtors." The substance of this petition is this,—

Lord *forgive* as *we* forgive. How many times we offer this prayer! Now, while you have an unforgiving spirit, we will suppose God answers it. What would become of you? You certainly would be lost, in answer to your own prayer. Not to be forgiven of God, is to take the penalty of the law we have violated, and be damned. You pray God to forgive just *as* you do; and you will not forgive, so you ask God not to forgive you. Do you wish to pray yourself down to perdition? Can you not reach there soon enough without asking God to send you there? Think of such a prayer! God will answer it at another day, if you persist in holding on to your unforgiving spirit.

Note another thing. Christ says, pray "*after this manner.*" He does not give you the privilege of asking forgiveness on any other ground. You have no right to even ask forgiveness on any other conditions. Lord forgive as I forgive. So you are shut up to these terms for eternal life. You must have God's smile and blessing on these terms, or not at all. Here is the difficulty why many in the church have no spirit of prayer. They have hard and wicked feelings towards those who have injured them. They live in that state of mind for years, and the heavens are brass over their heads. They will not make the least move to have that matter reconciled. God knows it, and he will not hear them. If there is one such here to-day, let me beseech you, as you value your soul, put away that wicked state of things, go and be reconciled to that offending brother or fellow-being, and then come and lay yourself on God's altar. He will hear, and pour his mercy richly into your soul. May God move you to do this work to-day!

4. In John xv. 7, is another condition introduced, with which we must comply to have access to God. " If ye abide in me, and my words abide in you, ye shall ask what ye will, and it shall be done unto you." How broad this promise! " Ye shall ask *what ye will*, and it shall be done unto you." It covers all our wants; and if they are not supplied, it is not because there is no promise that meets our case. But note the conditions of this promise. We must *abide in Christ*, and have *Christ's words abide in us*. The word *abide* means to dwell or live in a place. To abide in Christ is to dwell or live in Christ by faith, and have his words live and dwell in us. As the branch abides in the vine, and draws all its life, nourishment, and strength from the vine, so we are to abide in Christ, and draw our spiritual life, strength, and nourishment from him. The Christian can no more be in a healthy, living, flourishing state, cut off from Christ, than the branch can be in a living, healthy, flourishing state, when severed from the vine. How quick the branch withers and dies, when cut from the vine! So we wither, faint, and die, if cut off from Christ. We are perfectly de-

pendent upon him for our spiritual life and strength. Separate our hearts from him, and we have no strength. We are like Samson shorn of his strength. We must come into Christ and abide in him, if we would have access to God. What is it, therefore, to abide in Christ? The Bible frequently defines its own terms. When that is the case, we should always take its definitions as the best that can be given. God knows what he means by the phraseology he has used to express his ideas; and he is competent to define for himself. Let us turn to John's epistle, — John iii. 6, — and we have an answer to this question. Now remember, I am to give you John's answer, not mine. Hear him: " Whosoever abideth in him sinneth not." This is John's decision, and I suppose he understood this matter better than all the theologians of this age. To offer prevailing prayer, then, according to John, we must come and lay down *all*, ALL our known sins at Christ's feet, and give them up. On this same point let us hear David speak, — a good, sound, old-fashioned theologian, — Psalms lxvi. 18: " If I regard iniquity in *my heart*, the Lord will not hear me." Isaiah is another of these old divines. Isa. lix. 2: " But your iniquities have separated between you and your God, and your sins have hid his face from you, that he will not hear." I might multiply passages on this point, but these are enough. They settle the question, that to abide in Christ, and approach

God so as to prevail in prayer, you must give up all your known sins. This draws the line close, and is where we shall stumble and falter. There is but little prevailing prayer offered by the church, and why? Because she has so many sins she loves better than she loves an answer to prayer. She clings to them so that God will not hear. They are dearer to her than life, and they cause God to hide his face and leave her in a state of barrenness. Many of these sins are popular sins; and there are a class of individuals who are not troubled if they commit sin, if it is only popular. What a heart that must be! God hear such a being pray? He would hear the Devil as soon. What regard has such a heart for God or his authority? The question of right has no control over such beings, in any sense. All they desire is to have the multitude on their side, and the approbation of society around them, and they will commit any abomination. Such hearts, of course, have nothing but the form of prayer.

The dishonesty in trade at this day is a very common sin. How men will lie, deceive, and resort to all manner of trickery to make a few dollars, and then quiet their consciences with the thought that it is a common thing in business transactions. What! quiet your conscience because it is common! You will find it will be a very common thing for God to reckon with men, at another day, for such business transactions. God is an honest God, and requires of you to be honest, strictly honest, in all your dealings with your fellows. God hear that dishonest wretch pray? No, he will indignantly spurn him from his presence, until he shall repent and put away that sin. Such a man in Christ? Ridiculous! God would hear the thief pray as soon as he would hear such a being. Why not? The sin of dishonesty is the worst kind of stealing. The dishonest man takes away his neighbor's property without rendering an honest equivalent, just as much as the thief does; and then the thief has this advantage over him,— he did not add lying and deception in many instances to obtain it. But, you say, he had his neighbor's consent to take the property, and the thief had not. Admit it; but how did he obtain it? By lying and deception! He could not have obtained his consent without deception, any more than the thief could. There is something about the sin of dishonesty that is mean, contemptible, and devilish. God abhors it, and he will not hear the prayer of the heart that practises it. Have you been guilty of this sin, my brother? You must stop it. You must put away that iniquity. God will not hear you while you regard it in your heart.

The sin practised in politics is another popular sin, that shuts the soul away from God. What underhanded, low trickery men resort to in politics! What lying! what intrigue is practised! And church-members are in it as deep as others in many instances. When I think of it, my heart shudders, and I dread to meet a presidential election. There is lying enough in one such election to sink any nation, if God were not infinite in his long-suffering. Then see how our public men will falsify the truth in their public speeches, and in their public documents, — men in high stations. Read the speeches made in congress, only for one session of our national legislature. How sickening! Many of those speeches are but a tissue of falsehoods and misrepresentation of facts. Such speeches are called great speeches, and those who deliver them great statesmen. Great statesmen! A man is not worthy of the name of statesman, who will knowingly falsify the truth on one single point of public interest. A *great* statesmen is above it, nor will he stoop to such meanness. What do such men think? Do they suppose that the people elect and send them to Washington, and pay them for falsifying facts, and trying to deceive the nation? We, the people, ought to inquire seriously. Will this nation prosper under the influence and rule of such men? Are we not guilty for elevating them to stations of honor and power? Now these are sins, and *great* sins, but they are *popular* sins. They are sins at which the church wink, and many of her members participate in them. Others regard this iniquity in their hearts, — that is, they approve of it. God looks on and sees the whole, and remembers it when they come to the mercy-seat. God will not hear until they repent of such iniquity. You must become honest and upright in all your political and other movements. You must repent and put away popular and unpopular sins, as far as you know your heart, and thus come into Christ and abide there.

Look close here, my brother. Here is your difficulty, if you do not get access to God. There is some sin there. I have only referred to a few leading sins. There are a multitude of sins that we call little sins, which lurk in the heart, and shut us away from God. The sins of covetousness, selfishness, peevishness, and impatience; the sin of deception, which some persons practise almost constantly; the sin of lying *politely*, so as not to disturb your conscience. This kind of lying consists in stating certain things that are true, *literally*, but stated in such a manner as to convey a falsehood to the mind of the hearer. You withhold a part of the truth, enough to convey a false impression. That was what you aimed at. That you did, and you did it intentionally. That was a lie. But you ease off your conscience with the thought that what you said was literally true.

But what was the impression you left on the mind of the person addressed? You conveyed a falsehood to his mind, and you intended to do it. God always judges you by your intentions, and he writes *liar* on your soul in all such instances. Such kind of lying is the meanest kind, for it is the most artful kind of deception. The mind has to deliberate longer in forming it, and of course it is the most deliberate mode of falsifying the truth. This sin is practised by some people constantly, and can they offer prevailing prayer? God will not hear such an artful deceiver. Look close here, and come into Christ by abandoning all sin, and let Christ's words abide in you. Let his words be loved and cherished in your hearts daily. Let all their demands be reduced to practice. Then you may ask what you will, and it shall be done.

5. Let us turn our attention to yet another condition that must be complied with, if we would offer prevailing prayer. John xiv. 14: "If ye shall ask anything in *my name*, I will do it." How the subject of asking is kept up in all these passages, and each of them presents a new condition to be complied with! Christ intends to make the way to the mercy-seat so clear, that all may understand, if they will be governed by the teachings of the Bible. To ask in Christ's name is the condition to be complied with, in the passage now to come under consideration. What is it to ask in Christ's name? That is an important question, and should receive a correct answer. The truth involved in the answer must be reduced to practice, or our prayers will not be heard on high. This world is a rebellious province in God's empire. The human family have sinned,

all sinned. They have trampled under their feet a government which is perfect, pure, and good. They have trampled upon infinite rights, for they have trampled upon God's rights. Their sin is not a trifle, but a great crime, deserving of the deepest hell. They have forfeited all right and title to heaven. They deserve, from the hand of their Maker, a curse, and nothing but a curse. If such beings come to God for a blessing, and he deals with them according to their deserts, he will look them *quick* into hell. Strict justice would close heaven's doors, and bolt and bar them forever against all such beings, and against all their supplications. Now the question arises how can such beings approach their Maker, and have their prayers heard. Jesus Christ, by his death and suffering for man, has opened up a new and living way to God's throne. This new way is the way for unworthy sinners to come to God and be heard. Christ, by the atonement he has made, has purchased back for the human race all the blessings they forfeited by the fall. They forfeited heaven and eternal life; they can have them back through Christ. They forfeited the smile and approbation of God, but he can now smile upon and justify them when they approach him through Christ. They, by transgression, have exposed themselves to the fearful penalty of the divine law, and to all the agonies of the second death. They can be saved from the vials of its wrath by a free and full pardon, when they seek it through Christ. In a word, all that the soul needs for time and eternity, to supply its wants in this vale of tears and carry it triumphantly to heaven, exalt it high in glory, crown it with immortality and eternal life, is all embodied in Christ. To ask in his name, is to ask God to grant us these mercies, not on the ground of our worthiness, for we have none, but on the ground of his worthiness; not on the ground of our merit, for we have merited wrath, but on the ground of his infinite merit; not on the ground of anything we have done or can do, but on the ground of what he has done for us. It is to ask God to bless and save us, not simply that we may be blessed and made happy, and saved from wrath, but that Christ, this exalted High Priest of ours, may be honored, eternally honored in saving and blessing such unworthy, hell-deserving rebels as we have been. We base our plea wholly and entirely on the ground of the atoning sacrifice he has offered up in our behalf. When we offer prevailing prayer, we approach the cross, and look up and ask our heavenly Father to open his ears and listen to the groans of Christ: to open his eyes and behold the crimson tide poured out in our behalf, and then for his sake to hear and answer and defer not.

Now remember, any man who throws away the vicarious atonement of Christ, throws away the last hope, the only hope of this fallen world.

It is through that atonement alone that sinners have access to God. It is through that alone they can offer prevailing prayer.

The apostles and primitive Christians understood this great truth, which accounts for the fact that they hung their every hope upon the cross of Christ. "Christ and his cross was all their theme."

1 Cor. ii. 2: "I determined," says Paul, "not to know anything among you, save Jesus Christ, and him crucified." Why this determination on the part of Paul? For the simple reason that he knew that salvation by the meritorious death of Christ was the only hope of man; that it was the foundation-stone of *the Gospel*, that it was *the Gospel of God*. He understood full well that when the great truth of the atoning death of Christ was rejected, God's Gospel was thrown to the winds. And think you Paul would know or acknowledge any other system to have any saving power in it, or he have anything to do with a system that rejected the chief corner-stone of salvation, or he fellowship it in any form? He knew his duty too well. No, says Paul, I will know or acknowledge nothing as Gospel that rejects the cross of Christ. Take another passage from Paul, and see how he exhalts the cross, or the atonement of Christ; 1 Cor. i. 23, 24: "But we preach Christ crucified, unto the Jews a stumbling-block, and unto the Greeks foolishness; but unto them which are called, both Jews and Greeks, Christ the *power of God, and the wisdom of God.*"

How many wise Greeks we have here in Massachusetts! The preaching of the cross, or the meritorious death of Christ, is to them foolishness. How they ridicule the doctrine of the atonement! They expect to be saved by the law. They do not *fear* the law. When they have broken it, they say they expect and are willing to suffer its penalty. But this sacrificial religion they detest. So did the ancient Greeks. To them such a religion was foolishness. Paul here decides the character of all such beings, both ancient and modern. They are not of the called, or are not Christians. " But unto *them which are called*, Christ the power of God, and the wisdom of God."

To the real Christian, the preaching of the cross, or salvation by the sacrificial death of Christ, is the power of God, and the wisdom of God. He understands his ill deserts too well to even hope for salvation in any way except through the meritorious death of Christ. He understands full well that if he has access to God, it must be through Christ. You must keep this truth distinctly before the mind when you pray. You never will offer prevailing prayer when you lose sight of it. Let us therefore come to God through Christ, and ask in his name, and then he will hear, and we shall find this promise richly verified in our experience.

6. I will examine one condition more, and draw this subject to a close. You will find it de-

scribed in James i. 5, 6: "If any of you lack wisdom, let him ask of God, that giveth to all men liberally, and upbraideth not; and it shall be given him. But let him ask in faith, nothing wavering." The subject of asking is still kept up in this text, but a new condition is presented. "*Let him ask in faith.*" To approach God so as to be heard, we must come in faith. What is faith? It is credence of testimony, or taking God at his word. Faith takes hold of the promises of God, and expects God will do as he has promised. The man of faith expects to be heard; he looks for an answer. Take an illustration from Elijah's praying; 1 Kings, xviii. 42–45: He went up to the top of Carmel and cast himself down upon the ground, and commenced calling upon God. He sent his servant to look off upon the sea and watch for the answer. The servant returned with the report that the heavens were all bright, and there were no signs of an answer. Did this discourage Elijah, and lead him to give up the matter? Not at all. He expected an answer. Go up until the seventh time, he replies. The seventh time the servant returns with the report that a little cloud, the bigness of a man's hand, had made its appearance in the heavens. Did Elijah reply now,—well, if that is all there is to be seen after praying here seven times, we may as well give it up; it will not amount to much. This undertaking to force things, says he, is not the correct course. I believe in waiting God's time. What! we undertake to get up a storm any time we take it into our heads we need rain? I do not believe in such things. God will send us a rain in his own good time. Come, he remarks to his servant, let us go down and wait, and let God manage this matter. Was this the reasoning of Elijah? Not by any means. He expected a blessing. He looked for an answer to his prayers, and he knew it would come. He expected the little cloud would spread over the heavens, and that there would be a plentiful rain, in which he was not disappointed. Now notice in this case, as soon as this servant of God began to pray he began to look for the answer; he expected it. How his faith held on and did not waver amid discouragements, nor would he give it up until the answer came! This is faith. It needs a whole sermon to illustrate this point, but I must detain you here but a short time.

Let me direct your attention to one thing. When you go home, take up the New Testament and read the history of Christ as given by Matthew. As you pass along, observe how Christ, when on earth, always met men just on the ground of their faith. Take one or two instances as an illustration of this point. As he came down from the mount, after delivering that ever-memorable sermon, as recorded in the fifth, sixth, and seventh chapters of Matthew, a leprous man met and worshipped him, and said,

"Lord, if thou *will*, thou canst make me clean." Jesus replied, " I WILL; be thou clean!" and he was healed immediately. Please notice the faith of this man, how it takes hold of his ability. " If thou *will*, thou *canst.*" How Christ meets him right on that point! " I WILL," says he, and the work is done. Take another case : As Jesus entered Capernaum, a centurion met him, and said, " Lord, my servant lieth at home sick of the palsy, and grievously tormented." Christ replied, " I will come and heal him." He objected.. Why object ? Does he not wish his servant healed ? Let him answer : I am not worthy that such a holy personage should come under my roof; but speak the *word* only, and my servant shall be healed. Listen to his reasoning for a moment. How sensible! How forcible! I am a *man*, a *mere man*, Lord, says he. You are something more than a man. You are *Lord;* you are *God over all.* I am a man under other men; I am a man under authority. A centurion was an officer in the Roman army who had the command of one hundred soldiers. He was not the highest officer in the army ; he was a very inferior officer, under other men. Now, Lord, says he, *you* are not under authority; you are at the head of all things, and all things are under your control. But in *my* condition, being a man under other men, I can say to this man *go*, and he goeth, and to another *come*, and he cometh. Now, says he, diseases are but thy servants. Speak the *word* only, and my servant will be healed. You need not come to my house; only *command*, and say to the palsy *go*, and it will obey. Truly, says Christ, I have not found so great faith in all Israel. If your faith says a *word* can do it, go thy way,— a *word shall* do it. And his servant was healed from that moment. See how Christ met this man, just on the ground of his faith! Speak the word, he says, and it shall be done. Go thy way, says Christ, a word has done it.

Now, look the history of Christ through, and you will see that when on earth he always met men on the ground of their faith. He never turned a solitary individual away, who came to him in faith. All he wanted was to have them bring along their faith, and the blessing was theirs.

How much he complained of the unbelief of his disciples! There was hardly any sin that grieved him more, and for which he reproved them more sharply. O ye of little faith, he would exclaim, how long shall I bear with you? How long shall I suffer you?

The sin of unbelief is a very aggravating sin, as it calls in question God's veracity. Everywhere in the Bible God requires of us to have confidence in him and his promises; for without faith it is impossible to please him. Here is our sin in this age; we are full of unbelief. This shuts out our prayers, and God will not hear. Who of you before me to-day expects God will hear and answer your prayers daily? Do you look for an answer? Would you not rather be disappointed, if God should answer? When you arise from your knees, when you have been praying, suppose you stop and put this question to yourself: Now I have offered such and such petitions. Do I expect Christ will answer those requests? What would be the answer of your heart? Oh, you say, I do not expect God will hear my prayers. That settles the question for you, then. Your heart is full of unbelief. Where there is faith, the person *does* expect and look for a blessing. But why do you pray, and insult God with such unbelieving prayers? Because he commands me to pray. He does not command you to pray an unbelieving prayer, any more than he commands you to swear. An unbelieving prayer is sinful. God command you to sin? But God commands me to pray. That is true; but he commands you to pray the prayer of faith, and not an unbelieving prayer. A prayer coming from a heart full of unbelief he will not accept. It is wicked; he abhors it. The prayer of faith he loves to hear and answer; but the prayer of unbelief he hates, and will not answer. Now, why offer up a prayer that God hates? What would you have me do? stop praying? No; I would have you stop your unbelief, and pray in faith. Then the answer is yours. But I cannot exercise faith. I am not to blame for not having faith. But does not God command you to have faith? Yes, I suppose he does. And you break a command of God, and not be to blame? If you can break one command of God and not be to blame, perhaps you can all of his commands; and upon that theory you are not to blame for being a sinner at all. Where did you learn such a horrible theory as that? What! break any of God's commands, when you know they are his commands, and not be to blame? It is impossible. But faith is the gift of God. So is every other Christian grace. What does the Bible mean when it teaches that these graces are the gift of God? Does it mean that they are something that God does for you without your agency? That is impossible, for this reason: These graces are something that the Christian does. It is the Christian who repents, believes, and loves for himself, and not God who repents, believes, and loves for him. If it were so, it would be God's repentance, faith, and love, and not that of the Christian.

These graces, therefore, being something which the *Christian* does, *God* cannot do it for him without his agency. To have these graces at all, he must act. The question returns then, what is meant by their being the gift of God? This, namely, that these graces are a something which God's Spirit inclines, induces, or moves *you* to do; not a something which the Spirit does *for* you, nor a something which the Spirit *compels* you to do, — for compulsion cannot be applied here, as you are voluntary in the doing, — but it is a something which the Spirit inclines or moves you to do. For this reason the graces are called the gift of God, as you would never exercise them without this divine persuasion. That moving influence you have had more or less all your life, and resisted it. The Spirit always acts in harmony with the Bible, and the Bible demands them now. If we will stop resisting the Spirit and give ourselves up to do what the Bible demands, we shall soon find our hearts adorned with these graces. Now faith is something which God commands you to have. It is *your* exercise, and you are to blame for not having it. God condemns you for not having it; and when you throw the blame of your not having it upon God, and justify yourself in a state of unbelief by saying, Oh! faith is the gift of God; he does not give me faith, and I am not to blame, — that is horrible wickedness.

Now then, will you repent of all this wickedness, take the blame to yourself for being in a state of unbelief, fly to Christ for pardon, and begin from to-day to offer the prayer of faith? If you will live in that state of mind daily and habitually, God will answer.

I could add many striking incidents of answers to prayer, which I have witnessed in the revivals of the last twenty five years in our land, but as our papers, both political and religious, have been full of them, it is not necessary. I will now close this subject with a few

REMARKS.

1. What condescension on the part of our Maker to listen to a prayer coming up from this guilty world! Yet he bends his gracious ear to hear all who approach him in harmony with the directions he has given in his word. He is no respecter of persons. He has one set of rules for all to comply with. The high and the low, the rich and the poor, must come upon one common level when they pray. He has not one set of rules for the rich and another for the poor. The emperor upon his throne, to be heard, must stoop just as low as the beggar in the streets. All, all have sinned, and all must approach him by repentance of sin and faith in his Son. The man who is too proud to stoop as low as the beggar, is too proud to be saved, and in another world he may see the beggar exalted to heaven, while he himself is cast down to hell. God will subdue and take away all pride, and bring down all high looks before he will hear you pray.

2. We are indebted to the Lord Jesus Christ for this privilege. We forfeited the privilege of access to God when we sinned. This high privilege was purchased for us by the death-groans on the cross. How we ought to fall at Christ's feet, and pour forth

grateful hearts to him for opening a way by which we, poor sinners, may come to God and live! Have we sufficiently praised Christ for this great blessing? We are all guilty of ingratitude in this particular. Let us come to Christ with this sin to-day, and confess it and ask forgiveness. Let us offer up to him our united thanks for this unspeakable gift.

3. This subject will show us the difference between the true Christian, and a man who has never been converted. The true Christian prays because he loves to hold communion with God. It is the delight of his heart. He approaches God so as to secure an answer; but the man who has never been converted, if he prays at all, prays simply because he thinks he cannot be saved without. He has no love for prayer, but he wants to go to heaven ; or perhaps he wishes to convince others that he is a Christian; or he is a little gifted in prayer so far as words are concerned, and he wishes to show off; or he is resting on a false hope, which he wishes to maintain, and his conscience would not permit it if he should neglect the form of prayer; or perhaps some other selfish motive governs him. There is no true love for prayer in his heart, and he has no access to God. He draws nigh to him with the lips while the heart is far from him. Not so with the true child of God. His heart is in it. He has a spirit of prayer, and prevails. He is a man of faith.

Look close here, my brother. Do not deceive

yourself. Do you have access to God? If not, give up your hope; it is deceptive. Repent, and get a good one.

4. Finally. I have now spread before you this important subject. I have tried to show you how to approach God, so as to be heard. If you will all reduce these thoughts to practice, how God will come to this place and region!

Will you do it? No matter how plain the truth is preached, it will not benefit you unless you practise it. The clearer it is presented the more it will harden, if you resist it. These sermons will affect you, and you are to decide how. If you practise them, God will come in great power. If you reject this truth, you will grieve his Spirit. Will you decide the question now, what you will do? If you say, I will commence this work to-day, then throw yourself upon the arm of the Spirit, and plead for his presence until you are richly baptized. Rely upon it to make intercession in your hearts according to the divine will, and look for a great blessing; and if you come by faith, God will roll a wave of salvation over all this region.

VI.

POWER FROM ON HIGH.

"But tarry ye in the city of Jerusalem, until ye be endued with power from on high." — *Luke* xxiv. 49.

1. POWER SPOKEN OF IN THE TEXT. 2. WHAT IT WILL ACCOMPLISH. 3. HOW OBTAINED. 4. GUILT OF THE CHURCH IN NOT OBTAINING IT.

TARRY in Jerusalem. What! in that bloody city where they had put Christ to death? Yes, in that wicked city, the soil of which had just drank in the blood of the Son of God. Tarry there until you receive power from on high. He will have his disciples commence the work there, and build the first church under the gospel dispensation there, in spite of the Jews. They imagined they had effectually put down this new religion, that they had defeated Christ in his mission, that they had perfectly triumphed over him, when they nailed him to the cross, laid his dead body in the tomb, and guarded the sepulchre with a strong band of soldiers.

Their triumph, however, was but momentary. On the third day he scattered all their hopes to the winds. He came forth from the grave a triumphant conqueror, and commands his disciples to go back and tarry in this unrighteous city; to begin and establish this new religion on the very spot where they supposed they had subdued it. Is Christ to be defeated in his designs by a band of murderers? Not he. He will build up his cause in Jerusalem, in spite of the rage of his enemies. He will have a people to serve him even ,there. The gospel shall begin its victorious work there, and from Jerusalem it shall go forth to subdue and conquer the nations.

Tarry in Jerusalem, says Christ, until you receive power. Power from what source? From man? No, from on high. I am about to ascend to my Father and your Father, and I will send the promise of my Father upon you, which shall fit you for the great work before you. You shall be clothed with *power* that all your adversaries shall not be able to gainsay or resist. The weapons of your warfare shall not be carnal, but they shall be *mighty*. This power from on high shall make them mighty. They shall be mighty to bow stubborn hearts, to subdue stubborn wills, and uproot sin from the souls of men. Tarry in Jerusalem until you receive this power. Do not presume to undertake this work without it. *Your* power is all weakness. This power from above is all-subduing; it is the only hope of the church in building up Christ's kingdom. With it you have certain victory, sure success. Without it, certain defeat; all your efforts are a failure.

Now let me impress this truth upon this church. We are sure of a good work in this place, if we secure this power from on high. Unless we do secure it, not a sinner will be saved. What! Man save sinners without this power? No man on earth ever did or ever can do it. An angel could not do it. We must secure this power, or all go to hell. Will you set your faces to seek for it until it comes? Let this be a united work until we are all filled with this power, then how quick God will get to himself a name in this place! With your attention, I will proceed to show, —

I. What is meant by the power spoken of in this text.

II. What it will accomplish for the church, if she receives it.

III. How it can be obtained.

IV. The guilt of the church in living without it.

I. THEN I AM TO SHOW WHAT IS MEANT BY THE POWER SPOKEN OF IN THE TEXT.

The power referred to in this text is the Holy Ghost, or the third person in the Trinity. The whole verse from which the text is taken, reads thus: "And, behold, I send the promise of my Father upon you: but tarry ye in the city of Jerusalem, until ye be endued with power from on high." That is, wait in Jerusalem until I send this promise of my Father upon you. What was that promise? Turn to Acts ii. 33, and let Peter settle that question: "Therefore being by the right hand of God exalted," says Peter to the Jews "and having received of the Father the promise of the Holy Ghost, he hath shed forth this, which ye now see and hear." The promise of the Father then, was the promise of the Holy Ghost. This was the power for which they were to wait in Jerusalem until they received it. In obedience to this command of Christ, the Apostles and others did tarry in Jerusalem until they received this power, and then they went about God's work in earnest, and with wonderful success. The history informs us how they tarried. One hundred and twenty of them gathered into an upper chamber, and for ten days continued in prayer and supplication to God for the fulfilment of this promise. God, in answer to their prayers, and through the intercession of Christ, after he had arrived at the court of heaven, shed down this *power*. They were all filled with divine energy, and rushed out into the streets of Jerusalem to preach salvation and gather souls into the kingdom. Let us then imitate their example. Let us unitedly continue in prayer for this same power until we receive it. Then we are prepared for God's work. Then we can have success in leading souls to Christ. Will you do it? Will you begin to-day, and hold on until the blessing comes?

II. I AM TO SHOW WHAT IT WILL ACCOMPLISH FOR THE CHURCH, IF SHE RECEIVES IT.

1. It will cleanse your heart from impurities, from wicked thoughts and vain desires, and fit it to be a suitable temple for God to dwell in. " Know ye not that ye are the temple of God?" says Paul, in 1 Cor. iii. 16. God will not dwell in a polluted temple. He will first cleanse and purify it, and fit it to be the abode of his Spirit. Then he will take possession, and adorn it with every Christian grace.

2. He will take away your weak, vacillating heart, and give you a strong one. See how he accomplished this work for Peter. Before the wonderful refreshing on the day of Pentecost, Peter's heart was weak, and would fail him in the moment of temptation. Take an instance: Before Christ was arrested, he proclaimed to the Apostles one truth which, at the time, they could not believe. He declared that they would all forsake him in his hour of trial. Peter asserted, in the most positive manner, that if all the rest should forsake his master, he would stand by him to the last. *He* would not forsake him, if he stood alone. He even went so far as to affirm that he would sooner lay down his life than forsake Christ. I have no doubt that Peter, when he made this remark, was honest. He was not hypocritical in his pretensions of attachment to Christ. He did not, however, understand the weakness of his own heart. Christ understood

it, and revealed to him the fact, that that night he would deny and forsake his Lord. Peter could not believe it; but when the trial came, his life demonstrated Christ's prediction to be true. Christ was arrested and led away by the officer, to be put on trial for his life. Peter fell in the rear, but followed at a distance, to see the end of the matter. At length he was charged with being one of his disciples. He instantly denied it. "He is a stranger to me," says Peter; "I know not the man." What a lie! Being pressed further, he denied with an oath. He cursed and swore to save his own life. Peter, Peter, poor Peter! What a weak heart! How it gives way and is overcome in the hour of temptation! Now let us look at this same Peter after the day of Pentecost, and after he received power from on high. Every effort was made by the Jews and others to lead him to abandon Christ's cause. They threaten, arrest, imprison, and finally crucify him with his head downwards; but he is firm, and immovably fixed for Christ till his latest breath. What a heart now! How unchangeable! This power from on high has greatly strengthened his heart, and made it strong for God, so that it could not be overcome. How many in the church at this day have weak and vacillating hearts! How the hour of temptation overcomes all their good resolutions! They sin and grieve the Spirit, and bring leanness into their souls. How much they need this power to strengthen their hearts, and make them strong for the Lord. Tarry in Jerusalem, my brother, until you receive this power, and you will become mighty for Christ. How easy you will overcome temptation, then, instead of temptation overcoming you! Neither earth nor hell can lead you astray when your heart is full of the Holy Ghost.

3. This power from on high will illuminate your understandings, and greatly assist you in understanding the Scriptures. Sin has cast a veil over the mind, and blinded the eyes of our understandings so that we do not take hold of the truth with ease. This power tears off this veil, pours light in upon the soul, and helps it to take hold of the great things of Christ.

Referring to this power of the Spirit, Christ says: "When he is come he shall teach you all things, and bring all things to your remembrance." "If any man lack wisdom, let him ask of God." But why ask of God, unless he can somehow impart wisdom to the soul? Look at its effect upon the minds of the Apostles. Up to the day of Pentecost, up to the very time they received this power from on high, the minds of the Apostles seem to have been all in the dark in relation to Christ's spiritual kingdom. They were under the impression that Christ was to establish a temporal kingdom on earth, and that he was to reign here as a temporal prince. He had frequently said to them that his kingdom was not of this world, and explained the matter over and over again; but still their minds were in the dark upon this point. They would frequently dispute about who should be greatest in Christ's kingdom. One woman came to him with the request that her two sons might sit, one on his right hand and the other on his left, in his kingdom. He had frequently declared that the Jews would put him to death, but that he should rise again on the third day.

Notwithstanding all his teaching on this point, when he was crucified and laid in the grave, the last hope of his followers seems to have expired with him. Instead of looking for his resurrection, they made every preparation to embalm his body. How dark their minds! After his resurrection he fell in and conversed with some of them on their way to Emmaus. Not knowing who he was, they remark, " but we trusted that it had been he which should have redeemed Israel." But alas! as he was dead they had given up all hope. Christ now reveals himself to them, and they know for a certainty that he is risen from the dead. He associates with and instructs them for forty days, and then leads them out from Jerusalem to ascend up to the throne of God, and they come to him again with this old doctrine of a temporal kingdom. They put the question, " Lord, wilt thou at this time restore again the kingdom to Israel?" How their minds are still obscured in relation to the true nature of his kingdom! He sends them to Jerusalem to wait for this power from on high. After they receive it, that settles the whole matter. Not another word do we ever hear about a *temporal* kingdom. They understand the whole now. All is clear as heaven. Why? This power clears up this whole question to their understandings, and makes all simple. The Spirit imparted light they had never received before. One part of its work is to illuminate the soul, and help it to take hold of God's truth. If you wish a clear view of truth, get near to God. Let your soul be baptized with this power, and you will behold wondrous things out of God's law. The mind will not only see the truth, but the soul will love and feed upon it. Under its influence you will grow up into Christ, and become strong in the Lord and in the power of his might.

4. This power, when received, will take away and overcome in you the fear of man. Take Peter's case again as an illustration. When Christ was arrested, as we have before remarked, Peter and all the rest of the Apostles fled. " The fear of man bringeth a snare." How true this was in Peter's case. He thought, doubtless, that if he owned Christ, he too should be arrested, and perhaps put to death. To avoid this he lied, — denied Christ, cursed and swore, — being influenced by the fear of man. His courage and fortitude failed him

utterly; and, how timid he becomes in the presence of a female! Now look at the same Peter after he receives this power from Heaven. He then stands up in the presence of thousands, and not only owns Christ, but charges these very Jews, in a most public manner, with murdering the Son of God. How bold! How courageous! No timidity now. Henceforth, every opportunity he has he will preach Christ, even when he is before the highest tribunals in the nation. What a change! How is it brought about? This power has done up this wonderful work.

If you are troubled with the fear of man, go to Christ, and secure this divine influence, and how quick it will vanish! You can then meet any duty. You can stand before a world to plead his cause. What are kings or emperors to one filled with the Holy Ghost! You can meet all the men on earth, and all the devils in hell, and, looking them in the eye, own your Lord, and defend his cause in the presence of the whole of them. Such is the effect of this power upon the souls of men. How it nerved up the martyrs and made them strong in the Lord, and in the power of his might! It made Luther bold and courageous to meet all his enemies, and has imparted moral courage to God's people in every age of the world.

5. This power, when it is received, will overcome in you the love of the world. " Love not the

world, neither the things that are in the world. If any man love the world, the love of the Father is not in him," says John. This love of the world is eating out the very vitals of the church at this day. What a desire some beings have to be rich! Riches is their God. See them sacrifice ease, reputation, truth, honesty, and almost life itself to make money. They care but little *how* they get it, if they can only get it. Money, money, money, is the great thing that absorbs all their thoughts, all their time, and they will sell their eternal happiness, even, to obtain it. This love of the world must be broken up, or such souls will be lost. Such beings Christians? It is impossible! They are not Christians. So John affirms. The world is their God, and they will go down to perdition unless this love of the world is broken up. What can do it? This power can do it. Nothing short of this ever will do it. How it broke up the love of the world in the hearts of the primitive Christians! They sold out their entire estates and laid the whole at the feet of the Apostles, to promote and advance God's cause. What was money to them compared with the interests of Christ's kingdom? His kingdom was first and uppermost in their minds, and they were ready to sacrifice every thing to advance it. Let the church be baptized with the same power now, and it will produce the same effect. It will effectually break up this love of the world in the church, and draw out the soul in supreme love to God.

6. This power, when received, will clear up and present the great moving considerations, or motives of the Gospel, so strongly before the mind, that they will have an all-commanding influence over the heart and life. How it will make heaven stand out before the soul! How its glories will appear to the mind, and how infinitely desirable! How hell looks, how awful and how much to be dreaded! The mind's eye can almost see the smoke of the pit, and hear the wailings of the lost. It starts back from the world of despair. Eternity! How the mind dwells upon this great idea! How infinitely valuable the soul seems! The judgment, the great white throne is almost visible, and the individual feels as if he was hastening up to his final account. In a word, all the great truths of the Bible are made to stand out in such bold relief, that they become solemn realities, and move, melt, and subdue the heart under their sanctifying influence, and cause it sweetly to yield itself up to their control.

7. This power from on high, when it is received, will fill the soul with unutterable desires for the salvation of men. Paul, when under its influence, declared he had great heaviness, and continual sorrow in his heart for the Jews who rejected the Gospel. It will make you feel most intensely for others. It has always produced the same effect

in all hearts under its influence. A heart that has no deep feeling for the salvation of sinners is not under its influence. If it has ever had such feelings, but has now lost them, it is because it has grieved away the Spirit, and is now in a backslidden state. Such hearts should immediately repent, return to God and duty, and fly to the mercy-seat for a fresh baptism of the Spirit, which will restore to them this deep and ardent feeling for the salvation of men. The soul must be full of this deep feeling, to be successful in moving hearts. A cold, formal religion seldom gets further than the head, never reaches the heart. It is when the soul is full of love, full of compassion for others, that it moves and melts the heart of the sinner.

It is only when your heart is full of the Holy Ghost, that you have this godlike compassion, this compassion that has power in it. In times of revivals there will be members of the church who will be filled with it. Young converts will be filled with it. Why? Because at such times they have this power from on high. Now let the church live so as to retain this power with her constantly, and not grieve it away by sin, and what outgushings of soul you would see for the salvation of others!

8. This power from on high, when you receive it, will give you great power over men. Let a minister be full of it, and how he will chain and fix the attention of his hearers, and hold their minds to the

truth as if they were in the grasp of the Spirit. Some of his hearers will become excited, and manifest hatred towards him, and be ready to gnash upon him with their teeth; while others under the same sermon will be melted all down, completely subdued, and led to Christ for forgiveness. What power Peter had over his congregation on the day of Pentecost! How he held those murderers of Christ perfectly spell-bound, while he charged home upon them the blood of the Son of God! How they quailed under his preaching, and cried out in deep anguish of soul, "men and brethren, what shall we do?" Who was this Peter? Was he some highly educated man, — some wonderfully polished orator, that gave him such power over men? From whence did he graduate? From the fish-boat, some three years previous. He never saw an academy, college, or theological seminary. He was not blessed with such privileges. But he had applied to a higher source for wisdom: to the fountain head of all true knowledge. He had first received power from the heavens, and how the wicked were slain by its influence, and flocked in great multitudes to the Son of God, whom they had just murdered, for forgiveness and salvation! What power he had over men!

This power is to be attributed, not to Peter, but the God of Peter, who had shed down this divine energy from the heavens.

What power Luther had over men! How he

would march into the presence of his enemies, who were anxious to devour him the next moment, and bear his testimony for Christ, — holding them as if they were in the grasp of the Almighty! What a specimen at Worms! How he moved the world under his influence during his life! Why such power over men, and from whence did he derive it? From above, — from the Holy Ghost which worked in him mightily.

But we are not all Luthers, says one. That is true. But we can all have this power; and just in proportion as we have it, we shall have power over men for good. Just in proportion as the church are destitute of it, she will be powerless to lead the world to Christ.

9. This power from on high, when you receive it, will beget within you a spirit of deep and earnest prayer. It will break up your formal praying, and your soul will be solemnly in earnest when you approach the mercy-seat. It will help the infirmities of the flesh, and make intercession in your hearts with groanings which cannot be uttered. It will wake up in your soul desires that will be holy, deep, earnest desires, which will take possession of the whole heart, and draw out the whole spirit to God for help. It will make you feel that you must have assistance from Him, and you will cling to the mercy-seat and never give over until it comes. How manifest this is in times of revivals! What

praying then, what pleading, what wrestling with God! How the whole soul is then enlisted, and feels that it cannot be turned away empty! How the closet will be visited, and hours spent in pleading with God! How men will bend over their family altars, and with what fervor they will pray! What a rush to the prayer-meetings! How the petitions will be poured in, and presented with united, fervent prayer for help to the great God above! What faith! How prayer prevails! Why this state of things? This power from on high is at work among the people, and working up a spirit of prayer in their souls. Will you have it here, my brother? This is what you need. This is what you must have if there is anything done to save, that will produce any good and lasting results.

10. This power from on high, if you receive it, will give you a clear view of the great evil of sin. You will no longer view sin as a trifle. You will not say that it does not deserve to be punished endlessly. You will be amazed that you are out of an endless hell; that God could spare such a wretch thus long, and hold him back from the fires of the pit, which he so richly deserves. How distinctly this power will lead you to discover that you have trampled upon infinite authority; that you have broken a law that is holy, just, and good; a law if kept by all, would have secured the highest good of all; one that is as perfect as an infinitely wise

God could make it; that, added to this wicked violation of the law, you have rejected the Redeemer who died to save you; that you have unrighteously grieved away the Spirit that has been sent to your heart to renew and fit it for heaven.

This power will present these things so clearly before your minds, that you will have such a clear view of the great evil of sin, as to see that it would be just in God to send you to the deepest hell. Christ declared that when this power came, it would convince of sin. See how it led sinners to cry for help on the day of Pentecost! The same effect has been produced in all ages of the world, when it has been received. It has produced this same effect in Ireland. What a sense of sin those have who receive it! This is what we need. We shall not come to Christ without it. We shall be satisfied with the mere forms of godliness without the power; but when we have this clear view of sin, nothing short of coming to Christ for a salvation that can take away this abominable thing from the heart, will satisfy such an individual. How sinners will fly to the cross of Christ for deliverance under this view of themselves! If you wish to see this people moved generally, and all prostrated before God under a deep sense of their guilt, and all crying for help, and for deliverance from sin, take hold of this Divine help and plead until this power comes, and see how God will shake the place.

III. I am to show how you can obtain this power.

1. You must see and have a clear view of its importance. You must labor to bring your heart into that state. Stop and think here, how helpless you are, and how you struggled in vain to overcome your lusts and the influence of a wicked world over you; without it your resolutions fail, *all* fail, and the world overcomes *you*, instead of your overcoming the world. Your efforts to save your families and others are fruitless without the Spirit. How hard their hearts remain, notwithstanding all your care, watchfulness and instruction! *Look* at these things; let the mind dwell upon them; God will make you feel the importance of this great blessing before he will bestow it. You would not *value* it when given, unless he made you feel its importance. When you see its infinite importance, then there is one point gained towards your receiving it. In prayer ask God to make you see the necessity of this great blessing.

2. You must value this gift above everything else. God will have you view this matter in its true light before he will give you this power. To be blessed with the gift of the Spirit, is one of the richest blessings heaven has to bestow. When you receive it, you receive a preparation for heaven. It is the Holy Spirit which renews the heart and fits it for the heavenly world. Without this renovation

of heart, you are not fit to enjoy God, nor the society of angels. All that Christ has done for you is an utter failure without the Spirit, so far as your salvation is concerned. The atonement will save no one unless he sees his sins, repents, and has a new heart.

To convince of sin, lead to repentance, and renew the heart is the appropriate work of the Spirit. How valuable then this gift of God, and how important! You must prize it above everything else. If you value earthly things more than you value this blessing, God will withhold it. This is the trouble with the church at this day, in my estimation. She greatly undervalues this blessing. She prefers money to this power, for she will grieve the Spirit to obtain it. She prefers her own aggrandizement, her own gratification to this blessing, for she will grieve the Spirit to secure them. Now while you are in this state of heart, God will not give you this blessing. He will bring you into a state where you will value it above all earthly goods, before he will bestow it.

3. You must remember it is from God alone that you can receive this great gift. You are shut up to God here. This he will have you feel. Until you do feel and acknowledge it, he will let you struggle without it. To what other source can you look for this power? No other being has it, and consequently no other being can bestow it. No, you

must fly to God, and rely upon him, and upon him alone for it.

4. If you would obtain this power, you must feel deep down in your heart that nothing can supply its place. Here lies the difficulty of the church, in multitudes of instances. She leans upon other things to do the very work which this power was sent into the world to perform. In some cases, she will lean upon the minister,— his talent, his eloquence, his learning, or his influence. When a church has secured a man of her choice, then she is at rest. She expects he will build her up. What can a minister do unless he has this power to work with him? If he is as talented and eloquent as Gabriel, not a soul will be saved without this power. The church must feel this, and be on her face and plead with God for the Holy Ghost to work in and by him. If the church substitutes the preaching and talent of the minister, or leans upon *them* instead of this power, God will withhold this blessing, and let the church try it. Now, says God, lean upon and glorify the minister if you will; but the people will go to hell, and I will hold you accountable. He give this power to such a church? They would give all the glory to the minister, if he should. Again, the church can lean upon a series of meetings to save men. What can a series of meetings do, without this power? You may have meetings three hundred and sixty-five days in every year, and not a

soul will be saved, unless those meetings lead you to lean upon and look to this power for salvation. Again, you may lean upon prayer-meetings instead of this power. There is danger of this just now. These meetings have been wonderfully blessed in leading souls to Christ for two years past. Why? Because in them the church waited at the throne of grace for this power. Now, if you begin to lean upon these meetings instead of this power to save, God will cease to bless. They will become mere forms of godliness without the power, and the work of conversion in these meetings will cease.

Again; some seem to think if they can build a splendid church, and get a fine organ, with the best of singing, then these will draw the people under the sound of the Gospel, and save them. But, notwithstanding the churches in our cities have been experimenting in this way for a series of years past, the wicked have walked straight by our splendid sanctuaries on the way to hell. At length, when the church became alarmed at this state of things, and fled to God for help, how quick he opened the windows of heaven and shed down this power, moving the people to flock to the house of God, to cry for mercy and salvation. It takes this power from heaven to fill up your sanctuaries. If you secure it sufficiently, you will have to resort to the open field for meetings, as they did in the days of Wesley and Whitfield, and as they are now doing in Ireland.

Why will not the church learn wisdom on this point, and remember where her strength lies?

Again, the church leans upon a liberal education to fit ministers to preach, instead of this power, as she should do. Do not understand me to speak against an educated ministry. The more education the better, if you do not substitute that for the preparation which the Spirit alone can impart. If you do, it will fail you, and the ministry will not be prepared for their work. That young man has been through his ten years' course of study, and he now thinks, and the church feel, that he is prepared for the ministry. Prepared for the ministry! He is not prepared until he is baptized with this power from God. All the science this side of heaven cannot prepare him for this holy work, without this power. But let him be baptized with the Spirit, and he can use his education to good advantage. Without it he is powerless to save men. His preaching may please the ear, but it will not reach and move the heart. If you would obtain this power, therefore, remember you must cease to lean upon any of the means of grace to save men. It takes this power from on high *to accompany these means*, to make them effectual in saving the world. This you must feel and realize. When you do, and look to God for it, then the Gospel will be made effectual to save the world.

5. If you would obtain this power, you must feel

your indebtedness to Christ for it. We all forfeited it by sin, and therefore have no just claim upon God for it. If he should forever withhold it from us, it would be treating us according to our deserts. But Christ purchased it for us by his death. The Father promised it to him, as the context shows. He says: "Behold I send the promise of my Father upon you." This he will bestow in answer to Christ's intercession in our behalf. "I will pray the Father, and he shall give you another Comforter, that he may abide with you forever." One more: "But the Comforter, which is the Holy Ghost, whom the Father will send in my name."

These passages show that we are wholly indebted to Christ for this great gift. He purchased it, and in his name and in answer to his prayer the Father sends it. Therefore we must come to God for it through Christ. We must feel that it is a free gift of grace; and if we receive it, we shall be eternally indebted to Christ for it. Let us then look up to the Father for it through the cross, and hang our hope for it upon the cross, and he will hear. Christ will plead in our behalf and the work is done.

6. If you would receive it, you must be willing to give up everything for it. You may have some sins that are grieving the Spirit. If so, you must give them up. If you love those sins better than you love this great gift, God will not bestow it. You

must be willing to be guided and governed in all things by the Spirit.

7. You must seek it by prayer. Begin this work to-day; go to God in earnest for this blessing, and never give it up, until he hears and sheds upon you this power from on high. Will you do it?

IV. I AM TO SHOW THE GUILT OF THE CHURCH THAT LIVES WITHOUT THIS POWER.

1. She violates God's command, "Be filled with the Spirit." — Eph. v. 18. God demands it at the hands of the church, that she should live so as to be filled with this power. She violates this command of God every hour she is destitute of it.

2. The church throws away her usefulness while she is destitute of the Spirit. She has a mere *form* of Godliness without the *power*, which never results in saving men. When she is full of the Holy Ghost she will be useful, and you cannot prevent her doing good. Souls will come to Christ in great numbers, under her influence. How that wicked city of Jerusalem was moved under the influence of such a church! The primitive church swept all before it, and subdued the nations in a short time. Nothing could withstand her influence until she grieved away this power. What an influence this church would exert when filled with the power of the Holy Ghost! Now then, for all the good you could do if in that state, God will hold you strictly accountable. How

will you meet it, my brethren? Think of the enormous guilt here.

3. You are guilty of living in the dark in relation to God's truth. How minds are obscured in relation to many parts of the Bible! Some will undertake to justify and defend the chattel slavery of this nation, and many other sins, from that sacred Book. Defend this system of abominations by the Bible! Horrible! It is an insult to Heaven. If God's laws on slavery were carried into execution, you could not have a slaveholder in the nation. The Bible would put them all to death forthwith as unfit to live and associate with human beings, and hurl them into eternity. In Exod. xxi. 16, you have God's law on this point. Hear him for a moment in relation to this crime:

"And he that stealeth a man, and selleth him, or if he be found in his hand, he shall surely be put to death." 1. Here you have man-stealing, or the act of reducing a man to slavery. 2. Holding him as a slave if he be found in his hand. 3. Man-selling, or speculating in man as an article of property. God has put the whole upon one common level, and hurls death as a penalty at the head of each. Carry this Bible law into execution, and you would free the whole land of slavery in a few short weeks. Such a book in favor of slavery! It is absurd and ridiculous to suppose it. There is not a passage of all the Bible, rightly construed, that looks toward defending that system of abominations. It is a vile slander on the God of the Bible to pretend it. Such dark hearts not only love sin and are determined to practise it, but they wish to bring in the infinitely pure and holy One to indorse, and even authorize their crimes. That is the most aggravating part of their wickedness, as he will show them at a future day. Now the fact that we find men who pretend to defend such wickedness by the Bible, shows how much they need this illuminating power from above to scatter the darkness which beclouds their minds. While they live destitute of it they are guilty of shutting out truth and light from their hearts, that would do their souls good. There are other topics of vast interest to the church, where she needs light and would receive it, if she would but receive this power. What a change it would make in the state of things in the churches. Now, you have no right to live without this light; you are guilty while you do it, and wrong yourself and the world.

4. You are guilty of destroying your own peace of mind, while you live destitute of this power. Your conscience will reprove while you are grieving the Spirit. You know you are not right. You know there is something lacking. When you are filled with this power, you will have joy in the Holy Ghost. When Philip went to the city of Samaria and preached, the Holy Ghost came down and wrought wonders by him, and the good Book in-

forms us, that "there was great joy in the city." This holy power fills the soul with delight, and causes it to joy and triumph in God. While it feels intensely for the world, it at the same time feels intensely happy in God. In times of the outpouring of the Spirit, how Christians rejoice! When the heart is full of this power it will be happy. You may afflict the body with pain, but the soul will triumph. It will "rejoice with joy unspeakable and full of glory." Try it, my brother, and you will know by experience the richness of this blessing.

REMARKS.

1. We learn why the gospel produces so little effect. Ministers and laymen do not secure this power. They feel but little responsibility in relation to it. Let the minister cry out for it until his heart is full. Let the church follow his example, and how the wicked would be slain on every hand!

2. We see why the church has so little power over men. Her strength lies in having God with her. This she forgets, and consequently she cannot stand in the presence of her enemies.

3. We see how to obtain victory over the world, the flesh, and the devil. Secure this power, and you will come off conqueror, and more than conqueror. All earth cannot allure you, all hell cannot harm you.

4. We see the only safety of converts. The Bible informs us that they are kept by the power of God, through faith unto salvation.

God's power is your only hope. Be filled with this and you are safe. Be filled with this and you will grow up rapidly into Christ, and become mighty in the Scriptures, — you will be strong men for God. This age needs a race of such men, and then the world would move under their influence.

5. We see how much our theological schools need baptizing with this power. Until that takes place, we shall have a weak, sickly ministry, who will write and deliver, in a cold formal manner, little pretty pointless essays, with neither edge nor power in them to save the world. These young ministers need to be baptized with this power, and after having finished their education at the theological seminary, should be further instructed in the language of the text, — "tarry ye in the city of Jerusalem until ye be endued with power from on high." Then they can enter their pulpits and bring out truths that will burn. Hearts will be searched and moved to their very depths, and there will be a shaking among the dry bones of the sanctuary.

6. We see how hardhearted sinners can be reached and saved. How they trembled in Jerusalem, and cried out for mercy! Let the church be filled with this power all over the world, and the nations would move, and the world would soon come home to God.

Now, then, will you have it in this place? Will you to-day begin in earnest to plead for it, and give the Lord no rest until you receive it. Decide that matter now, and put every obstacle out of the way of your receiving it, and God will shake terribly this whole region.

INSTRUCTIONS TO THE WICKED.

VII.

THE CARELESS ONES.

Be troubled, ye careless ones. — *Isaiah* xxxii. 11.

1. CARELESS ABOUT GOD. 2. CARELESS ABOUT GOD'S LAW. 3. CARELESS ABOUT CHRIST. 4. CARELESS ABOUT DEATH. 5. CARELESS ABOUT THE JUDGMENT, HEAVEN, HELL, ETERNITY, SALVATION.

THE more I study my Bible, the more I am impressed with the thought that it is a singular book. It is totally unlike any other book I ever read. One of its peculiarities shall be noticed here, and, for want of time, only one. You take up any other book, even when the writer is undertaking to give you a description of human character, and while he may touch upon some of its leading prominent traits, you will discover his picture is strangely deficient. But when you turn your attention to the Bible, you have a perfect delineation of every character that ever has, does now, or ever will exist. There is not a development of human nature in this state, nation, or the world, that the Bible does not describe. Have you a thief in this community? The Bible describes him. Have you a liar, a covetous man, a fornicator, a malicious man, a man full of envy, murder, debate, deceit, malignity; a whisperer, backbiter, hater of God, despiteful, proud, a boaster, an inventor of evil things; one disobedient to parents, without understanding, a covenantbreaker, without natural affection, implacable, unmerciful, a hypocrite, a profane swearer, a sabbathbreaker, an atheist? The Bible describes them all. It affirms that the fool hath said in his heart, there is no God. Have you a good man? The Bible describes him. It is a perfect mirror into which every man may look, if he will, and see himself. He may examine his heart, and watch all its developments, and then go to the Bible and find it all described. There is not a thought, purpose, desire of the heart, or an act of the life, which is good, that the Bible does not demand; not a thought, purpose, desire of the heart, or act of the life, which is evil, that the Bible does not forbid or condemn. It covers the entire ground of right, demanding every possible act that the human soul can put forth that is good; and it also covers the entire ground of wrongdoing, forbidding everything evil; so that there is not and cannot be anything done by any man, right or wrong, but that the Bible describes it. This to me is one evidence that the Bible never was and never could be written by any man or men without divine help, divine inspiration. Here is the very impress of God upon this sacred volume, deny it who may. Think of it. In the brief compass of this one volume I hold in my hand, you have a complete, unerring picture of every character that ever will figure upon the stage of this world's history. Such a book written without divine aid, by a set of crafty priests, as infidels affirm? The thing was impossible, utterly impossible. When infidels make such charges, they pay too high a compliment to the priests, as they call them. They give them credit for an amount of intellect and originality they never possessed. There are things in the Bible that no human intellect ever could have originated without divine assistance. Do you ask for an instance? Take the one under consideration; and when you have disposed of that I will give you others. What finite mind can survey the whole world, and give a complete description of every human heart that ever will exist? It could not be done by an angel. There is but one being, — He who needeth not that any should testify of man, because he knoweth him altogether, — who could possibly perform such a task. It took a God to do it, and here you have his impress upon that book divine. There is a God here. Here is an infinite intellect, that has seen fit to unfold the great and glorious truths brought to light in that volume. I am amazed that Deists, and their half-brothers who talk so much about a liberal Christianity, the bigotry and narrow-mindedness of the orthodox, should not discover this fact. In their estimation, they are the only wise ones of this age. They can investigate and think freely, they say, without being trammelled by a creed. If they have such mighty intellects, let them account for this fact, if they can. It is one thing to cry out bigotry and narrow-mindedness, but quite another thing to meet facts and arguments, and meet them fairly. Let such men gird themselves for such a work, before they boast too much about their wonderful investigating powers. Let them show their strength here, for there is an ample field for it. Here is a book which has stood the test of a most rigid investigation for centuries; and notwithstanding the boast of infidels, in years gone by, that they would use it up, it still lives, and has a stronger hold upon the consciences of the community than all the other books of earth. Infidels have never fairly met the arguments upon which its inspiration rests, and they never can. There is not one solitary objection raised by this class of men that has not been completely annihilated over and over again, and still the young brood who are coming up at this day bring forward those old, stale things, as though they never had been replied to. I presume many of these modern objectors are so consummately ignorant on this point that they really think they have discovered some new difficulty, or some objection that never has been met. I would like to see some of the wise ones of this age bring forward a new objection, if they can. Before they boast too loud about their investigating powers, let them introduce one new argument against the inspiration of the Bible. When they will do it, they will probably find intellect in and among the very class which they denounce as bigots and narrow-minded, to meet anything they may bring forward. At any rate, infidelity has always found its match among the defenders of the Bible, and I presume it always will. You cannot present me with one solitary infidel writer who has not met with a successful reply. The Bible does not stand in fear of the most rigid investigation. It has stood this test for ages, and it will not shrink from it at this late day. It challenges investigation. One of its commands is, " *Prove all things.*"

It is not my object, however, in this sermon to defend the inspiration of the Bible. It needs no such defence. I only introduce the preceding ideas to prepare the way for another. The Bible is not only a singular book, but the trait of character brought to light in my text is a singular one: " CARELESS ONES."

When we look at the state of things which surrounds man in this life, how amazing this state of heart! To impress you with this thought we will suppose a case or two. Let an individual be taken from this congregation to-day, and transported at once to Heaven. He shall find himself upon its most lofty heights, and his feet shall truly tread its golden streets. He shall now be surrounded with all the hosts of that holy and upper temple. We will suppose for a moment that he can there survey each heart in that world of bliss, and see it just as God does. Among all the living ones on high, would he find this trait of character? What! A careless saint, a careless angel around the throne of God! Not one. In that happy world, all are awake. Every intellect is aroused and every heart is on fire. They look abroad and see God unfold his purity and holiness, and are lost in wonder and astonishment. They sing, shout, and praise him for his infinite excellence, and every soul is full of interest. No careless ones there. We will now suppose that the same being can enter at once into the world of woe. He shall find himself enclosed within the walls of that great prison-house of dark damnation. He listens to the groans, the gnashing of teeth, and the wailings of the lost. Here he can look at once into their hearts as he surveyed those in heaven. Would he find this trait of character there? What! a careless one with his head upon the pillow of the second death! A careless one in that world where their worm dieth not, and the fire is not quenched! A careless sinner in hell! Was the rich man in hell careless? Every soul will be awake there to its eternal interests when it is too late.

We will now suppose that he turns away from this scene of despair, and travels over the entire dominions of Jehovah, and surveys all worlds, and if they are all inhabited, probably not a solitary careless one would he find until he comes back to this earth. Here, where, as expressed by the poet, —

> "Lo, on a narrow neck of land,
> Betwixt two unbounded seas I stand,
> Yet how insensible!
> A point of time, a moment's space,
> Removes me to yon heavenly place,
> Or shuts me up in hell." —

Here in this world, where, between the cradle and the grave, the question is to be settled, eternally settled, whether the soul is to be saved or lost, man will settle down in a state of carelessness which is amazing. They will be careless, as if they had no souls; as if there was no God, no heaven, no hell, no eternal state; as indifferent as though nothing was at stake. Think of it, you careless ones! Here, under the Gospel, you fix your state in heaven or hell. Yet how insensible! Ah, sinner! you had better be careless in any other world than this. There would be more propriety in your being careless amid the shouts and glories of heaven, or amid the smoke of the pit and the lamentations of the damned, than to be careless here. You had better step up to the judgment even, and stand under the blazing eye of God, and be careless while you are listening to your final sentence than to be careless here. Remember, your destiny is not to be decided at the judgment, but in this world, while under the Gospel. Come, you careless sinners, here, to-day, pause, think, be candid for a season, and look at this state of heart. See its wickedness; on your knees, repent, shake off this indifference, and henceforth be *awake* about your eternal interests. May God arouse you now, and induce you to listen with interest to a few truths, and cause them to stir and move your inmost soul.

But, says one, do you call us careless sinners? I most certainly do. I lay that charge at your door, and I will make it good, if you will hear me candidly. But, if we are careless, about what are we careless? That is the very question to which I invite your most serious attention while I name some things of moment. The things about which you are careless are the things about which no being should be careless.

I. THEN YOU ARE CARELESS ABOUT GOD.

What a state of heart that must be, — careless about Jehovah! Sinner, reflect here. *Careless about your Maker!* How such a being would look in heaven, among that happy throng who are full of indescribable interest in relation to God! How all heaven would *scorn* such a wretch! How heaven would annoy such a soul! Let God turn and fix his holy gaze upon such a heart, and it would writhe as if under the agonies of the second death. What is it that interests your soul, — is it God? No. You know better. Some of you are interested in business matters, money speculations, &c.; others in political affairs; others still in balls, parties, theatres, gambling hells, or some other place of amusement, where they can have a good time. Introduce God to such beings, how quick they are silent! Upon that theme they do not wish to converse.

Sinner, if you say you are not careless about God, let me put a few questions directly to your conscience, and you ponder them well.

1. How much do you *think* about God? Such are the laws of your being, that when you are interested in any person or thing, that person or thing will become a topic of thought; it will occupy your thoughts just in proportion to your interest. If you are interested in money-making, you will think about it. If you are interested in your wife, children, or friends, you will think about them. If you are interested in the gratification of any appetite, or propensity of mind or body, you will think about it. If you are interested in God, you will think about God. How much do you think about HIM? When you awake in the morning, is God the first thought that occupies your mind? Do you think of the being who has kindly spread his wing over you during the night, and shielded you from harm? Does your heart flow out to him in thanksgiving and praise for his merciful care over you? Is God in all your thoughts? What say you to these questions? Is it not true that you crowd the thought of God

out of your mind? Your mind is engrossed almost entirely with earth's cares and pleasures, and you live as though there were no God. Is this true? I appeal to your conscience. *You* know. Can you deny it? If not, can you pretend that you are not careless about God?

Again, how much time have you spent for six months past in reading your Bible, to see what it says about God, so that you may have a correct knowledge of him? Now understand my question. The inquiry is not how much time you have spent reading the Bible for six months past, but how much time you have spent reading it to learn what it says about God. One great object of the Bible is to give us a true knowledge of God. Man, in consequence of sin, had lost a correct knowledge of God, as the whole heathen world demonstrates. Point me to any portion of the globe, destitute of this book, where they have any consistent knowledge of God! There is not such a spot on earth. Even the very Deist is indebted to the Bible he rejects, for all the correct views he has of God. The Deity understood this state of things, and in the Bible he has revealed himself to man. Now, how much time have you spent, during the last six months, reading that book to learn what it says about God? Have you spent an hour a week? Have you spent an hour a month? I presume there are sinners before me to-day, who have not spent an hour for a year in reading the

Bible for that object; can you deny it, or will you plead guilty. If you are guilty, will you, with this fact staring you in the face, pretend you are not careless about God? What! The only book which gives you a correct knowledge of God cast aside and neglected, and you not indifferent about him! The thought is absurd. If you were not careless about God, you would pore over its sacred pages, with deep anxiety, to see what it says about your Maker. You had better be careless about all the other beings in the universe, than to be careless about the Infinite One. Such a state of heart is wicked, supremely wicked. It wholly unfits you for heaven. No being can be saved in such a state of mind. Some of you church-members may be in this state. If so, remember you are not Christians. You are in the gall of bitterness, and will be lost, unless you repent. Oh, ye careless ones! careless about your Maker, — how can you be saved?

II. SINNERS ARE CARELESS ABOUT GOD'S LAW.

Were we not acquainted somewhat with the feeling of an impenitent heart, we should think this assertion almost incredible. We are all placed under God's law, and we cannot help ourselves if we would. God claims the right to enact laws to govern the human family, and he has done so. He is abundantly able and determined to maintain that right, and he will do it. He holds in his possession the means of enforcing his authority, and he will not neglect his duty. We may trample it under our feet, but we must take the consequences. His authority is of infinite worth to the universe. This he understands, and he will not see it trifled with, and trampled upon with impunity. We are perfectly in his power. What can we do when his hand takes hold on vengeance? Under such a king, such a ruler, will we trifle with his laws? Can we be careless about them? Still, sinners *are* careless about them. Sinner, what do you care about God's authority, God's laws? Go and show that profane young man, yonder, that God's law forbids his profanity. What does he care? He is so hardened he would almost look God right in the face and swear. Show that business man that God's law requires of him to love Him with all his heart, and his neighbor as himself. Ask him if he is doing it; he will throw up his head with an air of indifference, and reply, no, sir. Press him with another question: Will you do it? This is God's demand. I am not prepared to decide any such question, sir, he replies, — in a state of perfect indifference. He is as cool about the matter as if it were a perfectly trifling affair to trample infinite authority under his feet.

The human family will look at God's claims, admit them to be his, and, with their eyes open, they will go deliberately to the work of violating them. They will do it without feeling. What hardened wretches! What careless ones! Let men treat the laws of the land in the same way, how quick they would be imprisoned or put to death! God is long-suffering and waits to be gracious, but this carelessness cannot go unpunished, if persisted in.

III. SINNERS ARE CARELESS ABOUT CHRIST.

How can any earthly being be careless about Christ, the Saviour of the human race? Look at his character; how excellent, how pure, holy, merciful, and kind! Look at what he has done for man: He came to this earth, when he knew he should be wickedly slandered by the human family, treated with cold neglect, despised and rejected of men. He knew he would be arrested, tried at man's bar, condemned without evidence, and unrighteously put to death by the very beings he came to save. With his eyes open on this point, he came here and laid down his life to open a way by which we poor sinners could be saved. This you know; this you acknowledge. Now, sinners, how have you treated him? What do you care about Christ? How indifferently you have treated him! When he calls and invites you to come to him and live, you turn away with indifference. You heed not his invitations. If he should enter this congregation and weep over sinners here to-day, and entreat you to turn from your sins and live, you would probably scorn his message, trifle with his tears, and persist in your iniquity. Do you say, no? Think for a moment. Is he not here, although you see him not? Has he not poured out strong cries and tears for the whole human family? You sinners here were included in that number. How indifferent you have been about his agonies in your behalf up to this hour! Here you are in God's sanctuary now, careless ones. Careless about Christ your Redeemer? I will put the Life of Christ, as recorded by Matthew, and the Life of Washington into your hands to-day, and you will read the latter with tenfold more interest than the Life of Christ. But you will reply, Washington saved this nation. Saved this nation? Whom has Christ saved? Christ is the Saviour of the world. Then where did you get your Washington? Christ gave him to you, and gave him his intellectual powers, all his wisdom, and all his success. He watched around him on the field of battle; warded off the shafts of death; protected and carried him through all his trials. He is the author of every good and perfect gift. He supplies the wants of the whole human race. By his death in man's behalf, he brought life and immortality to light through the Gospel, so that all can be saved who will repent and believe in his name. He has gone up on high to prepare a heaven for you, and invites you all to be saved. Now, how can you be careless about such a being? Careless ones, you know you have treated Christ with perfect neglect all your lives. You are hastening to eternity in this state of heart. After treating him with such neglect, how can you look him in the face with any composure at the judgment? But you *must* meet him, and there look this matter full in the face under his holy gaze.

IV. MEN ARE CARELESS ABOUT DEATH.

There are several reasons why it would seem impossible that man could be careless about this event, connected, as it is, with each one's history.

1. Its certainty. There is not an individual in this congregation who can even hope that he shall not die. Death is on your track. It will overtake, arrest, and lay you low in the grave. The sentence, "dust thou art, and unto dust shalt thou return," is God's irrevocable decree. The high and the low, the rich and the poor, must fall under its power. Where are the generations that have preceded us? They are gone, all gone to the silent mansions of the dead. Take what course in life you please, surround yourself with the most skilful physicians the world ever produced, exhaust all earth's remedies to save life, and still death will enter your dwelling, or arrest you by the way-side, or in the bustle of business, and do up his relentless work of consigning you to the charnel house of all the living.

2. Death closes up all your worldly affairs. It closes your probationary state. Your plans of a worldly nature may be ever so important, and de-

mand your presence to see them executed successfully, and still death will snatch you from the whole. You may be in the high places of the nation; public interests may seem to demand that your life be prolonged; but if death calls, you must leave the whole to other hands. Your political history will then be ended, *eternally* closed up. When it calls, you must be torn from the circle of your friends, however dear to you, or however dear you may be to them. A wife and helpless children may seem to be dependent upon your daily labor to supply their wants; they may need your counsel, your watch, care, and your helping hand; but when *death* speaks, you must heed its voice, and look upon them for the last time in this world. When death comes, it closes up your probationary state, takes you from under the Gospel dispensation, and all the means of grace, and sends you to eternity. You have now heard your last sermon, listened to your last prayer, have seen the inside of the sanctuary for the last time, have received your last invitation to be reconciled to God; mercy's efforts to save are ended, and you go to your last and final account. How can any mind be careless about an event so important!

3. Not an individual in this house knows when he shall die. What man in this congregation knows he shall live a day or an hour? Sinner, do you even know you will live to reach your home? You may die in this house, before this sermon ends.

You may start for home and drop by the way-side. Should you live to reach your home and retire in health, your friends may find you dead in the morning. You know neither the day nor the hour when God will call you. So he affirms, so facts demonstrate. The world is full of facts showing that persons retire in health, and are found dead in the morning. Ministers fall in the sacred desk, lawyers in pleading at the bar, statesmen in the halls of legislation, business men in their counting-rooms. Men are killed on railroads, engulfed in the ocean by the hundred, swallowed up by earthquakes, swept into eternity by the tempest, struck down by lightning, and in a thousand other forms too numerous to mention. There is not an individual who knows when death will overtake him. It will come in an unexpected hour, and usher you into the presence of God.

But, says one, do you wish to frighten us? If looking at facts as they daily transpire before the eyes of the world will frighten, then you ought to be frightened. Facts are facts, and you should look them in the face; and every candid, reflecting man is willing to do it, and shape his life in view of them. All men should contemplate this event. They should do it daily. They should inquire often, am I ready to die? But the great multitude put it out of their minds. They are careless about death. The manner in which they talk about this event, their mode of living, settles that question. Would that man swear, if he thought death was by his side, ready to cut him down the next breath? How quick he would turn pale! Would those young people dance if you should place their coffin in one end of the hall, and hang their shroud in the other, with the knowledge that some or all of them must die at the close of the ball. Dance? They would say, *this* is no time to dance. Let death strike down one victim in every dance you have on earth, and how quick such amusements would be abandoned! The fact that men will spend their time in such places of hilarity shows they are careless about dying.

V. MEN ARE CARELESS ABOUT THE JUDGMENT, HEAVEN, HELL, ETERNITY, SALVATION.

They are careless about everything that pertains to another world; careless about God's glory, his wishes, his will. They are all interested in the trifles of the day; but the great end for which they are created, and for which all should live and act, is neglected and forgotten. The work of preparing for eternity is the topic upon which they are unwilling to dwell. They do not love to think about it or hear upon that point.

I will show *why* sinners should be troubled: 1. You should be troubled about the state itself. This state of heart is not only wicked, but it is alarming. The heart that is careless to-day, the strong probability is, will be more so a week or a month hence. This stupidity or carelessness about religious things generally increases with your age. This is the reason why young hearts are easily moved, while aged sinners are as hard and unfeeling as marble. If you are careless to-day, that should alarm you, and lead you to fly to God for his Spirit, to break up your stupidity.

2. You should be troubled about this state of heart, because it is so unbefitting your condition. God has surrounded you with scenes and events which ought to arouse a universe to the highest pitch of interest. You may look at your stupidity as an evidence of wisdom. An evidence of wisdom? It is an evidence of all but infinite folly. The greatest intellects in the universe are deeply interested in the scenes that surround man. God is awake. Angels desire to look into these things. How they shouted when the Saviour was born, who was to be your Redeemer! The repentance of one sinner here to-day would fill all heaven with acclamations of joy, such is the interest felt in the scenes that surround man, by the master spirits in the universe. They are all interest, and you careless. Such a thought should trouble you. How you would look among such beings! With such a heart, how unfit to mingle in such society!

3. You should be troubled about this state of heart, because God so abhors it. God, in his word

everywhere condemns this careless state. He condemns it in my text, and calls upon you in the most solemn manner to be troubled about it. How he condemns hardheartedness all through the Bible! God hates this state. He knows its wickedness; he knows how it endangers your eternal interests. No sinner ever repented in this state, and none ever will. Unless the Spirit can arouse you from this state, you will go down to hell. Sinner, you will be lost, if you persist in this state. You must lie down in sorrow.

This carelessness must be broken up. If the Gospel, the means of grace, and the striving of the Spirit to break up this state of heart, are all resisted, God will resort to sterner means at another day to bring you to your senses. Death, if you have your reason, will probably make you feel. You are unwilling to contemplate it now. God calls upon you to prepare to die, but you put him off. At length he will bring you and death face to face. It will lay its cold grasp upon you, and how you will shudder! Oh, how you will wake up when it places you in a condition where you must look over into eternity! You will then plead for time to prepare; but it will feel for that brittle thread, snap it, and you are gone.

2. The judgment! oh, how it will break up your carelessness! Take from the Bible one description of the state of feeling there will be among such sin-

ners, when that event takes place. Rev. vi. 15–17: "And the kings of the earth, and the great men, and the rich men, and the chief captains, and the mighty men, and every bondman, and every freeman, hid themselves in the dens, and in the rocks of the mountains: And said to the mountains and rocks, Fall on us, and hide us from the face of him that sitteth on the throne, and from the wrath of the Lamb: For the great day of his wrath is come; and who shall be able to stand?" What a description of the mental anguish of the great and wise ones of this earth when Christ shall come to judge them for this carelessness! How their carelessness will be crushed out at that hour, and their souls aroused when too late to repent! How they dread to look the Lamb in the face, after slighting and turning a deaf ear to all his calls, and spending a life of stupidity! How they tremble as they march up to his throne! Careless ones must look him in the face there. They must meet him, and render up their account for this strange stupidity. What a day that will be to you, careless sinner, when you will be compelled to listen to your final doom from his stern lips!

3. And finally, the pangs of the second death, as you lie down in hell's dark prison-house, will effectually break up your carelessness for a long eternity. Ages of unutterable anguish may roll away; but in the vast future that lies before you, your carelessness will never return.

REMARKS.

1. From this subject, we learn that the saints receive all their trouble in this life. In this world they may have tribulation, but it is momentary. When the pang of death is over, their troubles are brought to a perpetual end. All the future to them is peace and joy. Life, eternal life is their final reward.

2. From this subject, we learn that the sinner will receive all his consolation in this life. There will be trouble enough for him in the future. What an eternity, what an eternity, sinner! Poor sinner, will you not awake and shake off this carelessness to-day? Do not wait for death, the judgment, and hell, to break it up for you. Be troubled now about your sins, about this great sin to which I have called your attention in this sermon. Repent, and put away all your transgressions, and come to Christ for forgiveness; and then, when you close up earth, you shall spend an eternity at God's right hand, where all is peace.

VIII.

MORAL AGENCY.

I call heaven and earth to record this day against you, that I have set before you life and death, blessing and cursing: therefore choose life, that both thou and thy seed may live. — *Deut.* xxx. 19.

1. ATTRIBUTES OF A MORAL AGENT. 2. PROOF OF THE DOCTRINE.

Moses here affirms that he had set before the children of Israel life and death. The first inquiry which grows out of this text is, what does he mean by life and death? Does it have reference to the body? I answer, no, from the fact that, let the Jews pursue what course they would, their bodies must die. The text takes it for granted that if they obeyed God, they would escape the death here threatened. But they might obey God in all things, and still their bodies go to the grave. The sentence, "dust thou art," has passed upon all men, and that sentence is not to be revoked. Obedience to God will not set it aside. This settles the question that the terms life and death, as used in the text, have no reference to the body. To what then do they refer? I answer, that they refer to the life and death of the soul. The soul's life is its holiness and happiness; its death is its sinfulness and misery. Its happiness is the fruit or result of its holiness, and its misery is the fruit or result of its sinfulness. Now, says Moses, I have set before you life and death. I have pointed out to you the course which will secure you holiness and happiness, if you pursue it, both here and hereafter, and which is life, *eternal* life. Or I have spread before you the course which, if you pursue it, will be sinful and result in your death, *eternal* death. Now choose or decide which course you will adopt. God's command is to choose life.

From this text it is manifest that there are two agents active in deciding the destiny of man for eternity. There are certain things which God decides. His decision is already made up, and is as unchangeable as his eternal throne. It is this: If man will repent and obey all God's requirements, and pursue a life of obedience and holiness, its results shall be life, eternal felicity. But if man will disobey God's commandments and persist in a sinful life, it shall result in death to happiness, his eternal death. Thus far God decides. This is his unalterable purpose. These facts being revealed, God then submits this question to the choice of man, and he must decide which course he will pursue. His choice will now settle the matter and fix his destiny for eternity. This responsibility is now upon him. His fate is in his own hands, and God will neither take it out of his hands himself, nor suffer any other being to do it. Mark the objects of choice here presented. Will you lead a holy life, knowing it will result in happiness and bliss, *endless* bliss, or will you lead a sinful life, knowing it will result in misery and death, *eternal* death? Will you obey God, or resolve to have your own way? This is the question to be settled. Which course will you pursue? One of these courses you must pursue; that you cannot avoid. There is no neutral ground here. You cannot say, I will pursue neither. On that point you are not voluntary; you must pursue one course or the other. You are voluntary only in saying which. Here you cannot be forced. God will not force your decision either way, nor will he suffer any other being to do it. The question, which course of life you will pursue, is submitted to your choice. That question you *must* decide, and God will deal with you accordingly.

I will now draw from this text, and shall discuss in this sermon, the following

DOCTRINE:

MAN IS A MORAL AGENT.

I will examine this doctrine in the following order:

I. I will call your attention to the attributes of a moral agent.

II. Prove the doctrine.

1. WHAT, THEN, ARE THE ATTRIBUTES OF A MORAL AGENT?

1. To be a *moral* agent a being must be intelligent. He must have an intellect. We say heat is a powerful *agent*. It produces an effect, a powerful one, but there is no intelligence there. A moral agent must have the power of thinking, taking in the idea of God, seeing the relations which exist between him and his Creator, capable of studying his government, and laying hold of the great thoughts there presented.

2. To be a moral agent a being must have a conscience, or he must be capable of distinguishing between right and wrong. Conscience is that faculty of the soul which will decide between right and wrong, when you give it light. It cannot act without moral light or instruction, any more than the mind can see objects with the eye without natural light. A man may have a perfect eye, but he cannot perceive objects with it without light. The light is as essential as the eye itself. When you have both good eyes and light you can see. So with conscience; it wants moral light to be capable of seeing duty or distinguishing between right and wrong. It cannot decide duty without it. Conscience may exist and be perfect without moral light, as the eye may exist and be perfect without natural light. But to act, to point you to your duty, and bring in its decision in relation to your conduct, it must have light. It exists independent of light or instruction, as in the case of the infant.

The child has a conscience, but its faculties are not yet so far developed as to be capable of receiving moral light or instruction. As soon as it can receive light, and in proportion as it receives it, conscience says, this is the way, walk ye in it; that is wrong, refrain from it. When you decide to take the wrong course, conscience makes you feel guilty, — it condemns you. When you take the right course, it approves and approbates your life. That faculty of the soul which produces these effects, is the faculty I am talking about. Such a faculty is essential to constitute a being a moral agent. Where it does not exist there is no moral agency. The brutes are destitute of it, consequently are not moral agents, and not accountable for their conduct.

3. To be a moral agent, a being must have sensibility. He must be susceptible of pleasure or pain, or capable of happiness or misery. To this faculty motives can be addressed and the soul can be moved to action. Through it hope can be aroused, — hope for some good, — something that will advance happiness. Fear can be awakened, — fear of some evil that will produce pain. Through this faculty the soul can be aroused and moved to action.

4. To be a moral agent, a being must have a will, or the power of choice. The will is the monarch of the soul. It is the governing, controlling faculty. Its actions decide the whole destiny of man. It is *its* action which renders the soul holy or sinful, virtuous

or vicious. Temptations can be presented to the appetites or propensities of body or mind, but they cannot be indulged without the consent of the will. The *sinfulness* does not lie in the *appetite*, but in the decision of the will to indulge it at the expense of God's authority. The sin of Eve did not lie in her appetite for fruit, nor in her temptation by the serpent, but in the decision of the will to yield to the temptation. The appetite in that and all other cases was perfectly under the control of the will. Had she purposed not to indulge that appetite, where God had laid his prohibition, and had she remained firm and unchangeable in that purpose, she would have maintained her holiness, notwithstanding the appetite and the temptation. This establishes the fact that the sin consisted in the action or choice which the will made, and not in the appetite or temptation, so far as she was concerned. What was true in that case, is equally true in all other cases.

A moral agent, then, must have the power of choice. He must be capable of making a *holy* or *sinful* choice, or of choosing between right and wrong. What does such a choice imply?

1. It implies two courses of life presented to the eye of the mind; the one holy or right, and the other sinful or wrong.

2. It implies motives presented to influence to the right course, and motives to influence to the wrong course.

3. It implies power to resist all the motive that can be presented to move the will to select one of these courses in preference to the other. There is not motive enough in the universe to *compel* the will to make a holy or sinful choice. If there is, God will not present it himself, nor suffer any other being to do it; and I affirm it cannot be done by any being. It involves a contradiction in terms, and is a palpable absurdity; for a choice, to be holy or sinful, must be a voluntary choice. A forced act is neither holy nor sinful in the being forced to put it forth. If you array before the mind such a degree of motive that the will is forced to choose as it does, then it is not voluntary in its choice, and the act is neither sinful nor holy. A virtuous or sinful choice, let it be remembered, must be a voluntary choice of the will. If you apply an irresistible degree of motive, and force the will to choose as it does, such a choice (if you can call it a choice) is neither sinful nor holy. The will is not capable of putting forth a sinful or virtuous choice under an irresistible pressure of motive.

4. A virtuous act, then, implies the power to act in two ways. An agent who can act only in one way is not a *moral*, but a *necessary* agent. Water can act in one way: it can run down hill, but it lacks the power of turning about and running up hill. It is a *necessary*, and not a moral agent.

A moral agent has power to act in two ways. He

can do right or wrong. When he does right, it is not because he lacks the power to do wrong. When he puts forth a wrong act, it is not because he lacks the power to do right. He never can lose this power of acting in two ways while he remains a moral agent. Let him lose this power, and he would sink down from a moral to a necessary agent, and would no longer be capable of sin or holiness. The will, then, in making a holy or sinful choice at the time it puts forth such a choice, must have the power of choosing otherwise, if it sees fit to do so. It is a voluntary choice. The will cannot be forced in such a choice by any being. In fact, there is no choice without voluntariness. The very idea of choice supposes that the will cannot be forced in its decisions. This perfect independence of the will, to yield to or resist motive, to incline it in either direction, is absolutely essential as an attribute of moral agency. Without it, a being is controlled by irresistible power, and is a mere machine, not capable of sin or holiness.

Having submitted these remarks upon the attributes of a moral agent, I now proceed to the second proposition, which is as follows : —

II. Prove the Doctrine.

Under this head I present the following things :

1. Man possesses all the attributes of a moral agent. How do we go to work to prove that Christ is God as well as man? We prove it by showing that he

possesses all the attributes of God, and we pronounce such an argument sound. We say it cannot be successfully answered. I here present the same mode of reasoning to prove that man is a moral agent. 1. Man is an intelligent being. Look for a moment into the mechanical world. What a variety of useful inventions man has devised! What an amount of intellectual labor! Glance your eye over the literature of the world, and mark the quantity of books, papers, pamphlets, periodicals of all sorts and kinds. What a world of thought! Then survey the different governments of earth. Is there not an abundance of evidence of intellect here? Then there are your schools, colleges, and other means of education. Why all this machinery, if man is not an intelligent being? The fact is, man can be educated, and there are no limits to the expansion of his intellectual powers. They will expand endlessly, without doubt. 2. Man has a conscience. How constantly the human race are passing judgment upon their own conduct, in relation to its being right or wrong, and also judging their fellows upon the same point! It is an every-day occurrence. They talk about justice and injustice, sin and holiness, right and wrong. This has been true of all nations, how much soever their minds have been beclouded with darkness. Such conduct and talk settles the question that man has a conscience. Were it not for this fact, the idea of right and wrong would never have entered the breast of man. The beasts of the field have no such ideas. The fact that such thoughts are in the world, and all parts of the world, settles the question that man has a conscience. 3. Man has sensibility. He is capable of happiness or misery. This is something he feels and experiences. All men know this, and it is an idea out of which you cannot reason them. 4. Man has a will. He is capable of choice. He is choosing between objects every day of his life, and every hour in the day. Man chooses his business, his wife, his agents to do business for him, his goods, his horses and cattle, his farm. He chooses between right and wrong, — chooses this course of life because he thinks it right, and rejects that because he thinks it wrong; so that man is in the constant exercise of this and all the other attributes of a moral agent through his whole life. This is true of all men in all parts of the world.

I have now shown that man has all the attributes of a moral agent, — which completely establishes the truth of this doctrine. Man cannot have all these attributes and not be a moral agent, any more than the Deity can have all the attributes of God and not be God. I might rest this controversy here, and wait for the opponents of this doctrine to prove, if they can, that man does not possess these attributes. This they must prove, or this one argument is fatal to their theory. I have, however, other proofs I wish to present, for I intend to establish this doctrine beyond all successful controversy.

2. I present, in proof of this doctrine, the fact that God believes man to be a moral agent. God everywhere treats and deals with him as a moral agent, which would be wholly inconsistent in the Deity if this doctrine were not true. God has placed man under moral government, and by this act proclaims to the universe that he knows him to be a moral agent. If man is not a moral agent, he could not be governed by moral laws any more than the planetary system could be governed by moral laws. What would you think of God if he should issue a code of moral laws to govern the motion of the heavenly bodies? You would pronounce him destitute of all wisdom, and lose confidence in him at once. But why lose confidence? Because, you say, such laws are not adapted to the nature of the thing to be governed; the thing to be governed can only be governed by the law of force. If man is not a moral agent, he is not capable of being governed but by the law of force. Upon that principle, he is always governed by the law of force, and no other. He is in that case a necessary agent, and acts only as he is acted on by force. If he is not a moral agent, a moral government is no more adapted to his nature than it is adapted to govern the planets. God is not open to the charge of such folly. He knows man's nature, and the government adapted

to it. He knows full well that none but moral agents can be governed by moral laws. By placing man under moral government, therefore, he testified to the universe, by actions which speak louder than words, that he knows man is a moral agent.

Again, God praises and rewards man for doing right, and condemns and punishes him for doing wrong. Praise man for his action, if he is not voluntary! Why not praise the sun for shining, and the vegetables for growing? In that case they are just as voluntary as man is, and as deserving of praise. Condemn and punish him for his conduct! Condemn him for what? For what he is forced to do by an irresistible power? Why not condemn the tempest for levelling the forest to the ground, and the lightning for killing men? How quick you would charge God with folly, if he should do this! Why so? Because, you say, they are not voluntary. But are they not just as voluntary as man is, if he is not a moral agent? and is not the condemnation just as appropriate in the one case as in the other? Then punish man for doing wrong! Can a necessary agent do wrong? Can the earthquake do wrong? Can the volcano do wrong? Can the raging ocean, which ingulfs that steamer freighted with human life, do wrong? Who believes such nonsense? The common sense of every man teaches him better.

But if man is not a moral agent, his acts are no more deserving of punishment than the acts of the earthquake, the volcano, or the raging ocean. In that case he has no control over his action any more than these agents have over theirs, and he is no more deserving of punishment than they are. If there is any being who deserves to be punished in this matter, it is the being who applies the irresistible force, and not the being who is forced. Now, then, the fact that God does punish men for their actions is God's testimony, in the most convincing manner, that he knows him to be a moral agent; that he acts voluntarily, and not necessarily; that he might and ought to have done differently from what he has done; that his doing was voluntary, and deserving of punishment. Thus God testifies by his acts.

3. I present, as another evidence of the truthfulness of this doctrine, the fact that angels believe man to be a moral agent. Angels are holy, and, as a consequence, they cannot approve of any *wrong* conduct in any being. Angels are the constant observers of the Divine conduct. They watch with intense interest every movement of the Deity, particularly his dealing with the inhabitants of this globe. The Bible represents them as being desirous to look into his conduct towards man. When God condemns man for sin, and executes his judgments upon him for his wickedness, angels look on with deep and thrilling interest, and perfectly indorse and approve God's conduct. Let us turn to Rev. xvi. 5–7, for one moment, and hear their testimony: " And I heard the

angel of the waters say, Thou art righteous, O Lord, which art, and wast, and shalt be, because thou hast judged thus: For they have shed the blood of saints and prophets, and thou hast given them blood to drink; for they are worthy. And I heard another out of the altar say, Even so, Lord God Almighty, true and righteous are thy judgments." In the connection of this portion of truth, angels are represented as coming as messengers of God to execute these judgments upon man. While they are doing up the work of death, another class look on and proclaim, " Thou art righteous, O Lord, because thou hast judged thus. True and righteous are thy judgments." Here the conduct of God in executing those judgments is approved and applauded by angels in the most decisive language.

Now if man is a moral agent, and was voluntary in the wrongs for which God was afflicting him, then God was right in these judgments, as angels affirm. The conduct of God, and the indorsement of these angels upon that theory, is all consistent. But if man is a necessary agent, and was forced by his Maker to do just as he did do and he could not help himself, do you think holy angels can look on and pronounce the conduct of God just and righteous? What! force a being to do a thing, and then punish him for doing it! There is not a good being in the universe who would pronounce such conduct just, nor one who could approve of it. Just!—such conduct on the part of any being would be the height of injustice and cruelty, and all good beings must condemn it. But angels do not condemn this conduct on the part of God, they approve of it and point to it as evidence of God's justice and righteousness. The fact that they do it, settles the question, that angels know that man is a moral agent; that he was voluntary in his wrong-doing; that he might and ought to have acted differently; that he deserves to be punished for his crimes. Here then is the full indorsement of angels to the truth of the doctrine under consideration.

4. Another testimony in proof of this doctrine I will take from the conduct of the Devil. He believes man to be a moral agent. When he tempts man to sin, he most fully indorses the fact that he is capable of sinning. He could not sin if he were not a moral agent, any more than the sun could sin by shining. The Devil is not such a fool as to present temptations to the sun to sin. Why? He knows it is not voluntary in shining. It is not a moral agent, and of course not capable of sinning. In tempting man to sin he unwittingly indorsed the very doctrine under consideration. Perhaps I ought to apologize to his satanic majesty for introducing him into court, and extorting from him a testimony in favor of a doctrine he would gladly have man disbelieve. But we will make the whole intelligent universe testify in favor of this doctrine before we have done.

The Devil always uses moral means, and not force, in moving man to sin. He uses argument, persuasion, — motives which are applicable only to moral agents. If man is not voluntary, why resort to motive? Force is the only power that can move man, if he is not voluntary, and why not resort to it at once? Any being, therefore, who resorts to moral means to move man to act, bears testimony by his action that he believes the doctrine under consideration to be true.

5. Men believe each other to be moral agents. I will introduce into court those who deny this doctrine, and make them testify in its favor. In many instances they condemn their own conduct. How often they reproach themselves for many steps in their lives! What a fool I was for taking this, that, or the other step! But why a fool? If you are not voluntary, you could not help yourself. You had no power to do differently, — why reproach yourself? You do injustice to your own dear self by such reproaches, if you are not voluntary. But why this internal reproach? Take care, my dear man, that is the utterance of your inner soul, in proof of the very doctrine you deny. Thus your soul speaks out after all your efforts to stifle her voice. She knows you are a moral agent, and she will testify in favor of this doctrine every day of your life, in many forms. Let us hear her a little further, for she is one of the most important wit-

nesses we have on this point. Remember we are now taking the testimony of an adversary. The men who deny this doctrine in words, will praise and condemn the conduct of their fellows as much as other men. Watch their conversation for a season, and you will hear them speak in the highest terms of praise and approbation of some men. They will call it righteous, just, and holy. But stop, my dear sir. Why do you praise that man for his conduct? Why do you not praise the wind for blowing and fanning you with its gentle breezes? Why not pronounce it a holy and just wind? Do you ever do it? Do you talk about a virtuous or righteous wind? Do you ever pay such a compliment to the action of any necessary agent in the universe? You know you do not. But if man is a necessary and not a moral agent, he is no more praiseworthy for his action than the wind is for blowing. The fact that you praise him and speak of his acts as being virtuous, settles the question that you have an internal conviction of the truth of this doctrine, and by your action you indorse it as true.

Again, those who deny this doctrine are as much inclined to censure and condemn the conduct of their neighbors as other men. As a general thing, such men have a peculiar dislike to those they term priests and the church, and will denounce them as hypocrites and deceivers. But why censure them if they are not voluntary? They only act as they are acted upon by an irresistible power. They are not to blame, — they cannot help themselves. Why not condemn and censure the wind for blowing? There would be as much common sense in the one case as in the other, on the supposition that man is not a moral agent. To be consistent with your theory, if a man meets you in the street and knocks you down and forcibly takes your money, you should reply, Well, poor creature, you are not to blame, you cannot help it, you act only as you are acted upon, you are only a machine, I will not pursue you. How quick such men will abandon their own theory under such circumstances! They will not only condemn such a man, but, with an officer, will pursue, apprehend, imprison, and punish him. But why condemn or punish the poor fellow, if he is not voluntary? it would be unjust upon your own theory.

Now remember, every time you pass condemnation upon any man for his conduct, you indorse the doctrine that man *is* a moral agent. You may deny it by word, but by deed you proclaim to all men your belief in it.

It is evident that all men believe in this doctrine from the following considerations: All men put their children under moral training. They put them under moral government. They will lay down rules to guide them, command them to do this and forbid them to do that. They will praise them when they do right and blame them when they do wrong, reward them for obedience and punish them for disobedience. They resort to moral means to move them to right and wrong action. This is the uniform conduct of all the families of the earth. Here is testimony from every household, from all parts of the world and from every age of the world in proof of this doctrine. All families treat their children as voluntary beings.

Here is the testimony of *action*, which speaks louder than the tongue. It is the testimony of the whole world, speaking out of the honest convictions of the soul, and they all proclaim that they believe in the doctrine of moral agency. Take one other universal testimony from man. All the national governments on the face of the globe proclaim the truthfulness of the doctrine under consideration. They all treat man as a moral agent. These governments are moral governments. They all act upon the great truth that man is voluntary in his actions. Every law-making body under the whole heavens proclaims this fact, every court of justice proclaims the same truth. Every political and religious gathering, where moral means are resorted to, to prevail upon man to act in harmony with their wishes, indorses this truth. Some men who are active in politics deny this doctrine in words, but, at the same time, they testify by their actions that they believe their own tongue uttered a lie when it denied the truthfulness of this doctrine. You have a specimen in the case of Robert Dale Owen, in the noted debate with Campbell in Cincinnati, a number of years since, on the subject of the Bible as a divinely inspired book. He denied in that debate that man was a moral agent. He planted himself on the doctrine of fatalism, as Deists do generally. Some years after that, he was up before the community as a political man, and was elected to congress. After reading one of his speeches made in that body, I thought if I had access to his ear, I would inquire of him for what purpose he was in congress. He would doubtless reply, " To help make laws to govern the nation." But what kind of laws? I would further ask. " Moral laws, to be sure," would be his reply. Why make moral laws to govern man, if he is not a moral agent? Why not make moral laws to govern your horses and cattle? They are just as applicable to the one as to the other, if man is not a moral being. Now, the moment Mr. Owen had anything to do with politics, and the subject of law-making, his actions as a law-maker on the floor of congress testified to the nation and the world, that he believed what he said in Cincinnati, on the subject of moral agency, was false. Thus such men by their conduct deny the very doctrine they advocate with the tongue. Moreover they treat their children as moral agents, by rearing them under moral training. They treat the nation as moral agents, by being active in politics, and helping to enact moral laws to govern the people. In fact, no man can or does act upon the theory, that man is not a moral agent. All men, in their actions, indorse the truthfulness of the doctrine under consideration.

6. In proof of this doctrine I present your own consciousness. This is the highest possible testimony you can have on this point. I am just as confident that I am a voluntary agent as I am that I exist. I have the same evidence,— the testimony of consciousness. When I sit at my table to write, I know I could lay down my pen and stop writing if I saw fit. When I preach, I do it voluntarily. I know I could refuse, if I pleased. When you go to church, you go voluntarily. You could arise from your seats now and leave the house, if you felt so disposed. This you know from your own consciousness. All men are conscious they are voluntary. They *know* it. You may theorize to the contrary as much as you please, you have this internal conviction that you are a moral agent, and you cannot resist it or act upon any other theory.

I have now shown that the whole intelligent universe believes that man is a moral agent, not even excepting those who pretend, in words, to deny it. God knows it, holy angels believe it, fallen angels or devils believe it, and all men without exception believe it. We have no account of any other thinking, intelligent beings in the universe but the classes above named. Here is one uniform testimony from the whole, that the doctrine is true.

I will now admit it to be false, for the sake of argument, and look at its conclusions.

1. If it is not true, then all the intelligent universe are deceived in relation to man's true character.

2. If God *is* deceived, then he is not infinite in wisdom. Here is a point where he is laboring under a mistake, and of course does not know all things.

3. If God is *not* deceived, then he knowingly pursues a course which bears testimony to a false doctrine. In treating man as a moral agent, his action testifies that he believes in this doctrine. If, therefore, it is false, God is a false witness, which would militate against his moral character.

4. If man is not a moral agent, then the government of God is not adapted to man's nature. A moral government is adapted to govern moral agents, and no others. If man is a necessary agent, he is controlled by the laws of force, as much so as is the material universe. In fact, in that case, there is no other law adapted to his nature. So God, in placing him under a moral government, has made a great mistake.

5. If man is not a moral agent, then there is no such thing as sin or holiness among men; for none but moral agents *can* sin. So all this talk, in that case, about right and wrong, justice and injustice

among men is all delusive. You might as well talk about a sinful sun and moon, if this doctrine is false.

6. If man is not a moral agent, then all family and national governments should be thrown to the winds. All moral laws to govern human beings should be cast overboard. To be consistent with such a theory, you should break up your national council, throw away your courts of justice, tear down your prisons, and cease all your punishments, — stop your undertaking to punish man for what he cannot help. If men lie, steal, get drunk, swear, knock each other down, murder, and burn down houses, and do every other thing we have been in the habit of calling wrong, remember they are innocent in the whole. They are forced to do it, and are not to blame, any more than the wind for blowing down your house. Now, are you prepared to swallow down such absurdities? If not, you must fall back upon the theory that man is a moral agent. There is no other way of avoiding these conclusions. They are the legitimate inferences of the opposite theory. These considerations, I think, sufficiently settle the truthfulness of the doctrine I have drawn from this text, and put it beyond all successful controversy. A few remarks shall close this sermon.

REMARKS.

1. From this subject, we learn the nature of sin. Sin is the abuse of the power of moral agency. It lies in wrong action, or in disobedience to God.

2. We learn the nature of holiness. It is the right use of the power of moral agency. It is the voluntary conformity of the heart and life to God's law. It consists in doing his will.

3. We learn that man cannot be forced to sin or to be holy by any being. Cannot God force him to sin? asks one. I answer, no. The moment you apply force, you take away his voluntariness. His acts under the law of force would be necessary acts, and would be neither sinful nor holy. An act, to be sinful or holy, must be voluntary. It must be the voluntary choice of the will, so that force cannot be applied by any being.

4. We learn that OMNIPOTENT POWER could not keep sin out of the universe, and at the same time have a universe of moral agents. Moral agents can sin, and force cannot prevent it. To be a moral agent, one must have power to sin or be holy, and this must be left to his choice. He must have power to act in two ways, as we have seen in this discourse. Take away the power to sin, and we take away moral agency; consequently, there is no power that can force moral agents not to sin, and they at the same time retain their moral agency. A

universe of moral agents, therefore, can sin, and Omnipotence cannot prevent it. God understood this when he created moral agents. The question to be settled by the Divine mind, before the act of creation, was doubtless this: Shall I have a universe of moral, responsible agents, — beings who are capable of understanding my character and government, and voluntarily loving and adoring me, even if some of them do sin, — or shall I create a universe without such beings? The mind of the Infinite One preferred a universe of moral agents, even if the evil of sin was connected with it. He knew, when he created such a universe, that some of them would sin, and he could not prevent it; but, on the whole, it was best to call such a universe into existence.

5. We learn that God cannot convert men by physical power. The *Gospel* is the power to save, Paul affirms. But the Gospel is made up of moral power, — the power of motive, argument, and persuasion. The being to be converted is a moral agent, and God does not suspend or take away his moral agency in order to convert him. To convert him, you must change the governing purpose of his will. He now chooses to do his own will, and not God's. He must choose to do God's will, and not his own, to be converted. This change is brought about by the Holy Ghost presenting the motives of the Gospel so clearly before the mind, that the sinner voluntarily gives up his own will, and chooses God's

will as the governing, controlling principle for the rest of his life; and he consecrates his whole being to do God's will henceforth and forever. The change is brought about, not by physical power, but by the Holy Ghost applying moral power. During this change, the sinner is active. The change could not be produced without his action. *He* chooses; *he* yields his will to the will of God. He is voluntary in the whole transaction, and could not be converted without this voluntary act on his part. He acts, but he acts under the *constraining* influences of the Holy Spirit, but not under the influence or power of force.

6. We learn that sinners, being voluntary, can resist all that God can do to convert them, and go down to hell. God opens heaven, and spreads before you the glories of that bright world to allure. He opens hell, and thunders wrath in your ears if you persist in sin. He sends his ministers to preach and intreat you to flee from the wrath to come; his saints, to pray, warn, and invite you to Christ. He arranges his providences, and speaks through them. He sends his Spirit to convince of sin and move you to repentance. But all of these things you can resist. He does not apply any irresistible power here. He cannot do so, and permit you to remain a moral agent. You must yield to these influences to be saved, and you must do it from choice. You can resist the whole, and persevere in the way to death, and reap your reward in eternity.

7. Where any one gives a construction to any portion of the Bible that makes man a mere machine, you may know that that interpretation is false. Man is a moral agent, as we have proved in this sermon. The Bible was given to moral agents. When rightly interpreted, it does not falsify man's character. Here are two constructions to a passage, or to certain doctrines of the Bible : one makes man a machine, the other leaves him a free moral agent. The interpretation in harmony with the doctrine of moral agency is the correct one.

8. Sinner, you see from this subject that you have your destiny for eternity in your own hands, and you can and will decide it for yourself. If you will repent and obey God, you can be saved ; but if you persist in your sins, you must be damned. What a keen reflection it must be to you, if you lie down in hell, that you brought all your misery upon yourself. How it will pierce the soul through with ten thousand sorrows and regrets. You cannot, then, throw off your guilt upon another. You will know and feel, then, that it was your own voluntary conduct in rejecting the Gospel, which has brought all this anguish upon you. *Sinner*, SINNER, will you go thus madly down to ruin ? Will you deliberately leap into the burning pool ? Dying man, be entreated to turn to God to-day. Do you say a future time will do ? That future time may find your fate sealed, and your soul lost. Behold, now is the accepted time.

Let this day be a day of salvation to you. Before you is life and death. Choose life, says God. Hark! Do your hear him speak? *Choose life,* CHOOSE LIFE, *says God.* What say you? Will you choose life? Will you do it NOW? I pray God, as you go from this house, that the *Holy Spirit* may pursue you with these words: CHOOSE LIFE, CHOOSE LIFE!

IX.

GOD'S RIGHT TO GOVERN.

And Pharaoh said, who is the Lord that I should obey his voice? — Exod. v. 2.

1. DEFINITION OF GOVERNMENT. 2. TWO DEPARTMENTS IN THE UNIVERSE WHICH NEED GOVERNING. 3. GOVERNMENT SUPPOSES POWER EXERCISED OVER EACH DEPARTMENT. 4. BUT TWO KINDS OF POWER USED IN GOVERNING. 5. MORAL AGENTS NOT GOVERNED BY PHYSICAL POWER. 6. HOW FAR PHYSICAL POWER IS CONNECTED WITH MORAL GOVERNMENT, AND ITS PLACE. 7. THE NECESSITY OF MORAL AGENTS BEING UNDER GOVERNMENT. 8. THE BEING BEST QUALIFIED OUGHT TO GOVERN. 9. GOD THE ONLY BEING QUALIFIED. 10. GOD'S RIGHT AND DUTY TO GOVERN.

THESE words were the words of a proud, haughty monarch, who was then occupying the throne of Egypt. He was a wicked oppressor. He had trampled the rights of God's ancient Israel under his feet until they cried to God for help. He heard them from on high, as his ear is always open to the cry of the oppressed, and he came for their deliverance. The prediction that they should be evil entreated four hundred years was nearly fulfilled, the time was drawing to a close, and the day of deliverance was at hand. God appeared to Moses, and commissioned him, to be their leader back to the land of promise, from whence their fathers had migrated several generations previous. God commanded him to go to Pharaoh, the then ruling monarch of the nation, and demand of him to let his people go, — in other words, to emancipate them from the house of bondage. Moses and Aaron gained access to his royal presence, and spread this command of God before him. Hear them; they address him in the following language: " Thus saith the Lord God of Israel, *Let my people go, that they may hold a feast unto me in the wilderness.*" Now, mark this haughty monarch's reply, — " Who is the Lord, that I should obey his voice to let Israel go? I know not the Lord, neither will I let Israel go." What an impotent rebel! He did not believe in the " higher law " theory. What! Set up divine authority as superior to mine? Am I not the law-making power of this nation? My authority is the *supreme* authority of this land, and now you approach me with a " higher law." Who is your Lord, that *I* should submit to his dictation and authority? I know not your Lord, I acknowledge no higher authority in governmental matters than my own. I believe each nation and state has a right to regulate its own domestic institutions, without any reference to a higher-law theory. They have a right to enact such laws as they please, and when enacted, if ever so oppressive and wrong, I deny the right of any other authority, high or low, to interfere. I have my laws to govern this nation, and to govern Israel. They are my domestic servants, and I have a right to manage my own internal affairs in my own way. Now you fanatics, Moses and Aaron, come to me with your higher-law notions, and demand of me to let Israel go. You come in the name and by the authority of the HIGH GOD, as you pretend. I acknowledge no such authority, and I shall not let Israel go. Then, you clergy undertake to meddle with the affairs of government! What do you know about government matters? You should keep about your "appropriate work" of preaching the Gospel, and not step out of your "appropriate sphere" to dabble with politics. So reasoned the ancient Egyptian Pharaoh, — and so some of our modern American Pharaohs reason. But notwithstanding the reasoning of both ancient and modern Pharaohs, there is a higher tribunal than that of man, and one to which they are amenable, and the High God will make them feel it at a future day.

He is *King of kings* and *Lord of lords*. What does that mean? *King of kings*. What, king of legislative bodies? His authority higher than theirs? So he affirms, and so he will make them feel. He is King to rule over kings — to rule over all legislative bodies on earth, however high. He claims the right to dictate to them, to legislate over them; and when they call in question that right, they are ungodly rebels. But, says one, has not a state a right to enact such laws as it pleases, to control its own internal affairs? If it pleases to enact laws in harmony with God's law, it has, — and not otherwise. No state and no legislative body on earth has a right to enact an oppressive or wrong law. God allows no such right to any body of men. So, then, your whole modern theory, vulgarly called squatter sovereignty, is based upon a glaring falsehood. It calls in question God's right to dictate to legislative bodies, and is the very essence of Romanism. It exalts itself above God, sets aside his authority, is ruinous and corrupting in its tendency. If a state may enact any law it pleases, and make it of binding authority, then it may enact a law forbidding obedience to God under all circumstances, and the people would be under obligation to obey it, and wholly discard God and his authority. What a doctrine to be advocated in a nation that professes to be protestant in its faith!

What! A human tribunal with power, if it see fit to exercise it, to repeal God's laws and cast his authority overboard! This is your popular sovereignty theory, — and what is it but the Devil's sovereignty? It is what he has advocated for years, and what he would have all men embrace. This is the doctrine he taught Eve: has God said, you shall die if you eat of that forbidden fruit, or if you disobey him? God knows better, — I would pay no regard to his authority. I *would* eat. I would manage my own affairs. What! let God dictate you? Do not be such a silly fool, — be independent, — assert your own rights, — have your own way without any reference to God, or his authority. This is the Devil's sovereignty, and he would stir up all men to believe and advocate it. If he can induce men to advocate such doctrine in the halls of a nation, — all the better, as it will give it the greatest possible notoriety. This is the doctrine which some of our wonderful statesmen are advocating in the councils of the nation at the present time, for they deny the right of any higher law to control them. This was Pharaoh's doctrine. God undertook to dictate him about the children of Israel, and he denied his right at once, and refused to submit to it. This is the very feeling of a carnal, impenitent heart. It calls in question God's right to govern. Its language is, — who is the Lord that I should obey his voice?

In considering this text, we shall endeavor to examine and establish God's right to sit at the head of the universe, and dictate to all, high or low, — to all bodies of men, — and the corresponding duty of all men to acknowledge and submit to that authority. The topic of discussion, then, is *God's right to govern*. In considering it, I will —

I. Define the word government.

II. Show that there are two departments in the

universe God has created, both of which need governing.

III. Show that government supposes power exercised over each of these departments.

IV. Show that there are but two kinds of power which can be exercised by God, or any other being, in governing.

V. Show that moral agents cannot be controlled by physical power, so far as their moral actions are concerned.

VI. Show how far physical power is connected with moral government, and its place.

VII. Show that it is necessary that moral agents should be under government.

VIII. Show that we ought to have at the head of the universe the being who is best qualified to fill that station.

IX. Show that God is that being, and the only being who *is* qualified to fill that station.

X. Show that it is not only God's right, but his duty, to govern.

I. THEN I AM TO DEFINE THE WORD GOVERNMENT.

Webster defines government thus: 1. "Direction; regulation. 2. Control; restraint. 3. The exercise of authority; direction and restraint exercised over the actions of men in communities, societies, or states; the administration of public affairs."

Direction: The pilot at the helm of that steamer directs its course. He regulates and governs it, so as to run it into yonder port with safety. The conductor of that train of cars controls it. He rings his bell for it to stop; the hands apply the breaks, and it yields to their control. He rings again to have it start; the steam is applied, and off it goes;— he directs it; he governs it. The parent governs that child. He exercises authority over it; he marks out its course of life by his commands and prohibitions; he enforces his authority, and restrains it from wrongdoing by suitable rewards and punishments, which serve as motives to control that little mind.

The legislative bodies of different nations govern the people by enacting laws to mark out their duty; and enforce their authority by suitable rewards and punishments, to restrain them from vice, and to influence them to do right. This is restraint exercised over the actions of men in communities, or in their associated capacity in states or nations. This is government. It is control or restraint exercised over the thing governed.

II. I AM TO SHOW THAT THERE ARE TWO DEPARTMENTS IN THE UNIVERSE GOD HAS CREATED, BOTH OF WHICH NEED GOVERNING.

1. There is the *material* universe. Under this head we include all matter, whether in an organized or unorganized form; this earth on which we live, with all that pertains to it which is material; the whole planetary system connected with this earth,

and the ten thousand times ten thousand suns and worlds which roll on high; all the matter God has ever called into being;—all these need governing.

2. The universe of *minds*. Under this head we include the whole race of man, holy angels, fallen angels or devils. From what we can gather from the Bible, we think the word angel covers all the different orders of intelligent beings besides man. That there is an innumerable multitude of them is evident from such passages as the following;—Rev. v. 11: " And I beheld, and I heard the voice of *many* angels round about the throne, and the beasts, and the elders: and the number of them was ten thousand times ten thousand, and thousands of thousands." Such passages are not designed to point out a definite number, but an innumerable number. That there is a variety of orders of these intelligences, and that they inhabit the different worlds which journey through the immensity of space, is very manifest to me. This universe of thinking, rational, accountable creatures all need governing. They all belong to God's great kingdom.

3. That this great universe of mind and matter, which has been planned and called into existence by the wisdom and power of God, needs governing, is evident from the fact that an infinitely wise Being must have had some end, some great and glorious end, in view in creating it. To believe that God acted without an end to accomplish in this grand

display of power, is to believe that he acted foolishly. If he had an end to accomplish, government is absolutely essential to secure it. He sits at the head of this great universe of mind and matter, superintends all its parts, controls and regulates the whole, to develop the grand design of his heart. What confusion there would be in the material universe if God should exercise no controlling, regulating influence over it! The immensity of the heavenly bodies is such, and they fly through the depths of space with such incomprehensible rapidity, that, let them come in contact with each other, and what a work of ruin there would be! Let world be hurled upon world, and system dash against system; what confusion, what destruction, what a wreck of worlds! But with an Almighty God at the head of affairs, with his constant, superintending care over the most minute particle of matter, each of which fills its appropriate place, and each part moves in perfect harmony with the great whole, all is order, all is right, all tends to give us one great, grand, sublime idea of God. What an exhibition of his wisdom, power, and goodness!

III. SHOW THAT GOVERNMENT SUPPOSES POWER EXERCISED OVER EACH OF THESE DEPARTMENTS.

1. Define power. From Webster we have the following definition: 1. "The faculty of doing or performing anything. The faculty of moving or producing a change in something; ability or strength. 2. Force; animal strength."

1. That government supposes power exercised over this department, is evident from the very definition of the term government. We have seen that it is to direct and control. How do you regulate or control a thing? It is by applying power to it of some kind.

2. The exercise of power supposes a thinking, designing being, who has an end to accomplish, a plan to execute or carry into effect. The source of all power resides in the mind, in the will of some thinking being. Take an illustration from man. He wishes to erect a dwelling for his comfort as a place of residence. He first forms his plan. He then selects his materials. His will then calls into requisition his own physical power, and combines with that the intellectual and physical power of others, the power of animals which he controls, together with the power of machinery which mind has contrived and controls; and by this combination of power, the materials are moved on to the ground, formed, fashioned, and put together to his liking. Thus the building is erected by the application of power, in the controlling, regulating, and governing these materials. Government then is the application of power of some kind, to control the thing to be governed.

. IV. SHOW THAT THERE ARE BUT TWO KINDS OF POWER, WHICH CAN BE EXERCISED BY GOD, OR ANY OTHER BEING, IN GOVERNING.

1. Physical power or the power of force. This is applicable to move, control, and govern matter. The whole material universe is regulated and governed by the application of this kind of power. God and all other beings, when they wish to control matter, use this kind of power and no other. All the motions and changes of the heavenly bodies are produced by the application of the law of force. Every particle of matter is controlled by this law, and cannot be controlled by any other. Matter is inert; it has no power in itself of acting or resisting action. If moved or controlled it must be by force. It is passive, — perfectly so in its nature.

2. Moral power, or the power of motive or inducement. This is the power used to control mind, or the will of moral agents. Mind is the opposite of matter. To control it you must use another kind of power. Moral agents have power to act. They have power in themselves to resist power. To control them then, so far as this power to resist power is concerned, the consent of their wills, to be controlled, must be secured. For wise reasons they are constituted moral agents, and have the power of choice. In a previous sermon on the subject of moral agency, we have shown that in choosing between right and wrong, the will cannot be forced, — the law of force not being applicable. To control wills you must control them by moral power, or the power of motive or inducement. These are the two

kinds of power always used in governing. Each has its appropriate place in God's government, and in all other governments.

V. SHOW THAT MORAL AGENTS CANNOT BE CONTROLLED BY PHYSICAL POWER, SO FAR AS THEIR MORAL ACTIONS ARE CONCERNED.

1. Actions to be moral must be the actions of free will. They must be voluntary, as we have sufficiently shown in the sermon on moral agency,— consequently you cannot use irresistible power in this case. This is not its place in government.

2. It is evident that they cannot be controlled by physical power, from the fact that God does not thus control them. If moral agents could be forced not to sin, and forced to be holy, God would have used force and prevented their sinning. The very goodness of God would prompt him to do it, for he hates sin and loves holiness. He loves the happiness of his creatures and hates their misery. He knows that nothing but holiness can secure their happiness and prevent their misery. If by an act of his he could shut out all sin, and at the same time have a universe of moral agents, think you he would refuse to put forth such an act? It is an impeachment of his goodness and sincerity to pretend it. He professes to want all beings to be holy and happy, and if, by a purpose of his will, he could accomplish that grand end, what becomes of his sincerity while he withholds such an act? If he could

secure the holiness and happiness of all, by physical power, it would be done. But it is not done, — which settles the question that it could not be accomplished in that way. Physical power cannot force man to be holy.

VI. SHOW HOW FAR PHYSICAL POWER IS CONNECTED WITH MORAL GOVERNMENT, AND ITS PLACE.

1. It can create moral agents and give them their powers. There could be no moral government without such beings. They are indebted to omnipotent power for their existence, and for all their powers and faculties. In receiving existence, man is passive, — he has no control over that matter. In relation to the powers and faculties of his nature, he had no control over them. That is the work of Omnipotence.

2. Omnipotent power can sustain and uphold moral agents after it has created them, and they cannot help themselves. They cannot blot out of being themselves or each other. They may kill the body, but they cannot kill the moral agent. They may wish themselves out of existence, and blame their Maker for creating them, but they cannot uncreate themselves. The same irresistible hand which gave them being, can hold them in existence. They may try to flee from existence by the doctrine of annihilation, but God will not suffer it. His power created, and the same power will hold them in being endlessly. He upholds all things by the word of his power.

3. Physical power can fix their location and confine them there. It has fixed man's location here on earth, and holds him here by the law of force. He may long to visit other portions of the universe, but the law of force holds him here until it sees fit to liberate him. By his inventions he may pass up a little distance from the earth, through the atmosphere, but the law of force brings him down again.

4. Omnipotent power determines when, how, and where, man shall commence his existence. He causes some to commence their existence in this age, some in a previous one, some in America, some in England, others in Ireland, France, Africa, and others still in some other portion of the globe. This, Omnipotence controls. The being himself has no control over the place of his birth. How mean and wicked, therefore, to be prejudiced against a man because he was born in a particular locality. Whether born in Ireland, Africa, America, or any other place on earth, man has no control over that matter, and to think any the less of an individual on account of the place of his nativity, is all wrong.

5. Omnipotence connects mind with matter, or the soul with the body, and separates them at pleasure. It can break up this connection at any moment it sees fit, take the soul into another state of existence, and locate it at pleasure. When it wishes to do up this work, it waits not for the con-

sent of any man,—it does not even ask it. If the being himself with all his friends are opposed to this separation, it will make no difference. There is no resisting or controlling this power in this work. It strikes the stroke, and all the universe cannot resist or counteract it. The separation must take place at its bidding if it breaks a thousand hearts, and fills a whole nation with lamentation and woe. Omnipotence is not to be resisted, nor turned aside from its work here. There is no dodging that event,—it must come.

6. Omnipotence can control the circumstances which surround our being here. It can give us light or darkness, cold or heat, sickness or health. It can give us fair weather or foul, seed-time and harvest, or blast all our hopes. It can prosper us in our plans, or overturn them in a thousand forms.

7. When law is violated, Omnipotence can arrest and bring to trial, and execute penalty without any fear of opposition. It can defend its own rights, and the rights of the obedient subject of government, as it will do at a future day.

8. It can create a heaven for the righteous, and gather them into that happy world, and supply their every want.

9. It can create a hell for the wicked, and confine them there at pleasure.

10. But it cannot make beings holy. That is the work of moral power, and not of physical.

VII. Show that moral agents should be under government. The good of the universe demands it.

1. The end for which man was created calls for a moral government to secure it. That end was to glorify God and enjoy him forever. In creating moral agents, God intended greatly to augment the amount of happiness in the universe. All the bliss they will enjoy endlessly will be so much real happiness added, and which never would have been in the universe, had not God called moral agents into being. To promote his own glory, and greatly add to the amount of happiness, were two great objects God had in view in the act of creation. To secure these objects, moral government is a necessity. Man needs to be taught how to glorify God, he needs government to teach him how, and moral law to point out the way. To secure man's happiness, his holiness must be secured. Holiness cannot be secured without moral law. Holiness is the conformity of the heart and life to God's will, or to moral law. He needs the government to make known that will. He needs God's law to define God's rights, his own rights, and the rights of all other moral beings.

2. As man is a voluntary being, he needs all the restraints of government thrown around him to hold him in check from wrongdoing. Moral government is the means calculated to secure the moral order and harmony of moral beings.

3. Moral agents are capable of trampling upon each other's rights, of wronging each other, and the wronged party should have some tribunal to which it can appeal for redress. Moral government provides this tribunal, where all differences and encroachments on the rights of others can, and will be adjudicated, upon just principles, and the wronged party have his rights defended. When God has created a class of beings, and given them power which, if wrongfully used, they can harm each other, and trample upon each other's rights, justice demands that he should make some provision, by which and through which the wronged party can have their rights asserted and defended. Moral government meets this demand of justice. Without that, it could not be met. God understands this. He knows his duty, and has consequently placed moral agents under moral government.

4. The nature of moral agents is adapted to moral government, which shows its necessity.

5. In proof of its necessity, we have the experience of all families and nations on earth. They all resort to it, and thus bear testimony to its necessity. What nation on earth would be willing to try the experiment of dispensing with moral government? Not one would risk it. They know its necessity. They know public interest demands it, or why be willing to pay the enormous sums they now pay to support national governments?

6. The fact that God has placed the universe of minds under moral government, settles the question of its necessity. God is infinitely wise, and as a consequence, he never takes an unnecessary step. When he does a thing we know that it was absolutely necessary that such a step should be taken, or it would not have been taken. He knows perfectly the wants and necessities of moral agents, and by placing them under moral government, and subjecting them to moral training, we learn its absolute necessity to secure their highest good.

VIII. WE SHOULD HAVE AT THE HEAD OF THE UNIVERSE, AS GOVERNOR, THE BEING BEST QUALIFIED TO FILL THAT STATION.

Let me here give you the principle which should govern men in selecting public rulers. What is it? Look close, for this is an important thought. This nation, in selecting her rulers, is governed almost entirely by false principles. What *is* the thought that should control us in selecting our candidates for public stations? Should it be this,—does he belong to my party? That is the question which governs the great mass of voters. But that has nothing to do with the matter, and should not influence us in so important a step. If that man is elected, will he give me an office? That thought controls the vote and action of a great many in this nation. But a man whose vote can be controlled by such selfishness is wholly unfit to fill any office. While our public stations are filled by such men, the nation will be plundered and swindled, and the rights of whole communities bartered away for office. What do such miscreants care for the rights of men? Commit public interests to the hands of such men! You might as well commit your money to the hands of a thief for safe keeping.

Another class will be governed by this principle: Is he a northern or southern, eastern or western man? What has that to do with the matter? That is not the question which should govern us. What then is the principle? I answer, it is this: That man is the best qualified for the office, who will best protect and promote public interests; protect and defend the rights of all classes, high and low, and promote the highest good of the governed. To secure and promote the highest good of the governed is the true and legitimate end of government. In selecting rulers, therefore, we should select the men who are the best qualified to secure this great end of government, and who will exert all the power committed to their hands to carry out this design. Such men are *the* men. The interests of the nation can be safely intrusted to such hands. This principle should govern and control our wishes and desires in relation to the universe.

All moral agents should be interested in having at the head of affairs, the being who is the best qualified to fill that high station. The vast interests at stake demand it. The interest of each individual demands it. What a kingdom there is here over which some master mind should preside! It is not a temporary kingdom, it is a kingdom which is to be endless in duration. Here are interests at stake that are eternal. How they should be watched over and guarded with infinite care! Look at the extent of this kingdom. It is a government which extends not only over the race of man, the whole race of man, but it extends over all the intelligent creatures God ever has or ever will call into being. It is a government over all worlds. What mind can take in the vastness of this kingdom? To preside, then, over the destinies of such an innumerable multitude for eternity, needs the best talent in the universe. All eyes should be turned to such a being, all hearts should rejoice to see such a being ascend the throne and hold the reins of government over such a kingdom. Each heart should pay him homage and crown HIM Lord of all.

IX. SHOW THAT GOD IS THE BEING WHO IS BEST QUALIFIED FOR THIS STATION, AND THE ONLY BEING WHO IS FITTED AT ALL FOR THIS HIGH POSITION.

1. He is infinite in knowledge. This is an essential qualification for this vastly important work. He knows all hearts perfectly, and how to adapt his government to meet the wants of each. No se-

cret plot against his government can be formed and concealed from his notice. No new and unforeseen event can spring up for which he is unprepared, for he looks into the future and sees all that ever will or is possible to transpire. Not an event ever can take place, but that is now, and ever has been, distinctly before his infinite mind. How this wonderful knowledge perfectly fits him to be in readiness for any event that can take place in any world through all the coming ages of eternity! This knowledge fits him to see unerringly the best possible end to be secured by government, and the best system of government to secure that end. He can see distinctly, and define unerringly, his own rights, and the rights of all his creatures from the highest to the lowest. He can see and understand the wants of all in all worlds, and the means necessary to be used to supply them. What wisdom and knowledge is here! It is incomprehensible! This knowledge is underived; it is in himself. He is not dependent on, nor indebted to any other creature for it. What other being possesses this knowledge, and can bear comparison with God on this point? Not one. All other beings are limited in their knowledge; they are indebted to him for what they have, and for all their intellectual powers. We admire profound wisdom in a statesman. In God we have it in perfection, and in no other being.

2. He is omnipresent. He is present in all worlds, and in every part of the universe at the same instant. This is true of him at all times. This is not true of any other being. No created being could be in two places at the same time. An angel cannot be here and in heaven at the same moment. So, no being in the universe can compare with God in this particular. How this attribute fits him for this important station! Being everywhere, he can preside over every event in all worlds. He is present to witness all that transpires. All things take place under his eye, and under his special notice. He is present in all parts of the universe to act at any moment and to meet any emergency.

3. His power is infinite. This power is within himself. It is not derived from others, and cannot be taken away by others. We have some earthly monarchs whom we call powerful rulers. Their government we denominate a strong government. But what makes it strong? They manage to combine the wisdom, skill, and physical strength of other men with their own, to protect their thrones. But man is a changeable being. The men who will protect a throne to-day, may turn their weapons against it to-morrow, and drive its occupant into exile or imprisonment, or even put him to death. His power is not in himself. Moreover, all the power he and his subjects have is wholly derived from God, and he can take it away any moment. With

one glance of his eye he can look them all into eternity. God is not dependent upon any other being for his power, for it is in himself, and no being or combination of beings, however extensive, can take it from him. He could instantly annihilate the whole universe if they should rise up against him. How important this attribute to govern this great kingdom! No being could successfully sit at the head of the universe without it, and no being possesses it but God. How important to protect his throne against all combinations; to protect and defend the rights of all his subjects; when law is violated, to arrest and bring to trial and execute the penalty of a just law without fearing a rebellion that the governing power cannot control! In many governments, law cannot be executed when violated, for the want of strength in the government to control the rebels. The rebellious party becomes the most powerful, and overturns the government. Place any being, therefore, at the head of the universe who is not infinite in power, and it might, and doubtless would be ruined. Rebellion might break out that could not be controlled, and overrun all worlds, working infinite mischief. But with God at the head, all is safe, and no being would be safe without it. Rebellion is already in the universe, but an Almighty God will control it, and even cause the wrath of the rebellious to praise him. That which he cannot cause to praise him he will restrain.

4. God is unchangeable. "He is in one mind and none can turn him." A fickle government is always unsafe. It advocates one thing as right to-day, and condemns the same thing as wrong to-morrow. Such a government unsettles the confidence of its subjects in their rulers. How true this has been in this nation for a few years past! Its fruits none can fail to observe, who have watched our national affairs with any interest.

God being infinite in wisdom, can and does see the right. He takes his position for the right, and against the wrong, and remains there unchangeably for eternity. The subjects of government know where to find him. They know what and where his position will be a million years hence. Such a government is stable and commands respect, as it is unchangeably for right and against all wrong. No other being possesses this attribute. All other beings are limited in their knowledge. As new things transpire, a change in their views and feelings is produced, and they will change their conduct. God knows all things, so there can be nothing new to his mind to produce a change. All things are safe in such hands. His position, once taken for holiness and against sin, is eternally taken. Such a government is like himself, unalterable. Let all beings combine their influence to change his purposes and it would be fruitless.

5. His moral character is perfection itself. While

GOD'S RIGHT TO GOVERN.

he is infinite in his natural attributes, he is equally so in his moral. He is infinite in justice, mercy, truthfulness, goodness, and every other moral qualification which renders his character infinitely right and lovely. Is he all justice without mercy? No. Is he all mercy without justice? No. Mercy has *its* place in his government, and justice has *its* place, and everything else that goes to make up perfection in character. He is infinite in his loveliness, holiness, and goodness. He is so perfect in his moral character, that he is infinitely above all temptation to wrongdoing. This is essential to sit at the head of such a vast and sublime kingdom. Government affords many temptations to wrongdoing, temptations to injustice, oppression, and self-aggrandizement. These temptations lead to the sacrifice of public interests to promote private ends. Men become intoxicated with power, haughty, and overbearing. There is not a government on earth that has not been led into oppressive and wicked acts. Place any other being but God at the head of the universe, and his goodness might be overcome by temptation, and he might be led to wield his power for the destruction of public interests, instead of their promotion. But with him we are safe. He is infinitely above all temptation to wrong. What being but God is fit for this station? *Not one.* NOT ONE. To him all eyes should be turned, and all hearts should rejoice to place him on the throne and fall at his feet, and with holy reverence pray, THY KINGDOM COME, THY WILL BE DONE.

X. I AM TO SHOW THAT IT IS NOT ONLY GOD'S RIGHT, BUT HIS DUTY TO GOVERN.

1. He created this great universe, which gives him the right. It was contrived and called into being by his wisdom and power. All the material universe is his in the highest possible sense, and he has a right to dictate and control it. Every intelligent creature in the universe is his. He created body and soul, and gave them all their powers and faculties. They are all his, and he has a right to dictate and control them in the use of those powers. Can any other being claim such a relation to the universe? *Not one*. NOT ONE. This relation puts God lawfully on the throne. No other being can advance any such claim to the right to govern. This right is legitimate and cannot be called in question.

2. This relation which God bears to the universe, throws a responsibility upon him in relation to its welfare that cannot rest upon any other being. He was the cause of its having a being, and consequently has an interest in its destiny which no other being can have. This responsibility he cannot lay off upon the shoulders of any other being, and he has no wish to do so.

3. Public interest absolutely demands that God should govern. If he neglects this duty, the interests of this great commonwealth of worlds are

sacrificed. There is not another being in the universe fit for this high station, and not one who could fill it if he would. There is not another one who has powers adequate to the task.

If God should refuse to govern the universe, it would be utterly ruined, and the fault would partly lie at his door. In that case, such refusal on his part would be wrong, infinitely wrong, and would make him a sinner, an infinite sinner. Will he neglect his duty to the universe? No, never! He knows his duty too well, and is above temptation to neglect it.

4. The fact that God does govern, settles the question of his right and duty. He sits at the head of the universe, and proclaims his laws to govern both mind and matter. This he would not do if it were not his place. He knows his place, and he never will step out of it. He is so infinitely right, he never will do anything except what duty requires. The fact that he does it, is proof enough that he knows it is his duty and place to govern; and, being infinite in knowledge, he cannot be deceived.

The fact, therefore, that God does govern, settles the question that it is both his right and duty.

REMARKS.

1. With God at the head of the universe we have the highest possible guarantee that we shall have a wise and holy administration. Not a law will ever emanate from his throne that will be oppressive and wrong. The rights of all the subjects of his government, from the highest to the lowest, will be most sacredly guarded and protected. He understands that one great object of government is to protect the rights of all. He will not protect the rights of some at the expense of the rights of others. *Rights* are sacred in his eyes, and he will see that they are sacredly guarded.

Individuals who are trampling on the rights of any of his creatures in this world, will find themselves most wofully disappointed in the future, if they think to escape with impunity. God knows his duty to the subjects of his government, and he is too upright to neglect it. His laws are, like himself, perfect, pure and holy. His government is the result of infinite wisdom and goodness.

2. God's right to reign is universal. It extends to all worlds and all beings. It pertains to every moment of a man's history, in time and eternity. It covers every condition in which a man can be placed, every occupation or station he may fill, from the emperor upon the throne, down to the

most degraded beggar. It covers men in an associated capacity, as well as in an individual capacity. Whatever may be their condition, state, or employment, it is God's right to dictate and control them. They may disbelieve or deny this right, but God will hold them strictly accountable to him for all their conduct. Some men seem to imagine that when attending to political matters, and when acting in the capacity of a law maker, God has no right to dictate to them in such stations.

A little power in the hands of some men will bloat them up, and make them feel that they are above all dictation and control. This is nothing new. So Pharaoh felt, as we have seen. So other despots have felt, and God has been under the necessity of resorting to severe measures to teach them the higher-law doctrine. God drove Nebuchadnezzar from his throne and turned him out to grass for seven years, to teach and make him acknowledge the higher-law doctrine. Hear Daniel explain this matter to him;—Dan. iv. 25: "That they shall drive thee from men, and thy dwelling shall be with the beasts of the field, they shall make thee to eat grass as oxen, and they shall wet thee with the dew of heaven, and seven times shall pass over thee, *till thou know that the* MOST HIGH *ruleth in the kingdom of men, and giveth it to whomsoever he will.*"

These were severe measures to humble the pride of a haughty monarch, but they were effectual and brought him to his senses. Hear him, after this course of discipline; — Dan. iv. 37: " Now I Nebuchadnezzar praise and extol and honor the King of heaven, all whose works are truth, and his ways judgment: and those that walk in pride he is able to abase."

Thus God humbled his heart, and made him acknowledge his right to dictate to men in authority. It would probably be a blessing to this nation, if God should turn out to grass, not only seven years, but during life, some of its lordly legislators, unless they can learn that he has a right to dictate, and that they are accountable to him for every law they enact; that it is his place to rule and dictate to legislative bodies, and their duty to submit, and see to it, that they enact no law not in strict subjection and perfect harmony with the law of God.

3. This right and duty of God to reign, carries along with it a corresponding duty on the part of all beings to submit to his authority and obey all his requirements. We should study his word with care, to know and understand all his claims, and then make it the delight of our hearts to do his will. To call in question his authority to govern, is wicked; to refuse to obey any one of his requirements, is open rebellion.

4. Raising rebellion against this right of God to reign, is sin. A sinful heart is not willing to let God dictate; it wants its own way, and is resolved to have it. But remember God is upon the throne, — he is rightfully and lawfully there, and you must submit or take the consequences.

5. Sinner, remember you are under God's government, and you cannot escape from his dominions. He will hold you accountable for your conduct, whether you like it or not. You *ought* to like it. You ought to love his reign. The highest interests of the universe demand that he should reign. When you oppose it at heart, you are opposed to the best interests of the universe. How wicked such a state of heart must be! Stop! look at yourself for a moment. How little interest you have felt in God's right to reign! Perhaps you have been so indifferent about it, you have not examined that right in all your life. How indifferent you are to-day! How you trample upon his authority and defy his power! He will take you in hand at another day! In this state of rebellion and indifference you are hastening to his bar. How you will tremble when, at the judgment, he asserts and defends his right to govern! Will you not repent of this wicked state of heart now? Confess it all to him and ask forgiveness, and henceforth vote him upon the throne of your heart, give him

his place as King and Lawgiver, and take your place at his feet.

What say you; will you do it? Let that soul cry out to God now, " Thy kingdom *come. Thy kingdom come in* ME. Thy will be done by me henceforth and forever. AMEN."

X.

THE JUDGMENT-DAY.

When the son of man shall come in his glory, and all the holy angels with him, then shall he sit upon the throne of his glory: and before him shall be gathered all nations: and he shall separate them one from another, as a shepherd divideth his sheep from the goats: and he shall set the sheep on his right hand, but the goats on the left. Then shall the King say unto them on his right hand, Come, ye blessed of my Father, inherit the kingdom prepared for you from the foundation of the world: for I was an hungered, and ye gave me meat: I was thirsty, and ye gave me drink: I was a stranger, and ye took me in: naked, and ye clothed me: I was sick, and ye visited me: I was in prison, and ye came unto me. Then shall the righteous answer him, saying, Lord, when saw we thee an hungered, and fed thee? or thirsty, and gave thee drink? when saw we thee a stranger, and took thee in? or naked, and clothed thee? or when saw we thee sick, or in prison and came unto thee? And the King shall answer and say unto them, Verily I say unto you, inasmuch as ye have done it unto one of the least of these my brethren, ye have done it unto me. Then shall he say also unto them on the left hand, Depart from me, ye cursed, into everlasting fire, prepared for the devil and his angels: for I was an hungered, and ye gave me no meat: I was thirsty, and ye gave me no drink: I was a stranger, and ye took me not in: naked, and ye clothed me not: sick, and in prison, and ye visited me not. Then shall they also answer him, saying, Lord, when saw we thee an hungered, or athirst, or a stranger, or naked, or sick, or in prison, and did not minister to thee? Then shall he answer them, saying, Verily I say unto you, inasmuch as ye did it not to one of the least of these, ye did it not unto me. And these shall go away into everlasting punishment: but the righteous into life eternal. — *Matt.* xxv. 31–46.

1. ITS APPOINTMENT.   2. ITS OBJECTS.   3. ITS MAGNITUDE AND RESULTS.

THE theme of discourse suggested by this portion of divine truth, is one of deep solemnity and importance. It calls our attention to one of the great events connected with this world's history. This event is yet future, but is clearly revealed in the Bible, and made certain by the unalterable purpose of Jehovah.

A day of retribution is a topic to which we often refer in our conversation and intercourse with each other; and yet how few, if any, have a realizing sense of the fearful things that hang on the decisions of such an hour. The ushering in of this day will be the closing up of time to earth, and the introductory scene to eternity. It is earth's reckoning-day. The deeds of time must now be unfolded and reviewed by a scrutinizing God. His decision in relation to the merit or demerit of each heart will now be made known, and fix the character and doom of each and every individual forever. At this hour He will call the universe together, and in their presence give them such an exhibition of Himself, by unfolding and defending the great principles of his government, as will make heaven shout for joy and all hell groan with unutterable anguish. To this solemn hour we are all rapidly hastening, and yet how careless in relation to its results! Let us pause for a season, and think. "*Day of Judgment, Day of Wonders!*" Oh, what a day! It is the day of days. Sinner, sinner, think, oh, think! You are interested in that day, whether you believe it or not. You must be there; you cannot escape. God will send his angel for you, and you must appear and take your seat before your judge. But oh, you are not prepared for that fearful moment! You are a condemned criminal. You have violated the law of Him who will then be your judge. You have also rejected his mercy, and despised all his reproof. Up to this very hour, you have perseveringly refused to be saved by the only system that can rescue a sinner from the storm of divine wrath gathering over the path you dare to tread. *Stop, poor sinner;* STOP AND THINK. Remember this short but *infinitely important sentence*, DAY OF JUDGMENT! May God your judge write it upon your inmost soul, and never suffer you to lose sight of it until you repent and prepare for that great event. To impress your minds with the importance of this great theme, let me have your undivided attention to the consideration of the following propositions: —

I. I will show that God has appointed *a day* to judge this world in righteousness.

II. I will notice some of the *objects* to be accomplished by such an event.

III. I will call your attention to some things that will transpire in connection with that day, which will truly render it a *great day.*

I. First, then, I am to show that God has appointed a day to judge the world in righteousness.

In proof of this truth, I submit the following things: 1. A judgment-day is one of the necessary elements of moral government. By a necessary element of government, I mean there can be no moral government without it. Look for a moment at what such a government implies. Among other things, it implies the following : 1. A moral governor. 2. Moral subjects to be governed. 3. Moral law to govern such subjects. 4. A day set apart to call criminals to an account, and to execute the penalty of law upon transgressors. There can no more be a moral government, that amounts to anything, without a judgment-day, than there can be a moral government without law. One is just as essential as the other. Take away your courts of justice from this commonwealth, which are but judgment-days, and let the people trample upon law without calling them to an account, and what becomes of your government? Every reflecting mind must see that you have a government only in name, but not in reality. All your machinery for enacting and promulgating law, under such circumstances, is a mere sham. What does law amount to, if the rebellious are never called to an account? Adopt such a course of procedure, and the people are without government. Now, what would be true as touching this matter under a human government, would be equally true under a divine. Consequently, the doctrine of a day of judgment stands or falls with the doctrine of a moral government. Those, therefore, who would blot out this doctrine from the Bible would strip the government of God of one of its necessary attributes, and render it perfectly powerless to protect public interests. It is not surprising, however, that sinners and hypocritical professors hate a day of judgment, and would gladly overthrow this great truth. They are violators of the divine law, and are unwilling to believe they must be called to an account, and meet its fearful penalty. They feel, in relation to God's government, as criminals feel in relation to human government. There are multitudes of criminals on earth, who would sweep from the world every judicial tribunal, and hurl them all to the winds, rather than submit to have their crimes exposed, and be punished according to their deserts. And the same spirit reigns in the breast of man towards God's great reckoning day. This spirit manifests itself in the efforts that some make to reason themselves and others into the belief that the judgment is past, or that the human family are now standing before all the judgment-seat there is. Poor, deluded men! How your hopes will vanish when you start up from the grave, and behold Christ coming in the clouds of heaven, and you compelled to stand before that great white throne! What a moment! What a moment to the man whose delusion will then be broken up in an instant by the blast of the last trumpet!

2. A future judgment is evident from the fact that God does not distribute rewards and punishments in this life. God has seen fit, in infinite kindness, to place the human family under a just and good law, and to hold them accountable for their conduct. That law they have most wickedly violated. This, none will pretend to call in question. Under such circumstances the Ruler of the universe must call rebellious man to an account in this world or in a future state, or justice is sacrificed, and God's authority is trampled upon with impunity. The question therefore arises: Does God call men to an account in *this* world, and deal with them in *this* state of being according to the strict and stern demands of law and justice? If not, he most certainly will do it hereafter, unless they secure pardon by the system of grace, and even then they are not to escape the judgment. Is this state of being then a state of rewards and punishments? To this question I answer, unhesitatingly, no. And with this simple denial I might suffer the point in

dispute to rest until those, who have the affirmative of the question, present some proof to show that this world is a state of retribution. But I will not leave the matter in controversy here. I will call your attention to some difficulties that should be well pondered, before you embrace the absurd doctrine that God is dealing out to men in this world their full measure of justice.

First, then, I remark, that to me the Bible most clearly teaches, that immediately after the fall God introduced the Gospel system to save men. From that hour the human race have been under a merciful dispensation. The Gospel offers pardon, through the death of Christ, to all who will repent and return to obedience. It consequently lays over for this life the execution of the penalty of a violated law. Doubtless this is done to give the sinner sufficient time to think and make up his mind whether he will comply with these most reasonable terms, and be pardoned and saved, or whether he will reject this offer of grace, and throw himself back upon law to take justice without mercy at the hand of his Maker at a coming judgment. This suspension of penalty is further designed to give God an opportunity to use all suitable means to induce the human race to repent and accept of this offer of grace. To carry this, his noble purpose, into effect, he has commissioned his ministers to proclaim pardon and salvation through the death of his Son to all the nations of the earth, and this proclamation is to be continued until the closing up of time. Now while pardon is being offered, and the sinner is having a day of grace to decide whether he will comply with these terms and live, God is not at the same time executing the penalty upon the criminal. This offer of mercy necessarily holds back the execution of the penalty until the offer is withdrawn. Therefore, from the nature of the case, this world cannot be a place of rewards and punishments. This is mercy's world. It is the place where she has introduced her most costly sacrifice to save man, and where she exhausts every consistent means to reform and save the human race. Then comes the judgment; then comes the day of righteous retribution.

The above constitutes one difficulty, which must be removed before we can consistently believe that God is dealing with men, here, according to their deserts.

The second difficulty that lies in the way of our belief of such a doctrine, is the following: The Bible calls upon us to believe in a long-suffering God. The long-suffering of the Deity is one of those traits of character which stands out prominent in every part of its sacred pages. Its exercise is a noble exhibition of the great heart of Jehovah. What would become of the human race if they were deprived of such a God? In their condition he is just the God they need. Now a doctrine that takes from God this trait of character is a false doctrine, or the Bible bears false testimony. A man who believes in and worships a God who is not a long-suffering God, is not worshipping the God of the Bible. Let us look this matter fully in the face, then, before we embrace a doctrine that strips the Deity of this noble trait of character. Now I affirm that the doctrine, which teaches that God punishes men here according to their deserts, takes entirely away the long-suffering of the Holy One. That doctrine teaches that he smites the transgressor as soon as he sins, and to the fullest desert of his crimes. Now, admitting that to be true for a moment, I ask when and where and how in that case does he exercise long-suffering towards one solitary individual of the human race? It is false and absurd to pretend it. Consequently, the doctrine that God punishes men to the full desert of their crimes as they pass along through this life, and the doctrine that God is long-suffering, are perfect antipodes. They contradict each other, and cannot both be true. Now it is for you to decide which doctrine you will embrace, and whether you will love, reverence, and worship the God of the Bible or an anti-Bible God. A man whose object is truth will not be long in making his selection.

The third difficulty in the way, that must be removed before we can believe in the doctrine under consideration, is the fact that it contradicts some other plain declarations in the word of God. For brevity's sake I will call your attention to two only. Referring to the state of things in this world, Ecclesiastes ix. 2, affirms: "All things come alike to all: there is one event to the righteous, and to the wicked; to the good, and to the clean, and to the unclean; to him that sacrificeth, and to him that sacrificeth not: as is the good, so is the sinner; and he that sweareth, as he that feareth an oath."

Again, Ecclesiastes viii. 11: "Because sentence against an evil work is not executed speedily, therefore the heart of the sons of men is fully set in them to do evil."

These passages teach the three following things, viz:—

1. All things come alike to all in this life,—that is, that God is not, in this world under the merciful dispensation, rewarding men according to their deserts.

2. That sentence against an evil worker, in other words, the penalty of a violated law, is not speedily executed, but is laid over for the time being.

3. In consequence of this delay, the wicked have become bold, obstinate, and settled in their purpose to do evil. They have abused this kindness and mercy on the part of God, and perverted it to their ruin.

These doctrines are plainly taught in the above passages, and they most conclusively contradict the whole theory, that this world is a state of retribution. If we embrace that theory we must disbelieve this plain teaching of the word of God.

Now the question arises, which will you believe? The teachings of the Bible, or the theory that plainly contradicts it? That theory teaches that sentence against an evil work is speedily executed. The Bible declares it is not. Which will you adopt as your faith? Make your choice again.

Fourth. If we look at facts as they are daily spread out before us in the history of this world, we find another formidable objection to the theory that sin is punished in this life, and that virtue is rewarded this side the grave. Take one specimen from our own beloved land, which we hold up to the world as a land of liberty. Let us look in upon the dominions of slavery for a moment, where a man must be a large slaveholder in order to be a first class gentleman and rank high in society. Behold that professed owner of human beings! Mark how his eyes stand out with fatness, and he has all that heart can desire! Well may the Bible affirm concerning such beings, "these are the ungodly, who prosper in the world." They live at ease, journey at pleasure, roll in the lap of luxury, riot in their wickedness, and, in the language of Job, "They send forth their little ones like a flock, and their children dance." They hate God and everything that is good. But, ah! look again. Behold that slave bending low at his couch, and cringing like a whipped spaniel at his feet. He is a victim of his selfishness, tyranny, and love of power. His lordly master has robbed him of his liberty, his time, his right to be educated and worship God according to the dictates of his own conscience. He has torn from his embrace his wife and children, his only remaining earthly comforts, and sold them to the speculator in human flesh, and they are now to be separated, no more to meet on earth. Behold that downcast look, that agonizing countenance, that beating heart and heaving breast, and those streaming eyes, as he bids them a long and final adieu, and turns away to weep out his life. Truly he is a man of sorrows and acquainted with grief. His whole life is rendered wretched by the cruelty and injustice of a fellow-man. Now, is this an overdrawn picture? No one conversant with facts will pretend to deny that we have thousands of such cases in this land, which shouts LIBERTY! LIBERTY! loud enough to be heard from centre to circumference. The world is now and ever has been, since the fall, full of such specimens. Wickedness has rioted, reigned, and triumphed here for more than six thousand years. I would this were the only land where such facts were to be found, but alas! this is not true; villains have plotted together to grasp the reins of government in the different nations of the earth, and have rode to thrones and stations of power over the mangled bodies, and amid the groans and anguish of their dying fellow-men, whose lives they have wickedly sacrificed to promote their own wealth, ambition, and aggrandizement, and that of their families. In fact such rascals have managed to crush out and trample upon the rights of the great mass of human beings in every age of the world, and they have used their fellows as mere tools and beasts of burden to promote their own ends. No man conversant with history can call in question this position.

The good, the pious, the lovers of liberty and of mankind, the praying ones of earth, have been belied, abused, slandered, persecuted, imprisoned, tortured, and put to death by the thousand, so that a Paul could justly exclaim, "if in this life only we have hope in Christ we are of all men most miserable." Now in view of these facts I ask, where is an avenging God if this is a state of retribution? What becomes of his justice? No being could have confidence in his administration for a moment, if he is dealing with men here according to their deserts. Now I believe the foregoing difficulties are perfectly fatal to the theory that God punishes and rewards men in this world. Consequently a future judgment is necessary to set this matter right, and vindicate his character as a just moral governor.

Thus far in this discussion I have been giving you the testimony of reason upon this grave point. I now call your attention to the direct testimony of the Bible in proof of a future day of judgment. What saith the Scriptures upon this point? To the law and to the testimony, for if we speak not according to them, it is because there is no light in us. For the sake of brevity, I shall cite but a few out of many passages that might be brought forward under this head. 1. Then let us look at Rom. xiv. 10: "For we shall all stand before the judgment-seat of Christ." But how stand before the judgment-seat, if there is no judgment-day? Here is the solemn fact revealed, that there is a judgment-seat, and that we must all stand at that great tribunal. Notice the language. It does not read *we do all stand* before the judgment-seat of Christ *now*, as some would vainly have us believe. How the sinner, who hates the doctrine of a future judgment, would gladly think that he is *now* before all the judgment-seat there is. Poor man, why so infinitely foolish as to wish to deceive yourself on this grave point?

Read again, and may God write upon your inmost soul, as with the pen of a diamond, these dread words: "WE SHALL ALL STAND BEFORE THE JUDGMENT-SEAT OF CHRIST." Then remember that verse 12 gives you the object of this standing at the judgment: So that *every* one of us shall give account of himself to God. Here is the reckoning day for earth's conduct. Yes it will come. He shall give an account of *himself* to *God*. Notice the language, he shall give an account of *himself* to God. Not for his neighbor, but for *himself*. He could not control his *neighbor's* conduct, but he *could* control his own. Each shall give an account for the influence he could have exerted for good, and for the influence he did exert for evil,—which settles the question of individual responsibility. Another thing should be noticed. This account is to be given to God. This reckoning is to be with your Maker, the infinitely Holy One, against whom you have so often sinned.

Remember he is not a being who can be deceived, nor a man who can be bribed to connive at your iniquity. Neither can you escape his judgment. You must appear and answer to your name, and receive your fearful doom.

2. Let us look at Acts xvii. 31 : " Because he hath appointed a day, in the which he will judge the world in righteousness by that man whom he hath ordained." This passage teaches that a special day has been set apart, by the particular appointment of God, to try criminals who have sinned against their Maker in this earthly state; and this day is represented as being in the future,—which harmonizes with other portions of truth which we have examined. Particular attention should be given to the expression " IN THE WHICH HE WILL JUDGE THE WORLD." On this eventful day the *world* are to be assembled for trial. Such an assembling of the

world never has taken place, and never can until the last individual of the human family has commenced his existence. Then the world can be assembled for trial, and not before. How foolish therefore to hope that such an event is *past*, when the very phraseology of the passage under consideration settles the question, that from the nature of the case it must be future.

Another thought in the text should be observed: "He is to judge the world in *righteousness.*" Yes, says the sinner, 'I am thankful I am to be judged by a righteous being. You and all other beings ought to rejoice in a fact so vastly important. But you should remember, moreover, that *that* is a fearful truth for you. Pause for a moment and think, — you have done what? You have deliberately and voluntarily violated a law that is infinitely wise and good, the penalty of which is now suspended over your guilty head. God has opened a way by which you can be safely and honorably pardoned, if you will comply with the reasonable terms of the Gospel. He has given you time to repent, and besought you with all the compassion of a God, that you would cease your rebellion against his good government, and fly to Christ and live. Now, how have you treated this kindness on the part of your Maker? You have deliberately rejected every overture of mercy, and perseveringly refused to be saved by grace. In this condition you are hastening to the judgment to be judged in righteousness. But remember, a righteous judgment will hurl your guilty soul into a *deep* and *damning* HELL, "where their worm dieth not, and the fire is not quenched." One thought more and I will dismiss this passage.

He is to judge the world "*by that man whom he hath ordained.*" And who is that man? It is Christ, your compassionate Redeemer. It is the same being who spent his whole life in doing good to this ungrateful world. It is that Christ who was wickedly arraigned at the bar of man, charged with being an impostor, when he had given the world unanswerable evidence that he was sent from God for their special good. He was tried by man, condemned on false testimony, or rather without testimony, and publicly executed as a malefactor. That is the being who is to be your judge. It is not surprising, therefore, that when he makes his appearance, the Bible represents the wicked as crying to the rocks and mountains to fall upon them, to hide them from the face of this righteous being whom they have so wickedly abused. How can they look such a being in the face? The thought that will then rush into their minds, that they must now come to his bar, while their destiny for a long eternity is in his hands, would naturally fill them with the greatest possible consternation. The being for whose blood they had most unrighteously clamored, and concerning whom they had cried out, Away with this fellow from the earth, "CRUCIFY HIM, CRUCIFY HIM," is now to ascend the *Throne*. With what trembling fear the sinner will approach the tribunal of such a judge! But is he not *merciful?* asks the sinner. He is, but that mercy you have rejected, and refused to be saved by its terms. You have thrown yourself back upon *law*, and he now comes to deal with you according to *law*. His righteous decision will blot out your last hope, and consign you over to the great *prison-house* of the universe, for safe keeping during a long eternity.

One passage more, with but little comment, and then I will hasten to another branch of this subject. Let us look at 2 Cor. v. 10: "For we must all appear before the judgment-seat of Christ; that every one may receive the things *done* in *his* body, according to that he hath done, whether *it be* good or bad." We must appear before this high court of heaven. By earthly courts we frequently have a process served upon us, commanding us to appear at such a time and place, to answer to such and such charges that have been preferred against us by our fellows. Sinner, God, the mighty God will soon send his officers to serve a process upon you to appear at the supreme court of the universe, to meet the charge of rebellion against Jehovah's laws, and rejecting the Gospel of his Son. That command you must obey. That will be a searching investigation, but we must all meet it.

Please observe that this passage affirms again that, at that hour, you are to be dealt with and rewarded for the things done in the body; which confirms the position previously taken, that you are not receiving your reward for the things done in the body, while in the body. You will notice that this text does not read that we *have* all appeared before the judgment-seat of Christ, nor that we are appearing there *now*, and are receiving *now;* but that we *shall* appear, and *shall* receive, &c. O, sinner! you are not there to-day, but you must meet this passage at another day, and witness its fulfilment. Improve the present moment to prepare to meet that solemn hour. With these proofs, I now submit this part of the subject, and hasten to the examination of the second proposition in this discourse.

II. I AM TO NOTICE SOME OF THE OBJECTS TO BE ACCOMPLISHED BY SUCH AN EVENT.

1. It is to defend God's authority, and cause it to be respected. To command, is one thing; to make the subjects of government feel that, when a command is given, it must be *obeyed*, is altogether another. To produce that state of feeling in the hearts of the subjects of a moral government is of infinite moment. The main strength of a government to prevent crime lies in that one thing. Whatever produces that state of feeling secures a real good to the universe; whatever diminishes it endangers its happiness and its highest welfare. The

goodness of God will therefore lead him to guard that point most sacredly, and his wisdom will select the best means to accomplish it. While God has been exhibiting his mercy to the world in the introduction of the Gospel system, and staying his wrath to give sinners an opportunity to repent and live, the world have been drawing false inferences from this step on the part of God. They have abused, most wickedly abused, this grand display of divine benevolence. Sinners have drawn this conclusion from God's conduct: that sin, after all, is not so great an evil; that it is a mere trifle, if an evil at all; to trample upon God's authority is a small affair. In consequence of God's not executing upon them at once the just sentence for their crimes, their hearts have become fully set to do evil. Respect for Jehovah's authority is dying out under this merciful dispensation. God saw it would be thus, and proclaimed it in his Word. But still, the ultimate good of the universe demanded that this exhibition of God's character should be given, even if sinners *did* abuse it to their own destruction. But that feeling must be checked. Its spread through the universe would work infinite mischief. The question now arises, How can it be done? I answer, the judgment-day will do it. God will call the universe together. He will try, condemn, and execute the penalty of his law upon those who have trifled with his authority, and rejected the mercy of his Son.

Thus he will show that he hates sin, respects his authority, and that he is able, willing, and determined to defend it.

Oh, guilty sinner, think! God, being a holy God, must respect his authority. He knows its value to the great commonwealth over which he presides. You are a deluded man if you imagine he looks on with indifference while you trample it under your feet. Your doom at the judgment, which will then fall from his stern lips, will break up that delusion most effectually, and convince you, and not only you, but a gazing universe, that his authority must be respected.

2. Another object of the judgment, will be to defend the great principles of his government.

The Declaration of Independence, and the Constitution of the United States, we Americans say, contain great and noble principles which ought to be defended. Our fathers pledged their fortunes, their lives, and their sacred honors in their defence, and we honor them for it. Now, I affirm that there are still greater and more noble principles in the divine government that need defending. These principles are of immense worth to his great empire. They are embodied in the constitution he has instituted to govern all worlds under his control. They lie at the foundation of all good government. They define most clearly, and guard most sacredly the rights of all beings, from the highest to the lowest, throughout his jurisdiction. These principles, if respected by all, and their lives conformed to their holy dictates, would secure to his great kingdom the highest possible degree of perfection, bliss, and prosperity. Such principles must be infinitely dear to God. He could be neither wise nor good, if this were not the fact. Can he look on and see such principles disrespected and trampled upon, and never come forward for their defence? He would be unworthy the high station he occupies, if that could be true. Angels and men would lose all respect for him when that fact was known, and it would be unavoidable. But happy is it for the universe that such is not the fact. At the judgment, God will show most convincingly to all worlds and all beings, that these great principles of his government are infinitely dear to his heart, that the least disrespect for, or violation of them is not to pass unnoticed, that he will sooner sacrifice a universe than see them trampled upon with impunity, that he holds in his possession the means for their defence, and he will use that means in earnest.

3. Still another object of the judgment will be to explain his providential dealings with men.

There are many things about the divine providences that are mysterious in this world. That is to be expected. We are short-sighted creatures. We see not as our Creator seeth. He sees the end from the beginning. His government is over a vast universe. He sees the bearing of every step, over all minds, both in time and down through the distant ages of eternity, and arranges things accordingly. Many of his steps, from the very nature of the case, will look mysterious to us in this world.

He does not see fit to stop here to explain the whys and wherefores of all his great movements. If he should, it could not be done half so effectually here as it can be at the judgment. An event he permits to-day, which looks to us mysterious, may produce an important effect in his empire an hundred or a thousand years hence. That effect he can make us see much clearer after it has taken place than he could now if he should attempt it. He can and will explain all at a future day, so that every being will see that every step he has taken with any of his creatures has been just right, and just such as should have been taken under the circumstances, so that then every mouth will be stopped, every cavilling tongue perfectly silenced, and every objector to his providential dealings utterly confounded and put to shame and everlasting confusion. At the judgment he will show the bearing of every step of his providences upon the happiness of the universal kingdom over which he presides, that those steps have been dictated by infinite wisdom and goodness, that the moral system he has chosen is the best on the whole that could be selected, that he has done everything consistent to be done to secure its highest perfection and happiness, that the things which have been done, have been done at the right time and in the best manner. He will then show, doubtless, that, if he had taken any other steps to save the world, or to keep sin out of the universe, it would have been inconsistent with the perfections of his nature, and that some evil would have broken out in some portion of his immense kingdom as the consequence, which would have greatly overbalanced the good that would have resulted from such steps. Consequently, he will make it appear to all that he has selected, as the great end for which he lives and reigns, the highest possible good that could, on the whole, be secured, and that he has used the best and most effectual means to secure that end. He will show, moreover, that the sinner had no excuse for sinning, that he has exhausted all consistent means to save him, all of which has been refused, that now justice and the ultimate good of the universe demand that he should be shut up eternally in the great prison-house of God's kingdom, to prevent his doing further harm by his ungodly influence in running at large.

The Bible plainly intimates that God will make this point so clear, that every good being will most heartily acquiesce in the execution of the law upon the finally impenitent. They will rejoice, not in the misery in itself considered, but in the fact that the rights of the universe have been secured by the execution of the penalty of a just law; and it will be seen that they could not have been secured without it. Thus God, by the exhibition he will give at the judgment, will carry the conscience of the entire universe with him. His whole character will then be made to appear as it never has before. His wisdom, power, goodness, mercy, long-suffering, tenderness, truthfulness, faithfulness, and *justice*, will then stand out as visible as the heavens, and that vast assembly will be awe-struck and overwhelmed with the outgushing of holiness that will then and there beam forth from every footstep of his providence. He will challenge even a devil to put his finger on the most minute step with any being in any world, that has not been just as it should be. Oh! how he will cover his enemies with eternal shame at that hour, and how all his holy creatures will give one long, unanimous, and spontaneous shout of " GLORY TO GOD IN THE HIGHEST," as they gaze upon his infinite purity, as it will then shine forth! As he thunders forth from his throne that just sentence of the law, upon the guilty heads of those who have refused to be redeemed, " DEPART, YE CURSED, INTO EVERLASTING FIRE," how they will drop upon their faces and cry, " AMEN, JUST AND TRUE ARE THY WAYS, THOU KING OF SAINTS!"

4. Another object of the judgment will be to defend the rights of those who have been trampled upon in this life. The rights of all the subjects

of a government are committed into the hands of the governing power for protection. It is the duty of those in authority to see that this work is most sacredly performed. They cannot neglect this duty without forfeiting the right to govern. Each subject of the government has a just claim on it for protection. They have a right to look for it, and expect it, nor has the government a right to withhold it. The government that will look on with indifference, and see the rights of any of its subjects trampled on, high or low, rich or poor, learned or unlearned, and not come forward for their defence, is not worthy the *name* of a government. In fact it is not a government. The end of government is lost sight of entirely. In such a case it becomes most unrighteous tyranny. The right to govern does not include the right to oppress or take away rights. Its appropriate business is to *protect* rights and not take them away. No righteous government, therefore, is oppressive. It is tyranny that oppresses, and not rightful government. Oppression is the abuse of government. It is the perverting the great ends of government, and making it an instrument of immense mischief and misery, when it should be an instrument of good, and only good. It is absurd to say that God has authorized man, in an associated or individual capacity, to do wrong. If those who hold the reins of government are so ignorant of the object of government, that they have not yet learned that to protect the rights of all their subjects is their appropriate duty, and a duty they have not the right to neglect, they are most certainly too ignorant to govern. If they do know their duty in this particular, and have not principle enough about them to do it, they are too corrupt to govern, and the reins of government should be taken from such hands forthwith, and committed to hands that will do their duty. To keep such villains in power is to defeat the great ends of government, and put in jeopardy the highest interests of the nation. To vote men into office who will lose sight of this great end of government, is absolute wickedness. This is the great curse of this nation at the present time. We have committed the reins of government into the hands of men who have no respect for the rights of their fellows. This course persisted in a little longer, and the nation is ruined. God thunders out of heaven, and says: "*thou shalt provide out of all the people able men,* such as *FEAR GOD, men of truth, hating covetousness,* AND PLACE SUCH *over them to be rulers.*" — Exod. xviii. 21. The church and minister, instead of obeying God in this solemn command, vote for profane swearers, drunkards and slaveholders, who enact laws which rob millions in this land of their rights, instead of protecting them. There is to be a reckoning-day for this fearful wickedness, and I thank God for it.

The great lawgiver of the universe does not look

on with indifference and see one class in a community trample on the rights of another, and not come to their defence. They are the subjects of his government, and he knows his duty too well, as a public ruler, not to listen to the cry of his abused subjects. To his oppressed ones, he proclaims from on high, "*Vengeance is mine*, I WILL REPAY, *saith the Lord.*" Mark that pledge on the part of God, and tremble, ye abusers of mankind. His throne is committed, and he knows how to do his duty, and he will do it. Thank heaven there is a tribunal to which the oppressed of this land and world can appeal, to have their wrongs redressed, and be heard. The day of retribution is at hand. God will bring the oppressor before the great tribunal of the universe, and deal out to him the reward for robbing his fellow-man of his rights. The abused party will then have a patient hearing. The testimony, even of the colored man, cannot then be thrown out of court. It will be heard and weighed. There will be no suppression of testimony, nor covering up of facts, permitted in that high court. The slave's scarred back, and his debased mind, debased and kept in ignorance by slave laws, will then appear as a swift witness against the master; and for every tear he has wrung out of his slave by abuse, and for every hour he has compelled him to serve without wages, and for all the evils he has inflicted on his moral and intellectual nature, God will then and there deal out his just reward.

What a moment to the proud, haughty master, that will be, when he will be compelled to see, perhaps, the victim he has despised as a "nigger," exalted high in heaven, while he, by a righteous and indignant universe, will be hissed down to hell! Oh! you wrongdoers of earth, who refuse to repent and let the oppressed go free, you who fill high places in the government, and shut up your ears to the cry of the poor and abused of this earth, the hour is coming when you shall want help, and cry for it, but shall not find it. "Whoso stoppeth his ears at the cry of the poor, he also shall cry himself, but shall not be heard." — Prov. xxi. 13. Your day of triumph, prosperity, and misrule will be short; your day of reckoning is at hand, and your doom will be fearful. God is the avenger of all the abused parties of earth, and that vengeance you must meet, if you persist in your wrongdoing. May God open your eyes and lead you to repentance, before that fearful reckoning-day overtakes you!

5. Another object of the judgment will be to exhibit God's love of holiness, and his hatred of, and opposition to sin.

What is holiness? It is the voluntary conforming of the heart and life to God's law. What is sin? It is the transgression of that law. No finite mind can estimate the value of holiness to the universe. Holiness is the means, and the only means, by which the happiness of a moral agent can be secured. It is worth to the universe, therefore, all the endless bliss of every intelligent creature God has ever formed. Universal holiness would secure the bliss, the *endless* bliss of all. What finite mind can estimate the value of the happiness of even one being for a never-ending eternity. Think of it, — ENDLESS BLISS! You cannot take in the thought, as it includes the thought of eternity, which no finite mind can comprehend. It takes God's mind to estimate the value of the happiness of even one being. How infinitely valuable, therefore, must be the happiness of a universe of beings! As holiness is the means, and the only means which can secure this bliss, it must be infinitely valuable.

But sin is the exact opposite of holiness, and would produce just the opposite effect. Sin has destroyed the happiness of every being who has committed it. It is the cause of all the misery and death of our world. Let it become universal, and it would work infinite mischief in God's immense kingdom. Universal sin would produce universal misery, and endless sin, endless misery. What being can be happy and sin? It is impossible. A moral agent was not created for sin, but for holiness; consequently he violates the laws of his being when he sins, and misery is the necessary result. We should keep in view, that the universe over which God presides, is a universe of moral agents, consequently they are all capable of sinning. Angels have sinned, man has sinned. The tendency of sin is to spread. One sinner can do immense mischief. The devil led astray the whole human family. Let this great enemy of the happiness of beings overrun the universe, and its happiness is gone forever. As, therefore, holiness would secure universal bliss, and sin destroy it, God must, from his very nature, be infinitely in favor of the one, and infinitely opposed to the other.

That opposition to sin and love to holiness we should naturally believe he would exhibit in his government, if he is an honest being. God being infinitely holy, he must, from the nature of the case, be infinitely honest, frank, and open-hearted. His government, therefore, is but an exhibition, or laying open his great heart to the universe.

If God loves holiness with an everlasting love, we should expect that he would require of all the subjects of his government that they be perfectly holy, at all times and under all circumstances, in thought, word, and deed. This natural expectation we find fully met in his government. If he hates sin with an eternal hatred, as he must if he is a good God, then we should expect, moreover, that in his government he would forbid all sin in his subjects, at all times and under all circumstances. This expectation, also, we find fully met in his government.

Again, if he thus loves holiness and hates sin, we should expect him to do all he can, as a public lawgiver, to encourage and promote the one and prevent the other. His goodness will necessarily lead him to do this. The question therefore arises, What can God do? If the definition we have given of holiness and sin be correct, we see that he cannot force men to be holy, nor force them not to sin. Men are moral agents, and their sin and holiness lies in their voluntary actions. The moment you apply force, you take away their free agency, and then they are neither capable of sin nor holiness. What God does, therefore, to secure the holiness of moral beings, (and there are no others capable of holiness or sin,) he must do by moral means, or by the power of motive, influence, argument, and persuasion. This being the fact, his goodness would prompt him to embody in his government the strongest possible degree of motive to influence the one and to hold in check the other. Experience teaches us that moral agents are capable of being very strongly influenced by their hopes and fears, or love of happiness and dread of misery. God's government, to be a perfect one, must make the strongest possible appeal to these two great moving principles in moral beings. Now if he has not done this, he has not done all that could be done by the power of motive to promote holiness and prevent sin. What is the highest and strongest degree of motive that can be presented to these two great moving principles embodied in the constitution of all moral agents? I answer, a heaven of eternal bliss and joy on the one hand, as a reward of holiness, and a hell of eternal pain and anguish on the other hand, as a reward or penalty for sin. Now turn your attention to my text, and you have this view of the subject fully confirmed. " Come, ye blessed of my Father, inherit the kingdom prepared for you from the foundation of the world," says God to the righteous. " Depart from me, ye cursed, into everlasting fire, prepared for the devil and his angels;" "and these shall go away into everlasting punishment: but the righteous into life eternal." Here is the government and its motives, and here are its rewards. But in the face of these great moving considerations, men have sinned and refused to be saved by the blood of Christ. They have doubted God's word, and they will not believe he ever intends to put in force these plain declarations. It remains, therefore, for him to show by his action that he means what he says — that not one jot or one tittle of his word shall fail until all be fulfilled. At the judgment, in presence of an assembled universe, he will come forth to this stern work of justice. To the saints, at that hour, he will open wide the gates of bliss, and welcome them to seats in that heavenly world where their joys shall never end; but the wicked he will cast down to hell, — and thus by his action he will place a distinction between sin and holiness that shall be as wide as heaven and as deep as hell. The eternal songs of the righteous, as they rise high in glory, shall proclaim to the universe his everlasting love of holiness; while the wailings of the lost, and the smoke of their torment, ascending up unceasingly in the presence of all worlds, shall be a monument of his eternal displeasure of sin.

DIVISION NO. II.

I have already endeavored to establish the first proposition under our text, namely, that "God has appointed a day to judge the world in righteousness." Under the second head, I have noticed "some of the objects to be accomplished by such an event." And now —

III. I AM TO CALL YOUR ATTENTION TO SOME THINGS THAT WILL TRANSPIRE IN CONNECTION WITH THAT DAY, WHICH WILL TRULY RENDER IT A GREAT EVENT.

1. The human family will cease to multiply. The last child ever to spring from the loins of old father Adam will have been born and commenced his eternal existence. The number of the human race will now be completed; the number of the elect will have been gathered into his church, and God will close up the system of propagation forever. The cry of the infant shall no more be heard in all the earth. The care, anxiety, and training of little ones will have passed away, and all mothers must now

hasten to the judgment, and there learn the good or evil effects of their influence over their offspring, and render up their account to Him who will reward them for that influence according to its real deserts.

2. The probation of the earth under mercy's reign will now be closed up. This earth has had two probations: one under law, and the other under grace. The probation under law was very brief. Immediately after the creation of our first parents, God placed them under law, and offered them life on the condition of perfect and constant obedience. They soon forfeited their right to life by transgression. God wound up that probation under law by calling them to an account for their conduct, found them guilty, but laid over the execution of the penalty for the time being, for the purpose of introducing the merciful dispensation of his government. This earth was to be the theatre where God was to unfold one trait of his character, which had not been fully developed to the mind of his creatures up to this hour. Mercy's dispensation commenced immediately after the fall, and is to continue down to the judgment. God at once began to unfold this great system of grace, and to prepare the way to introduce his Son into the world, to die to redeem a race of lost beings. He caused salvation to be published to the world through this coming Redeemer, and pardon to be offered in his name to all who would repent and return to obedience. He brought the

earth under a curse, and introduced a class of reformatory providences, which are to be continued down to the judgment, for the purpose of bringing the human race to repentance. He commenced converting and commissioning men to publish this salvation through the death of his Son, thus using reformed criminals to coöperate with him in spreading this great scheme of redemption. In the fulness of time, his Son made his appearance on earth, and instructed the human family more fully in relation to this noble system of reform. He gave up his life as an atoning sacrifice for man, and was laid in the grave. On the third day he arose, appeared to his disciples, commissioned them to publish this salvation to an entire world, and ascended into the heavens, where he is to make intercession for the transgressors until mercy has done her utmost to reform the human family. This is the world of reform. In this world, where Christ died, where the Gospel is preached, and where the Spirit is poured out, mercy is to do all she ever will do to reform man. When Christ makes his appearance as a judge, he winds up this great effort of reform, and closes up earth's probation of grace forever. "Then shall they call, but I will not answer."

Oh, what a moment to the world, when God shall forever close up the reign of grace! Sinner, you are not in a world of despair to-day; you are in Mercy's world. How you ought to drop on your knees and thank and praise God that you are out of hell!

3. Another thing that will render this event a great one is the fact that the mediatorial throne at that hour is to be given up. 1 Cor. xv. 24: " Then cometh the end, when he shall have delivered up the kingdom to God, even the Father." The *end* referred to in this text evidently has reference to the end of the reign of grace. The throne to be vacated and given up at that hour is none other than the mediatorial throne. That is the throne that Christ occupies now, which he will then vacate. This mediatorial reign of Christ is a temporary reign, and is not to last forever; it lasts only while the merciful or reformatory dispensation continues. When that closes up, Christ will give up his mediatorial kingdom forever. The vacation of an earthly throne will, under certain circumstances, excite a whole nation most intensely. Let the Queen of England publish to that nation that she will vacate her throne in six months, who doubts that that whole nation would be agitated to the very ends of its fingers. But what is the vacation of a mere earthly throne compared with the vacation of the mediatorial throne of the Son of God over this lost world? That step might and would affect a small portion of the human family temporally; but the step we are contemplating will affect the whole human family eternally. Nay, more; its effects, I doubt not, will be felt by angels

as well as men; for they will not look on with indifference, and witness this great transaction. This one step, therefore, will truly render this day a *great* day.

4. The Gospel will then cease to be preached to the human race, and the ministers of Christ will all be called from the walls of Zion to lay down their commissions at Christ's feet.

One of the great instrumentalities God has seen fit to use in reforming the world, is the preaching of the Gospel by human lips. God understands full well the laws of the human mind, and the power one human being has over another, to move him to action by argument and entreaty. This power is acknowledged by all the political gatherings and speeches made throughout the world. Why these political gatherings all over our land at the time of our elections, and why this putting forward certain prominent men to make speeches to the rest? It is because the human family know, and thus acknowledge, that human beings have great power over each other, through the medium of speech, to move and mould them according to their wishes. God understands this power, and has called it into requisition in the great economy of grace. In every age of the world he has been raising up and qualifying men for this holy work. He has commanded them to go forth and expound and enforce the great principles of his government; to show the world their sins in the light of those principles, and offer salvation, through the death of his dear Son, to all who will repent and obey the Gospel. What a work, to offer salvation to fallen, sinful man, in God's name and by God's authority! In this world, under this proclamation of the Gospel, men decide their destiny for eternity, and God intends they shall. Sinner, think! You fix your own state in heaven or hell, by the decision you make while under the Gospel. That minister preaches, and you decide under his sermon not to obey now. You hear again and come to the same conclusion, go through life thus, drop into eternity, and God then saves or damns you in harmony with your own decision. What a responsible seat you occupy when under the sound of the Gospel! But will God continue the proclamation of this Gospel to this world forever? The good Book answers that question and puts it beyond all controversy, to those who are willing to be guided by its testimony. When the judgment shall sit, every minister will be called from the walls of Zion to lay down his commission at Christ's feet, and give up an account to God for his stewardship. How solemn the moment, when the last note of mercy ever to fall upon the ear of man has been sounded, and the Gospel-trumpet has been laid aside forever! This transaction, in connection with others, will truly render this a *great* day.

5. The resurrection of the body is also to take

place at this hour. Rev. xx. 13: "And the sea gave up the dead which were in it; and death and hell delivered up the dead which were in them: and they were judged every man according to their works." In this passage the resurrection of the body is connected with this great event. The sea is represented as giving up the bodies of those who have perished in its mighty waters; and death, or the grave, gives up the bodies of those who have been entombed upon the land; and hell, or the unseen world or world of spirits, delivers up the souls of the human family,— when the soul and body, thus reunited, comes to the judgment to receive its final reward.

The doctrine of the resurrection of the body is strictly a Bible doctrine. The question propounded by Job, "If a man die shall he live again?" cannot be answered by all the philosophers on earth.

The God who has power to lay the body in the grave, has power to hold it there eternally. If it is raised, it is raised by his power alone. Whether he will ever see fit to exert that power, can be made known only by a direct revelation. That revelation, blessed be God, we have in his word. I say *blessed be God* for the simple reason, that to me and to Christians generally, the doctrine of the resurrection is a glorious doctrine. Mankind generally love their bodies, and those of their friends. To see this noble piece of God's workmanship decay and die, and return to earth, is a melancholy picture indeed. This is evident from the care and anxiety of the human family to preserve the life of the body, and from the lamentations they make over it when they lay it in the grave. But how that lamentation would be intensified a thousand-fold, if the conviction was forced home upon us, as we stand over the grave's mouth to deposit the remains of those we love, and as we lay them away in the bowels of the earth, that they were to sleep there forever! Who could retire from such a scene of death without the gloom of despair gathering over his spirit, to oppress him beyond all description? The grave would be shrouded in eternal midnight. It would be a dark night, with no morn beyond it. The sun of life would set never to rise again. How thankful we ought to be, that God has not left us thus without hope. In the Gospel of his son, Christ is presented as the resurrection and the life. The resurrection of the body had a prominent place in the preaching of the apostles and primitive Christians. They dwelt upon it with enthusiastic delight. The hope of the resurrection was to them a glorious hope, when connected with the salvation of their souls. But at this day, how we forget or undervalue it! What a day that must be when God, by the voice of his angel, in a moment of time, shall call into life again the millions who now sleep in the dust of earth, — when the sea and the dry land shall deliver up the bodies of men which they have long held under their dominion, and all the sons of time find themselves congregated in one vast assembly, and march up to that great white throne to meet their final account! Such a transaction, in connection with this event, will truly render it a momentous one.

6. Another transaction connected with this event, which will truly render it a great day, is the destruction of this earth by fire.

The great fire in the city of New York, several years since, was so important, that it was a subject of conversation in almost every part of this, and even in other countries. The burning of the city of Rome was another event of such magnitude as to be recorded in history, and has been preserved and handed down from generation to generation to the present hour. But what would be the burning of a thousand such cities, when compared with the destruction of this whole earth by fire? Think of that fearful moment when every city, village, and hamlet on earth shall be in a blaze! — when the old ocean itself shall burn like so much oil, and send up one vast sheet of fire that will astonish the universe! — when every continent and island shall be wrapped in flames! — when the solid mountains will melt like so much wax, and the atmosphere which surrounds this earth, shall burn like so much gas! Think of it for a moment. The whole world on fire! Not a city laid in ruins, but a WORLD wrapped in flames! How God can do up things on a large scale! What a spectacle to angels and men, as they look on and see all the wealth of earth swept away in one general conflagration!—the labor and toil of ages consumed with one breath from the Almighty! How the alarm of fire, ushering in this great scene, will be sounded through the universe! Look, says an angel, the EARTH on fire! LOOK! LOOK QUICK!! Sure enough, says another; and with the velocity of light he flies, and cries out as he flies, FIRE! FIRE! FIRE! The EARTH on FIRE! FIRE! The different worlds catch the *alarm*, and send forth one general shout of "FIRE!" that shall be heard in the most distant corner of God's dominions. The inhabitants of all worlds will come forth, doubtless, to witness this grand display of God's displeasure at the sins and corruptions of earth. How the universe will be amazed and awe-stricken by this fearful event. Truly, this sublime scene will render this day a *great* day! But, says one, where is the evidence of such a scene? Turn to 2 Peter iii. 6-12, and you have God's word for it:

" Whereby the world that then was, being overflowed with water, perished: but the heavens and the earth, which are now, by the same word are kept in store, reserved unto fire against the day of judgment and perdition of ungodly men. But, beloved, be not ignorant of this one thing, that one day is with the Lord as a thousand years, and a thousand years as one day. The Lord is not slack concerning his promise, as some men count slackness; but is long-suffering to us-ward, not willing that any should perish, but that all should come to repentance. But the day of the Lord will come as a thief in the night; in the which the heavens shall pass away with a great noise, and the elements shall melt with fervent heat, the earth also and the works that are therein shall be burned up. Seeing then that all these things shall be dissolved, what manner of persons ought ye to be in all holy conversation and godliness, looking for and hasting unto the coming of the day of God, wherein the heavens being on fire shall be dissolved, and the elements shall melt with fervent heat?"

7. The manner of Christ's approach to the world, on this occasion, will render this event a *great* one.

In the formation of the human mind, God has given it a power which we denominate the imagination. All the powers of the human soul were given to be exercised, and the right use of them is always justifiable.

The imagination, when under the illuminating and controlling influence of truth, will greatly aid us in taking hold of the great things revealed in the Bible, and in bringing them home to the soul as living and solemn realities. Under the guidance of the good Book, therefore, let us give play to this faculty of our minds, for a season, in considering this branch of our subject.

Now come with me, for a moment, down to the end of time. Let us take a position upon some lofty eminence, which overlooks the earth. Now mark that scenery which lies at your feet, — how delightful! Notice that busy multitude, — how they rush hither and thither for the pleasures of earth, her honors, wealth, and places of power! How thoughtless, how careless, and absorbed in earthly pursuits! Tomorrow shall be as this day, is their general impression. Behold I come as a thief, is forgotten and out of the mind of the mass of people. But time has grown old and hoary, and her last hour has come. Look yonder in mid-heaven, and behold the approach of that mighty angel. What a being! He is clothed with a cloud, and a rainbow is upon his head, — reminding the earth that the God, under whose commission he acts, is a covenant keeping God. His face! Oh! his face is like the sun, and his feet are truly as pillars of fire. In his hand he holds an open book, that guides his every movement. Behold him as he places one foot upon the great rolling ocean, and the other upon the solid earth. How majestic! One would truly think it was God himself, were it not for the fact that *angel* is written all over him, and had not John given such a minute description of him in Rev. 10.

But mark how he extends that hand up to heaven, and then notice that solemn countenance, as he looks up to the throne of the infinite One. His very position and manner show that he feels the weight, the full weight of the sentiment he is about to utter. But listen. *He speaks, he speaks.* He swears by Him that liveth forever and ever, who created earth with all her inhabitants, THAT TIME SHALL BE NO LONGER! What an oath! What a voice! Those severe responsive peals of thunder! How they shake creation, and are heard to the remotest corner of earth! The sun hides his face to weep, and refuses to shine henceforth upon this guilty earth; the moon is obscured; the stars of heaven are blown out; the history of the earth is closed up forever, and her reckoning-day is now to be ushered in. This is one of the scenes described in the Bible, as connected with Christ's approach to the world, that will render it a momentous hour.

Let us take another scene, and then I will hasten to another thought. When Christ comes to judge the world, the Bible informs us that he will make his approach to the earth upon the clouds of heaven. At the time of his ascension, after his resurrection, he took his disciples from Jerusalem to the Mount of Olives, commissioned them to preach the Gospel to all the world, gave them directions how and where to commence, and then lifted up his hands and blessed them for the last time. As he blessed he rose up from the earth in their presence, passed up through the atmosphere, took his seat upon the clouds, and rode off, triumphantly, up to the throne of God. His disciples watched him as he went up, until he was completely out of sight; and even then they continued to look and gaze up into heaven, hoping to get one more glimpse of that blessed one. The object on which their supreme affections were placed had gone up on high, and how could they have their eyes turned off to any other object? While thus gazing into heaven, God sent down two angels to comfort them by proclaiming a great truth. Hear their testimony for a moment: "*This same Jesus which is taken up from you into heaven,*" they affirm, "*shall so come* IN LIKE MANNER *as ye have seen him go up into heaven.*" There are two things in this testimony of these angels to which I invite your particular attention. 1. They affirm that "*this same Jesus,*" who ascended in the presence of these disciples, shall return again to this earth. 2. When he returns, he shall come "upon the clouds of heaven." This is evident from the following words in their testimony: "*He shall so come in like manner as ye have seen him go up into heaven.*"

Now the question arises, How did they see him go into heaven? He ascended upon the clouds. When he returns to earth, therefore, he will return upon the clouds. So the angels testify, and they are competent and truthful witnesses. Now turn your attention to Rev. i. 7, and you have another testimony to the truthfulness of this position: "Behold, he cometh with clouds; and every eye shall see him, and they also which pierced him: and all kindreds of the earth shall wail because of him. Even so, Amen." Please observe from this passage the following things: 1. When Christ comes, as described in this portion of truth, it will be a visible appearing that can be tested by the senses of the human family,—"AND EVERY EYE SHALL SEE HIM." 2. That being the fact, it fully settles the question that this coming of Christ is yet future. I summon here the whole human race as witnesses to the fact that their eyes have not yet seen Christ come to this earth upon the clouds of heaven. 3. It is evident that the resurrection of the bodies of men must *precede* this coming, as all the kindreds of the earth are to witness it, including his enemies who pierced him. Now I affirm that this evidence sufficiently establishes the fact, to all who are willing to be convinced, that when Christ returns to earth he will come upon the clouds. That thought I present as one that will render this scene a *great* one, as the very manner of his coming will be truly sublime. Let us suppose for a moment that we are in a position to witness this great transaction. We look abroad in the heavens, and behold Christ surrounded with an innumerable multitude of the heavenly hosts, making his approach to this earth, the scene of his sufferings and death. He takes his seat upon the clouds, while the whole human family look up and behold this declaration of God's Word fulfilled in their presence. They wanted demonstration that was irresistible to prove this fact, and now they have it, and how the kindreds of the earth wail under its influence! They that pierced him now look and gnash their teeth with anguish, but they must approach his judgment-seat. He comes now not to be despised and rejected of men, but he comes in his glory. He comes clothed with the authority of a God. He comes as a judge. Mark his countenance; it is as the "sun shining in his strength." "His eyes are as a flame of fire, and out of his mouth goeth a sharp, two-edged sword." At his side "hang the keys of death and hell," and he now "opens and no man shuts, and shuts and no man opens." Oh, look and listen, and see how he rides triumphantly around the earth, amid the shouts and triumphs of his officers of state!

Such is the description the Bible gives of this grand approach of Christ to our earth, when he comes to judgment; and I submit that the very manner of his coming will render it a *great* day.

8. The multitude that will meet on that occasion is another thing that will render it a *great* event. We have some days on earth which we call great days, in consequence of the multitudes who come

together. Some great political gathering, the celebration of some great political event, or to do honor to some prominent statesman; the return from the battle-field of a successful general who has led on his fellow-soldiers to the fearful work of human slaughter, the crowning or burial of some mighty monarch of earth. On these occasions multitudes congregate, and consequently we look back to them as great days.

But what are all the gatherings of earth, when compared to the innumerable multitudes who will meet on this occasion? They are but as a drop to the ocean. Could you see all the inhabitants of this nation assembled on some vast plain,— what a multitude! Add to that all the living sons of earth, and you have only a small part of this vast assembly. Call up from the grave all who have been swept from the shores of time by death, and then add all who are yet to be born of human kind, and you have only one family of this immense assembly. We sometimes long for one family gathering. Our father, Adam, will have one such gathering. He shall stand at the head of his numerous progeny, and all the children shall look each other and their venerable sire in the face, and then part never more to meet. In addition to this great number, Christ is to come with *all his* HOLY ANGELS. The word angels, as used in this text, comprehends, doubtless, all the holy intelligences in God's great kingdom, aside from man. That they exceed the number of human beings, almost infinitely, I have no doubt. How can we come to any other conclusion, when we look at the vastness of God's works? I see no inconsistency in supposing that the human family bear a similar proportion to the great whole, that our earth does to the immensity of the material universe. I think all these millions of worlds that roll on high are but splendid mansions fitted up by the infinite Hand, that created all things to be the eternal abode of an innumerable multitude of intelligences, which he has called into being to explore his works and adore him eternally for his infinite perfections. Upon this occasion they are all to be present to witness his reckoning with the human family.

Now add to this one other class of beings, termed Devils, and you have the extent of this assembly. The good Book informs us that these are fallen angels, a great number of them, and that they are reserved in chains unto the judgment. They are also to be present at that day to receive their final doom. What a multitude! What a multitude of beings! What mind can comprehend them! God will have one great meeting with his creatures, that each may know something of the extent of the kingdom over which he presides, and give him an opportunity to unfold some of the great plans he has devised and carried into execution for the promotion of its highest good.

9. The investigation of character, to take place at that hour, will render it a great day.

When Professor Webster was put on trial, in Boston, for the murder of Dr. Parkman, he doubtless considered that an eventful day in his history. Such was the interest in that affair through the nation, that all eyes were turned toward old Massachusetts. Thousands waited, with intense anxiety, the result of that investigation. But, sinner, think.! At the day of judgment you will be on trial for life. Ah, yes, ponder it well! not one man on trial for *life* simply, but a *world!* The whole human race arraigned at God's bar! and *all on trial for life!* What a spectacle! What interests are now at stake! But, oh, think again! What is the *life* that will be pending then? Not the life of the body, which is but a vapor that passeth away, but it is the ETERNAL LIFE of both soul and body that hangs upon the investigation of that hour. Then think of the development of hearts that will be made at that day! All the abominations of earth are then to come out! Every unholy thought, with every secret iniquity. "For God shall bring every work into judgment, with every secret thing, whether it be good or whether it be evil." — Eccl. xii. 14. There will be no covering up of crime at that hour. All the pollutions of your heart will be laid open to the gaze of the whole universe. What shame, — what eternal shame will then mantle your guilty face, as all your unrepented deeds are made to appear! Oh, who can abide the day of his coming! Who can stand when he appeareth!

Think once more, — the history of the whole race written in blood! Their lying, deception, murder, robbery, profanity, cheating, slander, and hating one another; their licentiousness, drunkenness, forgetfulness of God; the murder of his Son; the abuse of his Bible; the rejection of his Gospel, and the grieving of his Spirit; — all, all must now be developed. What a picture! How angels will hiss at such conduct, and the human race hang their heads, covered with eternal disgrace! What an eventful day!

10. The solemn separation that will take place, is another thing that will render it a *great* day. There are separations in this life to which we look forward with deep interest in many instances. That son or daughter is to sail on a given day to a distant island of the sea, as a missionary. Those parents and friends have assembled in Boston to bid them adieu. Now mark the distress of those aged parents as they grasp their hands for the last time, and give them that last parting blessing, and then turn away and weep.

Look in upon that death-bed scene for a moment. There is a dear relative or friend panting for breath. With what intense interest those friends gather around that dying couch, and gaze upon that pale face, those sunken cheeks, and those glassy eyes! With what eagerness they treasure up that last word! and how their hearts gush out through their eyes, as they listen to that faint but final adieu! Oh! how that last death-stare goes through them, as the soul leaps from time into eternity! Such separations are painful, but they are not *eternal.* We shall meet once more, and then comes the *final* separation, which *will* be eternal.

At the judgment, God shall separate that vast assembly, the righteous from the wicked, "as a shepherd divideth the sheep from the goats." This separation will be final. Husbands and wives, parents and children, brothers and sisters, neighbors and friends then will part to meet no more. Oh! that last look, that final adieu, as each takes his place, the one at the right hand, and the other at the left of the great judge of all the earth! What weeping and lamentation will be there on the part of the wicked, as they fall back to the left hand of the Judge!

11. And finally. The fearful doom that will be pronounced upon the wicked will render this a *great* day. What deep solicitude was felt in Boston when Professor Webster was brought into court to receive his sentence, after he had been found guilty of murder! What a moment to him, when the judge arose to deliver, in his hearing, the dreadful words of the law, " You shall be taken to the gallows, *and hung*

by the neck until you are DEAD, DEAD, DEAD!" How his guilty soul must have felt, as they sank down deep into his heart! What horror shook his whole frame as that listening multitude gazed! How his spirit writhed under that gaze, as he exclaimed, "*take me away*, TAKE ME AWAY!"

But what was that doom when compared with the one that will be pronounced at the judgment? The tribunal before which he was arraigned, was man's tribunal. The sinner will stand before God's. The death pronounced upon him was the death of the body. The death that will be pronounced upon the sinner, at that day, will involve both soul and body in ruin. The pang of death which the law inflicted on him was momentary. The sinner's will be *eternal*. He met the indignation of man. The sinner will meet the wrath and indignation of God. Ah, guilty sinner! God has seen fit to write out your doom beforehand, and he has left it on record in my text, that you may ponder its awful import, and decide whether you will escape its fearful destruction by flying to Christ for forgiveness and salvation, while the door of hope is open before you. Read it, oh read it! "DEPART YE CURSED INTO EVERLASTING FIRE, *prepared for the Devil and his angels.*" *What words, falling from such lips!* Coming from such a tribunal, how they will blast all your future prospects, blot out your last hope for a long eternity, and draw over your mind the gloom of eternal despair. How you will gnash your teeth with anguish, as they fall upon your ear at this great tribunal, and a long eternity in hell explains to you their full meaning! Oh! may God open wide your eyes to your danger, and lead you at once to the only ark of safety!

REMARKS.

1. This subject affords encouragement to the righteous to be patient under the trials and abuses of this life.

Our trials in this state of being will soon be over. Life is short, and when it closes up, we close up all our troubles forever. Beyond this vale of tears there is a rest for the people of God. They may be slandered, abused, and robbed of their rights in this life, but the judgment will set that matter all right; and their light afflictions here will only work out for them a weight of glory hereafter,— for all things work together for good to those who love God, and are called according to his purpose of grace.

How patient we should be, therefore, under the ills of this life, and wait for our reward until Christ makes his appearance! At that day the Christian shall triumph over all his enemies. The cause he has loved and advocated; for which he has suffered, perhaps, the loss of all things earthly; the cause which the wicked have ridiculed, and rendered unpopular in this world, will then be exalted and honored. God and all good beings will then indorse it publicly. The despisers of Christ, his cause and his children, shall then become the "byword" and the "hissing" of every noble being in the universe. How they then will be covered with eternal shame, while the Christian will lift up his head and rejoice with exceeding great joy, as he beholds Christ approaching upon the clouds with power and great glory! Who would not be patient, therefore, and wait and watch for such a blessed day?

2. This great theme affords a strong motive to influence the Christian to do with his might, what his hands find to do for the salvation of the world. Our friends and fellow-men are hastening to this great reckoning-day. Unless they repent quick, they will stand condemned at that fearful tribunal. Can we endure the thought, to see them stand trembling at the left hand of the judge? In this world they decide their fate for eternity; and our life, prayers, entreaties, and efforts will do much towards influencing them to decide it aright. That being the fact, how we should exhort and entreat with all long-suffering and doctrine! That father, mother, husband, wife, son, daughter, brother, sister, friend, or neighbor may be lost if you neglect your duty. Speak quick, or they may be dead, and sealed over to the judgment. Oh, SPEAK! SPEAK IN EAR-

NEST! WORK, WORK, WORK while the day lasts. Time is rolling on, and the judgment is hastening apace. The angel will soon be in mid-heaven, and the blast of his awful trumpet will burst upon your ear! Oh! awake, awake, ye sleepy Christians, and look up! Behold the judge standeth before the door! Hark! He speaks and thunders,— WHY STAND YE HERE ALL THE DAY IDLE? To your *post*, to your *post*, until he calls you to the *skies*.

3. What a fearful event this will be to the unfaithful minister, and those who have deceived the people by preaching error! The responsibility of the ministry is fearful. They are moulding the souls of men for eternity. If "they cry *peace, peace,* when there is *no peace* to the wicked, saith my God;" if they preach error, and corrupt and pervert the Bible, and lead men to think there is *no* danger when there *is* danger; if they are what the Bible terms "dumb dogs that will not bark," unfaithful watchmen who refuse to give the people warning, blind guides who mislead the minds of their hearers,— what a fearful reckoning they will have to meet at this hour! How they will come up to this high court, covered all over with the blood of souls! How the lost, whom they have led to ruin, and an indignant universe, will curse them for their murderous work! If there is a hell of hells, if there is a double damnation that will fall upon the head of any being at this final reckoning, it will fall upon the head of that man who

has used the ministry for his own personal aggrandizement, or merely as a support for himself and family, while he has had no care or anxiety for the salvation of the souls of the flock over which he has been placed as a watchman. What a moment to him, when he shall be compelled to behold the work of death he has done up for himself and his fellow-men! How the curses of the lost will pursue his guilty soul, endlessly, through hell's dark dominions! and how he will gnaw that murderous tongue with eternal anguish, for the work of ruin it has done to human beings.

4. And finally, this subject affords a strong motive to induce sinners to repent without delay, lest the great day of His wrath should come and find them unprepared to meet their account. *Sinner*, SINNER, how thankful you ought to be that you are not already sealed over to the judgment! and that you have a space to repent before you go up to meet Christ in the clouds.

In these discourses, I have tried to settle your minds in relation to the certainty of this event. I have laid before you its objects. I have shown you that it will be a great event. I have dealt with you plainly, faithfully, and honestly, for the purpose of showing you your danger. I have appealed to your reasoning powers, to your hopes, and your fears. Now, before we go to our account, let me beseech you once more, kindly and affectionately, to prepare for that event. You are under God's government; you cannot escape from his dominions. You must meet him; you cannot disobey the summons when he calls you to his bar. But you are not prepared. No, NO! Your conscience bears me record that you are not ready for that hour. How you would tremble to meet him in your present state of mind! *Dying man!* Oh, JUDGMENT-BOUND SINNER, be entreated! STOP! REPENT NOW! REFLECT, DO REFLECT, upon this *great theme*. Find some retired spot, and drop on your knees before your judge, and confess to him your sins. Tell him, honestly, you are sorry you ever violated his law, rejected his Son, and grieved his Spirit. Give yourself up to him, and implore forgiveness through a *Mediator*. Be in earnest. Why should you not? God is in earnest; the whole Trinity are awake for your salvation. Heaven, yes, ALL HEAVEN is in earnest for your soul. Cry with every breath to God! Sue for pardon; give your Maker no rest until you are justified by grace, and then you can meet him in peace. Why not do up this work right here, before you leave your seat? When can you ever have a better moment? While Christians pray, let your heart flow out with ours, that the Infinite One would forgive and save you NOW. May God, by the Holy Ghost, help you to do up this work here, before you leave this house. AMEN and AMEN.

www.ingramcontent.com/pod-product-compliance
Lightning Source LLC
Chambersburg PA
CBHW032033220426
43664CB00006B/462